CLASS, RACE, AND MARXISM

CLASS, RACE, AND MARXISM

David R. Roediger

VERSO

London • New York

First published by Verso 2017
© David R. Roediger 2017

3 5 7 9 10 8 6 4 2

Verso
UK: 6 Meard Street, London W1F 0EG
US: 20 Jay Street, Suite 1010, Brooklyn, NY 11201
versobooks.com

Verso is the imprint of New Left Books

ISBN-13: 978-1-78663-123-7
ISBN-13: 978-1-78663-125-1 (UK EBK)
ISBN-13: 978-1-78663-126-8 (US EBK)

British Library Cataloguing in Publication Data
A catalogue record for this book is available from the British Library

Library of Congress Cataloging-in-Publication Data
Names: Roediger, David R., author.
Title: Class, race, and Marxism / David Roediger.
Description: New York : Verso, 2017.
Identifiers: LCCN 2016051237 | ISBN 9781786631237 (hardback)
Subjects: LCSH: Social classes. | Class consciousness. | Race relations. |
  Socialism. | Communism. | BISAC: SOCIAL SCIENCE / Discrimination & Race
  Relations. | SOCIAL SCIENCE / Social Classes. | POLITICAL SCIENCE /
  Political Ideologies / Communism & Socialism.
Classification: LCC HT609 .R634 2017 | DDC 305.5—dc23
LC record available at https://lccn.loc.gov/2016051237

Typeset in Adobe Garamond Pro by Hewer Text UK, Ltd, Edinburgh
Printed and bound by CPI Group (UK) Ltd, Croydon, CR0 4YY

To Adrian Gaskins, Josie Fowler, and Joel Olson

Contents

Acknowledgments

In a book gathering work done over the course of a decade but reflecting thinking about these matters for four, acknowledgments cannot ever be adequate. I err here on the side of brevity and apologize for omissions. Everything I have written on race and class is informed by mentoring long ago from George Fredrickson, Margaret George, and George Rawick. Learning from Sterling Stuckey came early and continues to only grow. Outside of universities the Chicago Surrealist Group and especially Franklin Rosemont, Paul Garon, and Penelope Rosemont have been constant presences. Where psychology and contemporary social movements are concerned, my sons Brendan Roediger and Donovan Roediger have shared insights. Research assistance from Zach Sell, John Marquez, Stephanie Krehbiel, Martin Smith, Kathryn Robinson, and Hannah Bailey has helped greatly as has work from Edward G. Lee on web matters. I have run drafts and ideas by countless people, including Rebecca Hill, Paul Gilroy, Kevin Mumford, David Camfield, Vron Ware, Alberto Toscano, Dianne Harris, Michael Mizell-Nelson, Rachel Gugler, john powell, Joel Helfrich, Jean Allman, Jonathan Garlock, Noel Ignatiev, Nell Irvin Painter, Moon-Kie Jung, Thavolia Glymph, Richard Seymour, Tricia Rose, Robin D.G. Kelley, Joel Olson, Mark Leff, Clarence Lang, Rod Ferguson, Ferruccio Gambino, Enoch Page, Abigail Bakan, Enakshi Dua, Rose Feurer, Chad Person, John Bracey, Susan Ferber, Shawn Alexander, and George Lipsitz. At Verso Sebastian Budgen, Sophia Hussain, John

Merrick, and Rosie Warren have been especially helpful. Coauthor on one of the pieces, as well as supportive and most perceptive critic on all, was Elizabeth Esch.

My research and writing benefitted from institutional support in the form of fellowships from the Illinois Program for Research in the Humanities, the Center on Democracy in a Multiracial Society at University of Illinois, the Center for Advanced Study at University of Illinois, the Mellon Foundation, and from residencies at University of South Carolina and University of London's Queen Mary University. Thanks especially to Lawrence Glickman and to Gerry Hanlon for arranging the two residencies.

The essays originally appeared in the venues below and both the editors and editorial collectives involved improved them greatly in each case. They are reprinted with thanks:

Chapter 1: "The Retreat from Race and Class." *Monthly Review*, 58 (July–August 2006), 40–51.

Chapter 2: "Accounting for the Wages of Whiteness: US Marxism and the Critical History of Race" in Wulf Hund, David Roediger, and Jeremy Krikler, eds., *The Wages of Whiteness and Racist Symbolic Capital* (Berlin: LIT, 2011), 9–36.

Chapter 3: "The White Intellectual among Thinking Black Intellectuals: George Rawick and the Settings of Genius." *South Atlantic Quarterly*, 109 (Spring 2010), 225–47.

Chapter 4: "Removing Indians, Managing Slaves, and Justifying Slavery: The Case for Intersectionality" in Sabine Ritter and Iris Wigger, eds., *Racism and Modernity: Festschrift for Wulf D. Hund* (Berlin: LIT Verlag, 2011), 117–30.

Chapter 5: Coauthored with Elizabeth Esch, "'One Symptom of Originality': Race and the Management of Labor in US History." *Historical Materialism*, 17 (2009), 3–43.

Chapter 6: "Making Solidarity Uneasy: Cautions on a Keyword from Black Lives Matter to the Past." *American Quarterly*, 68 (June 2016), 223–48.

INTRODUCTION

Thinking through Race and Class in Hard Times

In a recent symposium in the web publication *Syndicate* on his book *Seventeen Contradictions and the End of Capitalism*, the Marxist theorist David Harvey takes issue with one of his critics, the radical scholar of religion Alex Dubilet. Harvey objects to Dubilet's contention that the struggles against police violence, municipal courts, and white supremacy that have matured in and beyond Ferguson, Missouri after the murder of Mike Brown are "anti-capitalist" ones. "Frankly," Harvey writes, "I don't see the current struggles in Ferguson as dealing very much in anti-capitalism." Instead he finds those struggles likely to recapitulate the "long history in the United States . . . of making sure that the anti-racist struggle does not turn anti-capitalist." In characterizing what he regards as the most "fearsome" challenge in his book for the US left, Harvey adds, "None of these other struggles should transcend or supersede that against capital and its contradictions."[1] Harvey gets matters quite wrong, but he starts us in a direction that is extremely useful for thinking about how we might work across disagreements where study and struggle regarding race and class are concerned.

Harvey's position, featuring an iron distinction between antiracist and anti-capitalist (and elsewhere between "revolutionary feminist" and

---

1 David Harvey, "Response to Alex Dubilet," *Syndicate* (April 1, 2015), syndicatetheology.com. Many thanks to Zach Sell for advice on this introduction.

anti-capitalist), is especially difficult to defend regarding Ferguson itself. The best way to see the contradictions inhering in it is to watch Orlando de Guzman's riveting film *Ferguson: Report from Occupied Territory*, which follows the lives of the working poor in and around Ferguson.[2] By letting poor people speak and taking viewers into their homes to an extent very rare in US cinema, *Ferguson* shows the municipal courts, the warrantless searches later justified by finding warrants accumulated in previous instances of racial profiling, unpayable fines for petty offenses, and the brutal but self-satisfied behavior by the police that ruin the lives of African American workers. We see the vast expanses of closed factories and the abandoned neighborhoods lost to deindustrialization and unfair housing practices that provide a backdrop. Those interviewed in the film clearly understand their problems as those of the working poor and the deindustrialized, as well as of those victimized in schools, courts, and on the streets because of their race. Surely, then, these are pro-worker struggles, aimed at abolishing one key institution of the state, the municipal courts, and at limiting the power of the police. In doing so, this resistance also aims to end the practice of running a suburb by shaking down its working poor rather than by taxing the large Emerson Electric corporation headquartered there.[3] We are welcome to wish—I do wish—that people in Ferguson talked explicitly about ending capitalism, though no one with political visibility in the United States ever does. But to assume that that their struggles are therefore not anti-capitalist ones seems formalistic in the extreme.

Nevertheless Harvey's response to Dubilet refuses in an important way to politically pit race against class. He emphasizes—the verbs should be familiar from the first paragraph above—that "none of the political mandates" flowing from his analysis of the contradictions of capital "transcends or supersedes the importance of waging war against all other forms of discrimination, oppression, and violent

---

2   The film appeared in 2015 from Fusion and is online at youtube.com; for Harvey on "revolutionary feminism," "race theory," and anti-capitalism, see his "*Commonwealth*: An Exchange," *Artforum*, 48 (November 2009), 211.

3   Walter Johnson, "Ferguson's Fortune 500 Corporation," *The Atlantic* (April 26, 2015), theatlantic.com; Thomas Harvey and Brendan Roediger, "St. Louis County Municipal Courts, For-Profit Policing, and the Road to Reforms," in Kimberly Jade Norwood, *Ferguson Fault Lines: The Race Quake That Rocked a Nation* (Chicago: ABA Publishing, 2015), 57–74.

repression within capitalism as a whole." Here Harvey draws a distinction, found in his *Seventeen Contradictions and the End of Capitalism* and in the work of others, between on the one hand "capitalism," which he allows is permeated with race and gender oppression, and on the other hand "capital," whose logic can be examined without needing to examine those categories.[4] The substance of the exchanges, and the broader question of whether the production of difference is in fact part of the inner logic of capital, forms the subject of the last section of this brief introduction.

Also noteworthy is the tone of Harvey's remarks and those of his critics. By tone, here and below, I mean the author's attitude toward her or his subject matters and, in this case, opponents. Sharp differences are registered by Harvey and his interlocutors without total dismissal of the positions of others. The personal virtues of, and relationships among, the participants perhaps go some way towards explaining the healthy tone, but politics also matter. No participant in the symposium is intent on seeing race- (or class-) based initiatives described as diversions from the "real" struggle.[5] Moreover, actual social motion in the last decade, from the immigrant rights marches and general strikes of 2006 to the local mobilizations against police murders of African-American young people named nationally as the Black Lives Matter movement, has so clearly given oxygen to US social movements that marginalizing "race" struggles is now difficult, yet still not without its aggressive advocates.

On both sides, then, the symposium on Harvey's work indexes ways in which we are in a more hopeful place regarding the theorizing of race and class than we were a decade ago, when the first of the essays collected here were written. Harvey's desire to balance, if in praxis more than theory, the claims of class and of other forms of social oppression might even be considered the basis for a productive common front for those thinking through these issues from various viewpoints. Thus the exchanges on Harvey's work described raise the major concerns of this introduction: where we are in the study of

---

4 Harvey, "Response to Alex Dubilet."
5 See especially Alex Dubilet, "Dispossession, Uselessness, and the Limits of Humanism," *Syndicate* (April, 2015), syndicatetheology.com; F.T.C. Manning, "On the Inner Laws of Capital and the Force That Decides," *Syndicate* (April 3, 2015), syndicatetheology.com.

race and class; how tone matters; the grounds for hope and, within the hope, how we might measure the promise of a variety of recent and older work refusing to place race outside of the logic of capital.

In January 2016, I contributed briefly to a small exchange among radicals at the invitation of one of my sons. In it activists and lawyers for Law for Black Lives took up a fascinating question: "why aren't killer cops fired?" Some threads in the discussion had suggested that the "logic of capital" dictated that the state, as employer, could cut its troubles in the streets and its losses in lawsuits by sternly and quickly disciplining cops who kill. From this viewpoint instituting mechanisms for profiling the police who are most likely to kill and weeding them out proactively would also make sense. And yet, again and again we find that police who shoot people dead under the most questionable circumstances already have substantial records of abuse complaints before the killing and remain on the force after it. Cities so firmly in the hands of liberal Democrats that they scarcely have an opposition party sign contracts with police "unions" allowing for the destruction of records of police against whom misconduct complaints regarding use of force are lodged, making the assessment of individuals about to cross over into deadly violence all but impossible.[6] How would scholars of race and class make sense of such apparent irrationality?

The tenor of the exchanges appealed to me greatly, in that nobody seemed to possess a ready-made line explaining everything and nobody assumed that an answer had to be finalized before actions could proceed. The discussion seemed a perfect illustration of political scientist Michael Dawson's reminder that (re)building a Black left requires becoming "comfortable with trying to effect change without knowing all the answers in advance."[7] In this way it contrasted with too many academic debates.

I answered the question on the non-firing of killer cops initially as a Marxist and labor historian. Some prior comments had reflected on police unions as a source of soft-on-police-violence practices. I

---

6   Ken Hare, "Reforming Chicago Police Starts with . . . Saving the Misconduct Records," *Chicago Defender* (April 6, 2016).

7   Michael C. Dawson, *Blacks In and Out of the Left* (Cambridge, MA: Harvard University Press, 2013), 203.

argued that, as unions, police organizations were not very strong, though their power to forestall investigation of police violence is at times striking. Successful police strikes remain very rare and labor law is not on their side, even if in some places they are exempt from general onslaughts against unions of public employees. In Ferguson the police victimizing the Black community made nearly low enough wages that they would have benefitted from the triumph of a fifteen-dollar minimum wage, though conditions vary widely and opportunities for money on the side are typically present. The informal power of the police to avoid being managed is far greater than the power of their unions however. They ride around alone or in pairs, with guns, and without bosses present; the general level of managerial control is bound to be low. After that initial point, my response entered into the more familiar territory of trying to think about race and class together by questioning the premise that the "logic of capital" exists apart from the practice of countenancing and fostering often violent divisions among workers. Even so it took a while for me to get to race and white supremacy as specific modalities in which the logic of capital combines rationality and irrationality. My own work on whiteness seemed not worth mentioning, although I did recommend the historian Nikhil Singh's provocative and convincing "The Whiteness of Police."[8]

It would have never occurred to me, in that context, to say that other points of departure beyond those that I presented toward answering why killer cops often keep their jobs needed then to be discredited. The idea that the question itself reflects overthinking—that police simply are in James Baldwin's terms "occupying armies" controlling racialized populations within a system accepting the collateral damage that they inflict—is not wrong. The hyper-masculine, aggressively hetero, and militarized culture and outfitting of the police certainly matters as well in producing both violence and cover for the transgressions of others among the police. The blowback from the brutalities of imperial adventures abroad, which provide intimidating equipment, technologies of torture, and manpower to police forces, likewise does so. The luxury of the

---

8   Nikhil Pal Singh, "The Whiteness of Police," *American Quarterly*, 66 (December 2014), 1091–99.

exchange was to think about contributing one's corner of knowledge without rejecting all others.

This introduction asks why the ways that we think through questions of race and class, particularly in academic settings, cannot be more like that back-and-forth on killer cops. It, and the book itself, urges less dismissiveness towards opposing positions. It refuses to imagine that we achieve open debate by embracing positions advocating for the sidelining of the consideration of race or, as in the case of liberal multiculturalism, by neglecting questions of class. However it does urge, in ways involving self-criticism of even some of the reprinted essays included in the volume, a respect for the ways in which those from whom we differ are working to address difficult problems in hard times.

A specific need for self-criticism deserves elaboration at this early point. Anchoring the collection is a 2006 provocation that I wrote for a special "Class" issue of the venerable US Marxist journal *Monthly Review*. Titled "The Retreat from Race and Class," my essay scarcely avoids the problems of tone for which I skewer others both within it and below in this introduction. When I wrote it, the most polemically sharp of these collected essays, the critical things that I had to say about some people whom I like and admire gave me pause. In some cases they should have given me more pause. Such was especially the case with regard to Antonia Darder and Rodolfo Torres, whom I now see less perhaps as retreating from race and class analysis than as trying to move beyond Black and white in understanding those matters, and to Paul Gilroy. I was therefore pleased that as the article circulated Paul and I were able to communicate forthrightly about it. At one point in trying to contextualize our differences, and my respect for his position, I wrote to him that I thought much of the contention stemmed from those against whom we were trying to argue. In my case the quarrel has been with activists and labor history scholars whose "class first" claims reduce social divisions so profoundly as to miss both the gravity of race-based inequality and the reality that much social motion responds to that inequality not because of manipulation by "middle-class" activists, but because of a history of struggles and a present shaped by old and new incarnations of white supremacy. Views marginalizing race also too often embrace the wishful thinking that if the political field were cleared of all those arguing for organizing around opposition to white supremacy, all would be well.

In Gilroy's case, the confrontation he enters has been with a narrow nationalism on both the fascist right in Europe and parts of the left that take the tactical utility of mobilizing on racial grounds as a fact of life. Such views, he warns, find their ways into the wider swaths of antiracist politics, which too easily suppose that constructions of race will endure and that it is wrong to question what it hides. So forcefully does Gilroy's *Against Race* take this stance that it argues for the rejection, which he admits to be costly, of race-based mobilization not as an immediate cure-all enabling a return to class politics but as a necessary step to find new forms capable of addressing inequality with a goal of transcending race. One can—and I do—disagree with the prescription while acknowledging that the issues raised are profound. In that sense, while leaving my own essays intact as a part of a developing argument, it is necessary to acknowledge overstatements in characterizing, for example, my differences with Gilroy, Darder, and Torres.

Seeking, then, to raise questions of tone as well as substance, this introduction begins with a consideration of how a long period of defeats for both racial and class justice structures both our confusion and our bitter certainties. A second section considers, perhaps less graciously in terms of tone, how recent controversies over the Bernie Sanders presidential campaign and its opposition to race-specific demands help to measure the difficulties of class-first positions. Such positions, I will argue, reach into the thinking even of some who succeed much of the time in keeping race and class simultaneously in view. A third part argues that, nevertheless, there are substantial grounds for hope in newer approaches to race and class, including in approaches criticized elsewhere in the introduction. Especially promising is work attempting to argue that the production of racial and other differences is itself part of the logic of capital. A concluding section takes readers through the contents and origins of the book's six essays.

Our Period and Its Discontents

On the surface, it would seem easy to think about race and class together. Not too long ago, I would have regarded a challenging formulation in the 1963 edition of C.L.R. James's *The Black Jacobins* as giving an elegant, if a little vague, solution to the question of how we do so: "The race question is subsidiary to the class question in politics," James wrote, "and to think of imperialism in terms of race is disastrous." But, he immediately added, "to neglect the racial factor as merely incidental is an error only less grave than to make it fundamental."[9] The quote still resonates powerfully, but I now think of it as being more a statement illustrating how deeply our problems run than as a solution to them. James sees the two categories as distinct, separable, and needing to be ranked, in ways I no longer do. Nevertheless his vantage, like Harvey's, provides a good basis for mutuality and common work among those with differing inflections. Subtle balancing is required. The task is hard and not susceptible to being precise. As movements ebb and flow, existing struggles make one terrain, or perhaps inflection, seem more attractive at one moment, less at others. Pretense regarding a mastery of the calculus James calls for is regularly humbled. It ought, then, to be possible to differ about the specific emphases on race and class across time and place while not vilifying each other.

Just after a 1984 conference on the future of labor history had been held at Northern Illinois University, I ran into my informal mentor George Rawick in St. Louis. George, an important thinker on race and class who is the subject of one of the essays in this volume, took care of me around the fact that I had not been invited to the conference, despite being a graduate of Northern Illinois. He offered accounts of lots of the papers, but shook his head, often suggesting that they could only be so good and were fated to descend into acrimonious, petty disputations. The whole idea of the event was, he repeated several times, a mistake: "Can you imagine holding a conference on the future of labor history when there are no strong social movements to tell us where it should go?" We might hesitate, and at other moments George would have hesitated, to stake so much on the connection between upsurges in social motion and clear thinking by intellectuals. Antonio Gramsci, Walter Benjamin, and Stuart Hall, for example, thought through important ideas in periods of profound political defeat. But mostly, Rawick was right in

---

9   C.L.R. James, *The Black Jacobins* (New York: Vintage Books, 1963), 283.

terms of substance and he was distinctly on to something in terms of the difficulty of maintaining a comradely tone during periods of social quiescence.

Rawick's comments speak to why it has not been easy to play nice and be clever when theorizing race and class during the long decline of the civil rights and labor movements. What used to be called the "nature of the period" has been favorable to posturing and unfavorable to both charity and clarity. The largest context structuring acrimony is that it has been for a very long time difficult to talk meaningfully about the ebb and flow of either struggles against class oppression or of those contesting racial injustice. For nearly half a century in the United States, we have overwhelmingly experienced ebbs and awaited flows. Nearly fifty years ago, when I first encountered the words quoted from James, US labor strikes of over 1,000 workers averaged 300 per year, sometimes reaching well over 400. In 2009, five such strikes occurred, in 2014 eleven, and in 2015 twelve. Today when the words "strike" and "US" are paired we think of drones. Union density, the traditional measure of labor's decline, has hit unions only a little less hard, with a third of workers organized in the mid 1960s and a tenth—far less than that in the private sector—in 2015. I still wear a faded old T-shirt opposing a "generation of givebacks" in union contracts, but persisting unions are now in the third generation of defensive struggles.

That same period witnessed the end of great advances of the Black freedom movement and a turn to struggles to keep 1960s measures in force. Since the 1980s, the movement has played defense by attempting to slow the timetable of the dismantling of affirmative action and by preserving voting rights. When I wrote the introduction to *How Race Survived US History* just a decade ago, I did so with a post-it note near my computer with "7x" twice written on it, reminding me of the social facts that young African-American men were imprisoned seven times as often as whites and that white wealth outpaced African-American wealth sevenfold. Today that latter figure is a factor of sixteen.

The disorienting impact of such a long period of defeat can hardly be overstated. In the 1950s and 1960s, a period of intense and constant struggle for gains by workers and by the civil rights movement, the permeability of the categories of race and class emerged in sharp relief. The expanding horizons created by the movements against racial oppression made all workers think more sharply about new tactics, new possibilities, and new freedoms. The spread of wildcat strikes across color lines is one example. The high hopes Martin Luther King Jr. invested in both the Poor People's Campaign and the strike of Black sanitation workers in Memphis remind us of a period that could test ideas in practice and could experience, if not always appreciate, the tendency for self-activity among people of color to generate possibilities for broader working-class mobilizations.

Optimistic thinking proclaims that things have recently turned around. *It Started in Wisconsin* was the title of a fine book on the mass struggles there against anti-union legislation in 2011, but those struggles were defensive, ultimately electoral, and soundly defeated. Or perhaps "it started" with the 2008 sit-in at the Goose Island facility of Chicago's Republic Windows and Doors, but that was a defensive struggle against a plant closure, involving 200 workers, and the plant closed. Or, how we hoped, Occupy "started it" again in 2011.[10] "It started" is interestingly most often applied to movements seen as presenting class demands, but the quality of such movements remains very far from turning into quantity. Spectacular workers' protests have occurred, especially those of the immigrant rights marches and general strikes of 2006 and of the recent local mobilizations of Black Lives Matter.[11] These struggles have won gains in some instances, but they are too easily considered as nonclass, mobilizations simply based on identity. Meanwhile the "labor" struggle most able to sustain itself, that of the Chicago Teachers Union, has been also the one with the most sophisticated and energetic anti–white supremacy politics.[12]

---

10   Mari Jo Buhle and Paul Buhle, eds., *It Started in Wisconsin: Dispatches from the Front Lines of the New Labor Protest* (New York: Verso, 2012); Kari Lydersen, *Revolt on Goose Island: The Chicago Factory Takeover and What It Says about the Economic Crisis* (New York: Melville House, 2009); Writers for the 99%, *Occupying Wall Street: The Inside Story of an Action That Changed America* (Chicago: Haymarket Books, 2012).

11   Nicolas De Genova, "The Queer Politics of Migration: The Politics of 'Illegality' and Incorrigibility," *Studies in Social Justice*, 4 (2010) 101–26; Jamala Rogers, *Ferguson Is America: Roots of Rebellion* (St. Louis: Jamala Rogers, 2015).

12   Micah Uetricht, *Strike for America: Chicago Teachers against Austerity* (New York: Verso, 2014).

One result of living inside of difficult circumstances not of our own choosing is that it has been too easy for some to suppose that our difficulties have been caused by paying too much attention to race, to gender, or to sexuality (where mass movements have also effected some significant reforms), and not enough attention to class. When these arguments press furthest and most simplistically—for example, in the writings of the literary scholar Walter Benn Michaels—we are presented with the view that neoliberal elites countenance demands based on race, gender, and sexuality in order to divert attention from the real inequalities of class.[13] Such a conspiracy theory trades on the kernel of truth that elites, bureaucracies, and the judiciary do persistently attempt to shift the terms of struggles against racism, sexism, and homophobia/transphobia into soporific vagaries regarding "diversity" and "multiculturalism." Corporate embraces of the "value of diversity" are, it is true, not antiracist. Multiculturalism does instead regularly mask desires for the surplus value produced by diversity. But this hardly makes popular antiracist struggles irrelevant or inimical to addressing class oppression.

Benn Michaels's move courts at least three major problems. First, it loses track of the extent to which working-class people participate in and shape initiatives such as immigrant rights, trans rights, and antiracist mobilizations and therefore misses working-class victories as momentous as those won in 2006 mass actions by immigrant workers. Second, it substitutes denunciation for patient attempts to define the terms of a coalition encouraging those oppressed in differing ways to come together and deepen the demands of all. Last, it locates the causes of the failures of organized labor and of labor politics outside and inside the Democratic Party as exogenous to those movements themselves, imagining that doing more of the same will work out fine, or would if multiculturalism were only defeated. The failures of the labor leadership are much better understood as fail-

---

13   Walter Benn Michaels, *The Trouble with Diversity: How We Learned to Love Identity and Ignore Inequality* (New York: Holt, 2006). For a particularly regrettable encapsulation of Benn Michaels's position, see his "Against Diversity," *New Left Review*, 52 (July–August 2008), newleftreview.org. For an important and careful study of how diversity operates inside and against concrete struggles, see Ellen Berrey, *The Enigma of Diversity: The Language of Race and the Limits of Racial Justice* (Chicago: University of Chicago Press, 2015).

ures of the labor leadership than the result of being outfoxed by multiculturalists.

According to Benn Michaels, the proof that demands for racial justice now function as mere covers for maintaining class inequalities dramatically surfaces when antiracists allow that in their ideal society poverty and inequality would continue and merely be evenly distributed across racial lines. The evidence that this is in fact a widely expressed position among antiracists is very scant. But, to be clear, the achievement of the equality amidst oppression so ridiculed by Benn Michaels is, though impossible without a broader social transformation, not actually a goal that anti-capitalists should sneer at as providing merely "victories for neoliberalism."[14] Since capital produces difference in its own interests, its continued sway limits progress towards eliminating racial inequality. By the same token, inroads in that regard do challenge the logic and limit the room for maneuver of capitalist management. As the London-based socialist thinker Sivanandan has observed, "in recovering a sense of oppression," white workers must confront their "alienation [from] a white-oriented culture" and "arrive at a consciousness of racial oppression."[15] Struggles for racial justice are sites of learning for white workers, of self-activity by workers of color, and of placing limits on capital's ability to divide workers.

Class-splaining: Ta-Nehisi Coates, Tone, and Race-Specific Demands

A revealing example of the difficulties of tone and substance associated with the Benn Michaels position, and with its partial embrace by some whose work in other ways usefully challenges class reductionism, followed on an early 2016 Ta-Nehisi Coates contribution to *The Atlantic*. The article, "Why Precisely Is Bernie Sanders against Reparations?" concerned the failure of the Sanders presidential campaign to consider demands for the payment by the US state to African Americans of reparations for slavery, Jim Crow, and more

---

14 Benn Michaels, "Against Diversity" ("victories for neoliberalism").
15 Ambalavaner Sivanandan, *A Different Hunger: Writings on Black Resistance* (London: Pluto Press, 1982 [1974]), 96

recent injustices. Recently a recipient of the prestigious "genius" grant from the MacArthur Foundation and of the National Book Award, Coates had previously argued for reparations, but, in this instance, he further asked why Bernie Sanders's campaign so preferred "universal" race-neutral strategies for combatting inequality over a combination of such remedies with other, race-specific policy changes.

Coates reported the position of the Sanders campaign to be not only that reparations were impossible to win but also that they were "very divisive" and a wrong choice given that people of color are so disproportionately poor. Thus reforms like a $15-per-hour minimum wage or free college education could function as economic demands that serve racial justice without dividing people. Coates confessed remaining unpersuaded, doubting that racial inequality, created by long patterns of racial discrimination in law and property, would yield to remedies that did not address the past and present of such practices. The article as a whole straightforwardly lamented that the Sanders campaign felt so little need for race-specific strategies to alleviate inequality. Coates also stressed the absence of strong support for affirmative action in Sanders's program, underlining that the grand universalist strategy deployed by some socialists, and not only the controversial specifics of reparations, was at issue. There was not a hint that the article opposed socialism itself. Far from delivering paeans to Hillary Clinton, Coates gloried in the fact that "radicals expand the political imagination and, hopefully, prevent incrementalism from becoming virtue."[16]

The responses to Coates's little five-page article came with astonishing speed, repetition, and imbalance. They reflected a mixture of support for Sanders, of unfounded judgment, and of unseemly resentment regarding Coates's awards. The often insightful radical historian Paul Street, with seventeen pages in *Counterpunch* a day after Coates's article appeared, blamed the heresies of Coates on the " 'bougie' sensibility" of the latter. He meant this not in the slangy cultural sense in which Coates has playfully applied the term to himself. Instead Street insisted that the

16   Ta-Nehisi Coates, "Why Precisely Is Bernie Sanders against Reparations?" *Atlantic* (January 19, 2016), theatlantic.com.

"foundation-certified genius," by virtue of his MacArthur grant and book royalties, is somehow actually—the italics are Street's—"*bourgeois*", and therefore embraces a "bourgeois world view" that "denies the central importance of class oppression."[17]

A day later, the political scientist Adolph Reed Jr. edged from mere bitterness to ugly accusations when the economist Doug Henwood devoted his radio show to Reed's views on Coates. It was unclear from the dialogue whether Coates was charged with being an agent of the US state, or of the capitalist class, or just of the Hillary Clinton presidential campaign. Reed reported that Coates "sneers at programs of material redistribution," as Coates had not done, when in fact reparations is such a program. "When I was working in the GI movement, when people like that would come into the meeting," Reed added, "I'd just ask them 'So which branch of military intelligence are you assigned to?'" Reed also, as a Sanders supporter, sniffed out a more immediate conspiracy: "The idea that Bernie Sanders becomes the target of race-line activists now, and not Hillary Clinton, is just beyond me and it smells. It smells to high heaven." For him, Coates's perfidy also directly reflected a class position, but this time the enemy was not bourgeois but the "professional-managerial class" that allegedly forwards the issue of reparations while Black working people, equally allegedly, do not. Coates's stature, on this view, derived not from his writing and thought but from his utility to elites. Henwood asked: "This sort of stuff plays very well to guilty white liberals, doesn't it?" Reed responded, "A friend, whom I won't out, observed to me a while ago that one of the things that really irks him (and he's a professor) about Coates is the way that white liberals gush over him and my inform-ant said that it reminds him of the way that upper-middle-class liberals fawn over the maid's son who has gone to college and 'made something of himself.'"[18]

The slightly later response to Coates coauthored by Kenneth Warren and Benn Michaels accused Coates of purveying a

17   Paul Street, "Race without Class: The 'Bougie' Sensibility of Ta-Nehisi Coates," *Counterpunch* (January 20, 2016), counterpunch.org.

18   Henwood's interview with Reed on his KPFA-Berkeley "Behind the News" show (January 21, 2016) is at shout.lbo-talk.org.

"right-wing fantasy" because reparations would not do away with capitalist markets.[19] Such pro-Sanders critiques of Coates ironically came at a moment in the campaign when it became clear the African-American vote was going overwhelmingly to Clinton and would be instrumental in securing her the Democratic nomination, arguably making the rejection of race-specific demands as questionable as political strategy as it is as theory.[20]

By far the most coherent, though rancorous, response came from the often perceptive political scientist Cedric Johnson, writing in *Jacobin* in early February 2016. Perhaps his editors gave the piece its mean-spirited title, "An Open Letter to Ta-Nehisi Coates and the Liberals Who Love Him." However, the piece itself did regard the historical role of not only Coates but also and remarkably of James Baldwin to be "assuaging white guilt." Alongside a particularly strident attack on reparations, Johnson held that Coates "updates the Cold War, anti-socialist canard that any attempt to build social democracy on US soil will inevitably be hobbled by racism." However, his own article showed that social democratic reforms certainly were so "hobbled" even at their highest points during the New Deal.[21]

Johnson criticized the "handful of Black Lives Matter protesters" who interrupted Sanders events as forwarding the anti–"social democratic" position. He lamented, "But I've grown weary of this position—repeated with startling unanimity by students, activists, academic colleagues, social media commentators, and career pundits, who frequently reject any talk of a universal, broad-based leftist project." To frame matters thusly threatens to read out of existence the whole strand of fighters like James, Claudia Jones, and Dr. King, all of whom very much believed in universal projects *and* antiracist demands. The problems of Johnson's position in this regard were

19   Walter Benn Michaels and Kenneth Warren, "Reparations and Other Right-Wing Fantasies" (February 11, 2016), nonsite.org.

20   For an electorally engaged response, see Bill Fletcher Jr., "A Letter to the Bernie Sanders Campaign," *New Pittsburgh Courier* (January 28, 2016), newpittsburghcourieronline.com; see also Brian Jones, "The Socialist Case for Reparations," *Jacobin* (March 1, 2016), jacobinmag.com.

21   Cedric Johnson, "An Open Letter to Ta-Nahesi Coates and to the Liberals Who Love Him," *Jacobin* (February 3, 2016), jacobinmag.com.

dramatically revealed when Coates announced that he was in fact a Sanders supporter, and declared himself to be delighted that socialism was gaining a popular hearing, despite his reservations on Sanders's understanding of white supremacy. As he wrote in a specific rejoinder to Johnson, "But I do not believe that if this world [of social democratic reforms that he supports] were realized, the problem of white supremacy would dissipate, any more than I believe that if reparations were realized, the problems of economic inequality would dissipate."[22]

Again and again, contemporary debates on race and class involve characterizations like Johnson's of the supposed state of the existing discourse and policies as hopelessly tilted towards race at the expense of class. We need to bend the stick in one direction, it is said, because everyone else, or perhaps just liberals and neoliberals, so bend it in the other. So many well-positioned writers imagine that an increased emphasis on class can only come by toning down the race and gender talk that it is hard to see how they maintain the stance that they are lonely figures sacrificing to tell the truth. Academic emphases and those of NGOs are said to structure race-first distortions. Injecting a word about class becomes an act of extraordinary freethinking courage, defying a deck stacked against any such mention. No matter how repeatedly such mentions occur they get to count as speaking truth to power—itself perhaps an overrated practice.

On one level, as a Marxist who began writing in the 1970s when it was somewhat easier to be one, I get it. But we are hardly without platforms. Moreover, perceiving such a tilted-towards-race status quo sometimes creates too easy an alliance between those who wish to combine emphases on race and class and those who would rather see race off the agenda altogether on the theory that the poverty of people of color means that they can benefit from class-based reforms without the need for specific antiracist demands.

Consider, for example, the activist-scholar Keeanga-Yamahtta Taylor, her recent study *From #BlackLivesMatter to Black Liberation*, and her reaction to Johnson's attack on reparations. Her book is an

22 Ibid., and Ta-Nehisi Coates, "The Enduring Solidarity of Whiteness," *Atlantic* (February 8, 2016), and "Ta-Nehisi Coates Is Voting for Bernie Sanders Despite the Senator's Opposition to Reparations," *Democracy Now* (February 10, 2016), democracynow.org.

estimable effort to take race and class struggles seriously. She argues well that without an emphasis on critically important questions of class only limited motion to toward racial justice can occur and a good society cannot take shape. Her book rehearses well some figures on racial disparities in wealth as well as disparities within the African-American population. Her knowledge of Black Lives Matter is as impressive as her respect for Black self-activity. The book is a cause for optimism that "race or class" sterilities might give way.[23]

However, at times, Taylor seems to so believe that Marxism is locked in an uphill battle to be heard that unexamined certainties interfere with her analysis, and even her fact-checking. A pat review of the objective character of class, for example, sees her school her book's readers to the effect that "whether or not a group of workers has reactionary . . . consciousness does not change its objective status as exploited and oppressed labor." She then moves to specifics: "Just because white workers may at times fully accept reactionary ideas about African Americans does not change the objective fact that the majority of the US poor are white."[24] But it isn't. In 2013 just short of 20 million whites suffered in poverty while the combined Black, Hispanic, Asian-American, and American-Indian poor numbered 27 million.[25]

On social media, Taylor posted Johnson's attack on Coates and on reparations with a headnote describing it as the "essential reading for today." The post extracted a pull-quote highlighting exactly the passage in which Johnson expressed how put upon he felt in the face of race-forward positions "repeated with startling unanimity by students, activists, academic colleagues, social media commentators, and career pundits."[26] Since Taylor elsewhere avowed support for reparations, the attractions of the aggrieved tone would seem to override the disagreement with the central political issue actually raised by Johnson in this instance.

---

23 Keeanga-Yamahtta Taylor, *From #BLACKLIVESMATTER to Black Liberation* (Chicago: Haymarket Books, 2016).

24 Taylor, *From #BLACKLIVESM[ATTER to Black Liberation*, 213–14.

25 US Census Bureau, *Income and Poverty in the US: 2013* (September 2014), 12–14, census.gov.

26 The Facebook posting generating the threads described below is from February 3, 2016.

But the aggrieved tone itself is unproductive and at best half-convincing. The fuller story, as suggested above, is that substantive discussions of ending racial oppression and of ending class oppression both fight for a hearing against daunting odds. At the level of policy it cannot be said that demands for racial justice have had a sufficient presence in the program of Democrats over the last forty years to so stifle discussion of class. What would those demands be? At best, retreats from a half-hearted defense of affirmative action programs have typified Democratic practice, leavened by allegedly brave, and disgusting, attacks on family values among African Americans. That was the Bill Clinton approach, which advocated an "It's the economy, stupid" rhetorical emphasis on the fortunes of the middle class as the unifying issue that would be jeopardized by appeals to (Black) special interests.[27] Racial justice has, at the level of national politics, been marginalized in the service of lamentably vague class talk, even as nebulous talk about racial justice has sidelined debates over class.

As I argued at the start of the Bill Clinton years in a *New Left Review* essay titled "The Racial Crisis of American Liberalism," timid and duplicitous race politics perfectly complement timid and duplicitous class politics.[28] If—and I have held no illusions that this is ever to be in the cards—the Democrats were to have advanced militant departures from center-right politics on race, they would almost certainly have had to offer something to organized labor to keep a coalition together. To build support for strong forms of affirmative action, for example, in the 1980s or 1990s would have almost necessitated commitment to rewarding union support with labor law reform. It is hard to say which the party hierarchy wanted less. If Sanders were—again the whole paragraph here deals in hypotheticals—to have taken Coates's advice and supported reparations, it would have been wise to offer reforms creating conditions for rebuilding unions and to take up directly how to build a movement to win such demands. Race and class demands, on this view, do not exist in a zero-sum relationship. Increased boldness in class demands

---

27   David Roediger, *How Race Survived United States History: From Settlement and Slavery to the Obama Phenomenon* (London and New York: Verso, 2008), 207–11.

28   David Roediger, "The Racial Crisis of American Liberalism," *New Left Review*, 196 (November–December 1992), 114–19.

is not gained, as the attacks on Coates assume, by hitting the mute button where race talk is concerned.

Where Work on Race and Class Is Going and Might Go

Admittedly, so far the introduction has not been a model of a positive, open-to-everything tone. Where attempts to sideline thinking about specificities of racial oppression are concerned, I suspect that letting "a thousand flowers bloom" cannot be the watchword, though willingness to work and debate together across difference can. I do stand by the idea that all of us should approach the difficulties for thinking about race and class generated by the difficult period in which we live with humility and frank admission that we cannot know where things will go. Happily, there is much in recent scholarly work and in recent struggles that offers glimmers of possibility. Indeed, some of the best insights in politically engaged recent work comes from some writers whom I have criticized above as too ready to suppose that class analysis best thrives when the field is cleared of over-emphasis on race.

In particular, three areas of promise deserve emphasis. The first involves how the critical study of whiteness might best respond to profound changes in the working class itself. The second measures the importance of anti-police, anti-racist movements and of recent work addressing inequality within the African-American population and to the increased visibility of what might be called "rulers of color." The third brings us back to the introduction's beginning, taking up the ways in which recent work challenges the view of David Harvey and so many others that race sits outside of the logic of capital.

With regard to the critical study of whiteness, the left scholarly project with which I have been most involved, the grounds for possibly productive auto-critique seem clear. I approach matters as someone who doubts that how we attach labels matters much against the weight of social relations. "Black or African American?" produced for a time interesting debates, for example, but in the longer run things shifted, and it became clear that academics and even activists do not get to determine popular usages, and social relations mattered more than names for them. Nevertheless, I think that we may be due for discussion on whether "white privilege" now serves us well in naming patterns of white advantage inside a system in which most people are miserable.

This question struck me forcefully during a 2015 visit to Rochester, New York. The historians Joel Helfrich and Jonathan Garlock had taken me on a wonderful tour of Rochester's past struggles and present deindustrialized crises before I appeared on a Rochester Public Radio show. The host asked much about "white privilege." It is not a phrasing I use often but neither has it ever been one I objected to. In this instance, I did note the extent of joblessness and foreclosure across the color line in Rochester and wonder aloud if "white advantage" might be a less loaded term."[29] This reservation registers the fact that the Marxist coinage of "white privilege" (or "white-skin privilege") by Theodore Allen with Noel Ignatin in the 1960s seems to have become less the popular meaning of the term today than non-Marxist variants. Allen theorized "white privilege" as the package of mostly petty preferences offered to all whites and especially to poor whites, in order to create a cross-class, elite-dominated political coalition policing (enslaved) Black labor and keeping propertyless whites out of mobilizations challenging the wealthy. Why "privilege" became Allen's noun of choice remains a mystery. Whatever the derivation, as used in Allen's writings "privilege" cannot be read as anything but ironic and bitter, with the benefits of the crumbs from masters' tables being pitiable and fully worth rejecting.[30]

Today though discussions of the privileges attached to whiteness, whether in the useful writings of Peggy McIntosh and Stephanie Wildman or the less fresh formulations of Tim Wise, refer to what whites get away with interpersonally, especially within social movements and to what small affronts they do not have to worry about

---

29   "Evan Dawson Interviews David Roediger," *Connections*, WXXI Rochester (April 2015). Available in podcast at wxxinews.org.

30   Michael Staudenmaier, "The White Skin Privilege Concept: From Margin to Center in Revolutionary Politics" (unpublished paper, 2007) and Chapter Two below. See also David Camfield's excellent "Elements of a Historical Materialist Theory of Racism," *Historical Materialism*, 24 (2016). For the classical Marxist uses of privilege, see Engels, "England in 1845 and 1885" written March 1, 1885, marxists.org; Eric Hobsbawm, "Lenin and the 'Aristocracy of Labor,'" *Monthly Review*, 64 (December 2012, originally 1970), monthlyreview.org. Correspondence with Noel Ignatiev (formerly Ignatin) has yielded no firm clue as to what Allen drew upon. Jeff Perry, Allen's literary executor, intends to write a future article on the subject.

facing. In such writing white privilege is to be rejected in the name of racial justice but not necessarily also so that working class whites can fight for their own broadest interests.[31] This usage will continue whether or not it is championed by historical materialists and I wonder if we on the left might be better off with a different terminology, perhaps focusing on white advantage, though with the same credit to Allen.

Critical studies of whiteness also have anchored—mea culpa—discussions in a framework that imagines race as overwhelmingly involving Black and white people as its subjects. This is true of both activist and academic writing on the subject. Rooted in an explanation of the origins of whiteness as bound up with racial slavery, it has been less than curious about settler colonialism's role in shaping the creation of a white identity. The explosion of fine new work on settler colonialism and race, especially Aileen Moreton-Robinson's *The White Possessive: Property, Power, and Indigenous Sovereignty*, challenges older studies of whiteness profoundly.[32] The sociologist Moon-Kie Jung's brilliant *Beneath the Surface of White Supremacy: Denaturalizing U. S. Racisms Past and Present* specifies the task of retaining older emphases and taking on new ones in its closing words: "Once we realize that we are, or side with, Indians and Blacks, pledging allegiance to Old Glory is no longer an option. Instead it becomes incumbent on us to adhere to a variation on one of [James] Baldwin's famous lines: As long as we think we're Americans, there's no hope for us."[33]

With regard to race and nonwhite immigration the critical study of whiteness has certainly helped to inspire very important studies, including those of Neil Foley, Natalia Molina, Ian Haney-López, and Kornel Chang.[34] However, the most-cited studies have not made

31   Tim Wise, *White Like Me: Reflections on Race from a Privileged Son* (Berkeley, CA: Soft Skull Press, 2011); Peggy McIntosh, "Unpacking the Invisible Knapsack of Privilege," *Peace and Freedom* (July–August 1989), 10–12; Stephanie Wildman, *Privilege Revealed: How Invisible Preference Undermines America* (New York: NYU Press, 1996).

32   Aileen Moreton-Robinson, *The White Possessive: Property, Power, and Indigenous Sovereignty* (Minneapolis: University of Minnesota Press, 2015).

33   Moon-Kie Jung, *Beneath the Surface of White Supremacy: Denaturalizing US Racisms Past and Present* (Stanford: Stanford University Press, 2015), 181; see also Aziz Rana, *The Two Faces of American Freedom* (Cambridge: Cambridge University Press, 2010) and Glen Coulthard, *Red Skins, White Masks: Rejecting the Colonial Politics of Recognition* (Minneapolis: Universty of Minnesota Press, 2014).

34   Neil Foley, *The White Scourge: Mexicans, Blacks, and Poor Whites in Texas Cotton Culture* (Berkeley: University of California Press, 1997); Kornel Chang, *Pacific Connections:*

non-white immigrant labor central to theorizing whiteness. We have in the United States nothing like Satnam Virdee's methodologically pathbreaking study of the United Kingdom, *Racism, Class and the Racialized Outsider*. On balance the study of whiteness has contributed, even among its critics, to keeping left attention focused on Black and white.[35] Thus, when Taylor wishes to make the case that Black liberation requires alliances with the working-class movement, she decisively concludes in the familiar setting of a critique of "whiteness studies" rather than an engagement with the question of Black–immigrant solidarity. At a time when there are probably more—figures are necessarily unreliable—undocumented workers in the US labor force than private sector members of labor unions, we have been very slow to realize what working-class unity, and struggle, now means. In this area the critical study of whiteness has too often helped more to recapitulate dated discussions than to generate new ones.[36]

The second set of gathering trends in life and letters inspiring work on race and class concerns the challenges and possibilities raised in the recent past by militant African-American anti-police and campus protests, coinciding as they do with the most visible ever presence of "Black faces in high places." The ways in which those protests focus on terror, take psychology seriously, and feature jobless, female, queer, and trans people ready to participate, lead, and bring their own demands encourages us to consider ways in which identities, including class identities, are multiply made. Frank Wilderson's forceful 2003 critique of reductionism, "Gramsci's Black

---

The Making of the US–Canadian Borderlands (Berkeley: University of California Press, 2012), esp. 91–96; Natalia Molina, *How Race Is Made in America: Immigration, Citizenship, and the Historical Power of Racial Scripts* (Berkeley: University of California Press, 2014), 2–7; Ian Haney-Lopez, *White by Law: The Legal Construction of Race* (New York: NYU Press, 1996).

35 Satnam Virdee, *Racism, Class and the Racialized Outsider* (Houndsmills, Hampshire: Palgrave Macmillan, 2014).

36 For an important work charting new directions see Molina, *How Race Is Made in America*. On the statistics, see Pew Research Center, "Share of Unauthorized Immigrant Workers in Production, Construction Jobs Falls Since 2007" (March 26, 2015), pewhispanic. org, and Bureau of Labor Statistics (US Department of Labor), "Union Members—2015" (January 28, 2016), pewhispanic.org. See also Taylor, *From #BLACKLIVESMATTER to Black Liberation*, esp. 184–219.

Marx: Whither the Slave in Civil Society?" could almost have been written for today's movements against police violence. Wilderson insisted that any theorization in which "racism is read off the base, as it were, as being derivative of political economy . . . is not an adequate subalternity from which to think the elaboration of antagonistic identity."[37] Written much more squarely within the Marxist tradition, but taking account of the simultaneity and materiality of strands of identity, the Canadian sociologist David Camfield's elaboration of an "anti-racist queer feminist historical materialism" deserves to change how we think about race, class, and more.[38]

In 2006, when I wrote critically of the "retreat from race and class," few would have predicted that an African-American liberal would hold the most powerful political position in the world two years later. Certainly, a few Black leaders occupied already very visible leadership positions in the cabinet and armed services and on the Supreme Court but they were then largely Republicans. The Congressional Black Caucus (under)represented African Americans in Congress, and Black mayors at times had the unenviable job of running cities in crisis. The election of Barack Obama posed the issue of Black and particularly Black liberal roles in running an oppressive system with new force. Allied with the growth of significant wealth at the top of the African-American community, this trend has given rise to exciting new scholarship on intra-racial class politics and on intra-racial economic inequality in the last five years. Or to be more self-critical, perhaps my 2006 critique was too harsh in examining work that already was attempting to account for inequality within the Black community and the inadequacies of African-American liberal leadership, though in ways that I still think ended being insufficiently attentive to either race or class.

The most stylish and emblematic book among several taking up these problems in the recent past is the political scientist Lester K. Spence's *Knocking the Hustle: Against the Neoliberal Turn in Black*

37   Frank Wilderson III, "Gramsci's Black Marx: Whither the Slave in Civil Society?" *Social Identities*, 9/2 (2003), 225 and 226–40. For a challenging recent history of politics and Freud, especially connecting psychoananlysis and race, see Eli Zaretsky, *Political Freud: A History* (New York: Columbia University Press, 2015), 38–79.

38   David Camfield, "Theoretical Foundations of an Anti-Racist Queer Feminist Historical Materialism," *Critical Sociology*, 42/2 (February 2014), online before print.

Politics. Racism, Spence argues, "still shapes the lives" of African Americans, but "it cannot explain why some blacks . . . have a lot of resources and some have few." He adds, "Racism cannot explain why there are some black populations we as black men and women are willing to fight for, while there are other black populations we are willing to let die." Like Taylor, whose book also exemplifies the usefulness of apprehending race and class together, Spence notes tremendous inequalities among African Americans.[39] Indeed if we add also Dawson's extraordinary *Blacks In and Out of the Left*, with its emphasis on the changed contours of social relations under neoliberalism, its vigorous defense of reparations, and its discussion of a Black middle class that is both important and threatened, a fascinating range of agreement and differences is emerging in the new literature on race and class.[40]

One barometer of the understandably unsettled nature of contemporary approaches to race and class is the regularity with which remarkably lucid and eloquent accounts of the centrality of race emerge from accounts generally arguing for universal, class-based approaches and against identity. Thus, in Johnson's "Open Letter to Ta-Nehisi Coates and the Liberals Who Love Him," after a flat statement that "racism is not the principal determinant of material conditions and economic mobility for many African Americans" comes a very sharp observation on the role of racism in the entire system. "Social exclusion and labor exploitation," Johnson writes, "are different problems, but they are never disconnected under capitalism." He continues, "Both processes work to the advantage of capital. Segmented labor markets, ethnic rivalry, racism, sexism [and] xenophobia . . . all work against solidarity."[41]

Johnson's point regarding the "never disconnected" relationship of race and class is occasionally stated with equal force and subtlety by Adolph Reed. Writing recently with Merlin Chowkwanyun in *Socialist Register*, Reed proposed "jettisoning the hoary, mechanistic race/class

39   Lester K. Spence, *Knocking the Hustle: Against the Neoliberal Turn in Black Politics* (Brooklyn: Punctum Books, 2015), xxiii ("let die"); Taylor, *From #BLACKLIVESMATTER to Black Liberation*, 7–9 and 75–106. See also Karen E. Fields and Barbara J. Fields, *Racecraft: The Soul of Inequality in American Life* (New York: Verso, 2014).

40   Dawson, *Blacks In and Out of the Left*, esp. 178–88 and 196–97.

41   Johnson, "An Open Letter to Ta-Nahesi Coates and to the Liberals Who Love Him."

debate entirely," favoring instead "a dynamic historical materialist perspective in which race and class are [only] relatively distinct—sometimes more, sometimes less, sometimes incoherently related or even interchangeable within a unitary system of capitalist social hierarchy." The essays collected here would lead us to call the unitary system "racial capitalism," following Cedric Robinson, rather than simply capitalism, a point so far eluding the meticulous but largely atheoretical and not-so-new-as-imagined set of studies undertaken under the rubric of the "new history of capitalism."[42] Indeed in the recent past, compelling new studies of capitalism have overwhelmingly been ones focused on both class and other forms of difference.[43]

The simultaneity and interpenetration of race and class remarked on by Johnson, Taylor, Reed, and Chowkwanyum takes us to the last area of promise for current possibilities in radical scholarship. The most dynamic new work often calls into question the easy distinction that Harvey makes between capital, whose logic is said to exclude racial divisions, and capitalism, which has on his view happened to hold sway in a long epoch littered with such divisions. In making this distinction Harvey retools the theorist and historian Ellen Meiksins Wood's contention that "Class exploitation is *constitutive* of capitalism as gender or racial inequality are not." While Wood's shorthand has provoked criticism from within Marxism, hers and Harvey's view remains broadly the dominant interpretation.[44]

42 Adolph Reed Jr. and Merlin Chowkwanyun, "Race, Class, and Crisis: The Discourse of Racial Disparity and Its Analytical Discontents," *Socialist Register*, 48 (2012), 169 ("hoary" and "relatively distinct") and 149–75; Darryl C. Thomas, "Cedric Robinson and Racial Capitalism," *African Identities*, 11 (2013), 133–47. On the "new history of capitalism," see Peter Hudson, "The Racist Dawn of Capitalism: Unearthing the Economy of Bondage," *Boston Review* (March 14, 2016), bostonreview.net and Seth Rockman, "What Makes the History of Capitalism Newsworthy?" *Journal of the Early Republic*," 34 (Fall 2014), 439–66.

43 For some examples, see my "Freedom Breaks," which reviews the work of Chandan Reddy, Jodi Melamed, Roderick Ferguson, and Grace Kyungwon Hong in *American Quarterly*, 64 (June 2012), 37–44 and Manu Vimalassery, "The Wealth of Natives: Toward a Critique of Settler Colonial Political Economy," *Settler Colonial Studies*, 3 (2013), 295–310.

44 Ellen Meiksins Wood, "The Uses and Abuses of 'Civil Society'" in Ralph Miliband and Leo Panitch, eds., *The Retreat of the Intellectuals: Socialist Register 1990* (London: Merlin Press, 1990), 76 (emphasis original); Reed Jr. and Chowkwanyun, "Race, Class, and Crisis," 168; Alexander Aneivas and Kerem Nisancioglu, "The Poverty of Political Marxism," *International Socialist Review*, 94 (Fall 2014), isreview.org.

When Elizabeth Esch and I began ten years ago to take up these questions in a *Historical Materialism* essay (reprinted in this volume) and then in *The Production of Difference*, the most developed arguments that capitalism not only encountered but also sought, exploited, needed, and created difference came from scholars extremely well-versed in Marxism but not necessarily identifying as Marxists. These included Cedric Robinson, Dipesh Chakrabarty, and Lisa Lowe, from whom we took the phrase "production of difference." Especially important to us was the work of the Marxist economist Michael Lebowitz in his 2006 article "The Politics of Assumption, The Assumption of Politics," a piece based on his talk as recipient of the Deutscher Prize. Lebowitz held that "the tendency to divide workers" functions as "part of the essence of capital, indeed, an essential aspect of the logic of capital." To paraphrase Harvey, Lebowitz argued that racism was part of capitalism, and of capital, but not of *Capital*, as Marx left the production of difference untheorized in a way that we cannot afford to.[45] Lebowitz's contribution very much helped Esch and myself to argue our case within Marxism.

Although the radical geographer F.T.C. Manning is probably right that the Harvey-Wood position remains the "easy, well-trodden, obvious Marxist/leftist path," other roads are becoming a little more traveled. In some ways the tenor and quality of online exchanges on race and the logic of capital reminds me (absent the internet) of the late 1980s when many of us realized we were writing similar books critically studying whiteness in response to the historical moment of Reaganism. For example, Manning's acute response to Cinzia Arruzza's "Remarks on Gender" offers much on the ways in which race and gender are analogous and different in relation to capital, and a firm stance against the idea of an "indifferent capitalism" without an interest in the production of difference. But the response can only be so critical in part because Arruzza's own article

---

45   Dipesh Chakrabarty, "Universalism and Belonging in the Logic of Capital," *Public Culture*, 12 (Fall 2000), 653-78; Lisa Lowe, *Immigrant Acts: On Asian American Cultural Politics* (Chapel Hill: Duke University Press, 1996), esp. 28; Michael A. Lebowitz, "The Politics of Assumption, the Assumption of Politics," *Historical Materialism*, 14 (2006), 29-47. See also Elizabeth Esch and David R. Roediger, *The Production of Difference: Race and the Management of Labor in the United States* (New York: Oxford University Press, 2012) and Chapter Five below.

provides a striking critique of Wood's position. That Harvey so clearly acknowledges what Manning calls the "primacy of race and gender despite their structural contingency" gives critiques room to work. Dubilet roots his challenge to Harvey's arbitrary distinctions between "what is internal and essential to the contradictions of capital, and what is an externality, merely belonging to capitalism as a social formation" with the example of Ferguson. In thought and life, the idea that to consider difference as fundamental to the capitalist era places one outside of Marxism occupies a far more defensive position than when Wood wrote a quarter century ago. Indeed, we may soon be debating, as Chris Chen's work perhaps suggests, how admitting white supremacy as being within the logic of capital can allow us to also theorize the social "relations of terror" and a logic of white supremacy in materialist thought.[46]

The Book

The book itself is divided into two parts. The first roughly half gathers three essays on how we write about race and class. The first selection is the occasionally too fierce *Monthly Review* piece on the "retreat from race and class" discussed above. The two other essays in Part One manage to be more restrained. The first of these, "Accounting for the Wages of Whiteness: US Marxism and the Critical History of Race," speaks crucially to the overall themes of the volume. Published originally, and perhaps somewhat obscurely in Germany in 2011, the work originated out of frustration. Puzzlingly, liberal and too many left opponents of recent histories taking seriously race, and particularly

46 F.T.C. Manning, "Closing the Conceptual Gap: A Response to Cinzia Arruzza's 'Remarks on Gender,'" *Viewpoint Magazine* (May 4, 2015), viewpointmag.com ("indifferent capitalism"); Cinzia Arruzza, "Remarks on Gender," *Viewpoint Magazine* (September 2, 2014), viewpointmag.com; Manning, "On the Inner Laws of Capital" ("structural contingency"); David Harvey, "Response to FTC Manning" (April 3, 2015), syndicatetheology. com; Manning, "Same Path, Different Weather," (April 11, 2015), syndicatetheology.com ("well-trodden"); Dubilet, "Dispossession, Uselessness, and the Limits of Humanism" ("internal and essential"); Chris Chen, "The Limit Point of Capitalist Equality," *Endnotes*, 3 (September, 2013), endnotes.org.uk.

"whiteness," have managed to miss the fact that, more perhaps than in any other historical subspecialty, work on whiteness has been produced by Marxists. Connecting as they did the wave of study of whiteness in the 1990s to Ernesto Laclau, Chantal Mouffe, postmodernism, the "linguistic turn," liberalism, and "identity politics"—indeed to all manner of things other than the historical materialism at its core—dismissive critiques finally seemed worth a response.

This problem hardly seems behind us where the critical study of whiteness is concerned. The current Wikipedia entry on "white priv-ilege," for example, samples the volubly anti-communist historian Eric Arnesen as delivering a "Marxist critique" of the study of white-ness, somehow linking his position to a 1972 essay in *Proletarian Cause*. In so doing, Wikipedia repeats an error still made in more scholarly, and activist, venues. Taylor's recent book makes the admit-tedly increasingly hard-to-take recent writings of Tim Wise stand in for the whole field of the critical study of whiteness, which then can be attacked as anti-Marxist and reformist.[47]

The final article in the book's first half, "The White Intellectual among Thinking Black Intellectuals: George Rawick and the Settings of Genius," first appeared in a special "Thinking Black Intellectuals" issue of *South Atlantic Quarterly* in 2010. It portrays an unlikely figure who fashioned a heterodox, supple, and psychoanalytically informed Marxist approach to race and class after long apprentice-ship in Trotskyist groups not always nurturing in any of those regards. Rawick, a mentor of mine, had the good fortune to encoun-ter the Trinidadian Marxist C.L.R. James, the militant Black work-ers of Detroit in the 1960s, and the voices of ex-slaves whose stories had been collected in a Great Depression project funded by the federal government in making his escape from rigidities.[48]

The book's second half, also gathering three essays, speaks to matters of tone and to questions now being debated under the rubric of race and the "logic of capital." The first of the pieces in Part Two,

---

47   "White Privilege" in Wikipedia (accessed March 12, 2016), wikipedia.org; Taylor, *From #BLACKLIVESMATTER to Black Liberation*, 210, 211, and 214–15.

48   See also David R. Roediger with Martin Smith, *Listening to Revolt: Selected Writings of George Rawick* (Chicago: Charles H. Kerr Publishing Company, 2010).

published in a small book of essays in honor of the sociologist Wulf Hund, is "Removing Indians, Managing Slaves, and Justifying Slavery: The Case for Intersectionality." It briefly attempts to think about how critical both settler colonialism and the gendered social reproduction of the enslaved labor force were to producing a slaveholder-led cross-class alliance that undergirded the expansionist capitalist state in the United States before 1848. The second, originally appearing in the Marxist journal *Historical Materialism* in 2009, reflects the breadth and confidence born of my collaborating in writing it with the historian of transnational Fordism Elizabeth Esch. Titled "'One Symptom of Originality': Race and the Management of Labor in US History," it argues that US capitalist management both exploited and reproduced racial division as part of processes of expansion, production, and accumulation.

The final selection, "Making Solidarity Uneasy: Cautions on a Keyword from Black Lives Matter to the Past," comes back to questions of tone. It emphasizes how precious, but also how understandably fragile, broad solidarities are among groups who are oppressed but oppressed in very different and divisive ways. Originating as my 2015 presidential address to the American Studies Association and first published in *American Quarterly* the following year, it reconstructs the checkered history of the origins and uses of the word *solidarity*. It also analyzes the urgencies and silences surrounding how we memorialize, remember, and experience instances of solidarity, which we urgently need to desire and to question.

PART ONE

INTERVENTIONS: MAKING SENSE OF RACE AND CLASS

CHAPTER I

The Retreat from Race and Class

As the twentieth century started, indeed at almost exactly the same moment that W.E.B. Du Bois predicted that the "color line" would be its great divide, Eugene Victor Debs announced that the socialist movement that he led in the United States could and should offer "nothing special" to African Americans. "The class struggle," Debs added, "is colorless." As the century unfolded, the Marxist left, schooled by struggles for colonial freedom and by people of color in the centers of empire, increasingly saw the wisdom of Du Bois's insight and tried hard to consider how knowledge of the color line could illuminate, energize, and express class struggles. We would find in Debs the striking historical insight, "That the white heel is still on the black neck is simply proof that the world is not yet civilized. The history of the Negro in the United States is a history of crime without a parallel."[1]

---

1 The books discussed in this essay are Paul Gilroy, *Against Race: Imagining Political Culture beyond the Color Line* (Cambridge, MA: Harvard University Press, 2000) and Antonia Darder and Rodolfo D. Torres, *After Race: Racism after Multiculturalism* (New York: NYU Press, 2004). Pierre Bourdieu and Loïc Wacquant's, "On the Cunning of Imperialist Reason," and the debates surrounding it can be found in *Theory, Culture, and Society*, 16 and 17 (1999 and 2000). See also Mark Alan Healey, "Powers of Misrecognition: Bourdieu and Wacquant on Race in Brazil," *Neplantla: Views from the South*, 4 (2003), 391–400 and Robert Stam and Ella Shohat, "Variations on an Anti-American Theme," *CR: The New Centennial Review*, 5 (2005), 141–78. For Patterson, see his "Race Over," *New Republic*, 222 (January 10, 2000) and "Race by the Numbers," *New York Times* (May 8, 2001). On Reed, see his "Class-ifying the Hurricane," *The Nation*, 281 (October 3, 2005) and "The Real Divide," *Progressive*, 69 (November, 2005). For Debs, see his "The Negro in the Class Struggle," *International Socialist Review*, 4 (November, 1903), marxists.org.

But we would also find him too often unable to act on that insight.

As the twenty-first century starts, the idea of a colorless struggle for human progress is unfortunately back with a vengeance. Such is of course the case on the right in the United States, where what the legal scholar Neil Gotanda and others have called "colorblind racism" has underpinned attacks on affirmative action and even on the collection of the race-based statistics necessary to show patterns of discrimination. The high-minded, ostensibly freedom-loving names given to such initiatives—"civil rights initiatives" to do in affirmative action and "racial privacy acts" to undermine the amassing of basic knowledge regarding the impact of race—have contributed mightily to attempts to recapture the moral high ground by those thinking that a society in which white family wealth is about ten times that of African-American family wealth could possibly be a colorblind one.

Nor are such instances confined to the United States. With the blood scarcely dry from white Australian riots against Arab beach-goers in 2005, that country's neoliberal leader John Howard reacted to press headlines screaming "RACE HATE" and "RACE WAR" by loudly declaiming that he heads a colorblind society. When the French interior minister Nicolas Sarkozy, leader of the ruling party there and leading candidate to replace Jacques Chirac as president, recently suffered criticism on race issues, he quickly planned a late 2005 trip to Martinique to emphasize how little color matters in the French colonial world.

Sarkozy stood out at the time as especially harsh in his response to the rebellions of Islamic youth in France against police violence. He failed to join the president and prime minister in distancing them-selves from a recently passed law requiring that French textbooks "recognize in particular the positive role of the French presence over-seas, notably in North Africa." Sarkozy was so thoroughly unwel-comed by Martinique's great politician, poet, and theorist of libera-tion Aimé Césaire and others that the publicity stunt had to be cancelled. But within France the pernicious role of long-established "colorblindness" operates so strongly that Sarkozy can remain a top presidential contender. The legislative left did not originally raise a serious protest against passage of the pro-colonialist textbook legisla-tion and the nation adheres to the no-counting-by-race policy that racial privacy acts seek to enjoin in the United States. Ironically Sarkozy himself has recently called for limited "discrimination positive" (affirmative action) as a carrot operating in tandem with deportations and immigration restriction to quell French rebellions. But to put any "positive" measures into practice remains a problem. As the *Economist* recently put it, the French minister for equality remains practically alone at the top levels of government in advocating for finding a way to even "measure the presence of the children of immigration" in political structures, the bureaucracy, and the labor force. The prevailing logic is summed up by the nation's prime minister: "We don't want to take into account colour."

Against Race but Not for Class:
Raceless Liberalism, Postcolonialism, and Sociology

What is distressingly new, or at the least resurgent, is the extent to which indictments of antiracism, and even of the use of race as a concept, come now from liberalism and from the left. Electorally, of course, one hallmark of efforts by the Democratic Leadership Council to move the Democratic Party still further to the right has been an attempt to distance itself from specific appeals to, and identification with, people of color. Thus the constituencies most aware of both race and class inequities are marginalized in the name of appeals for "universal" programs, even as universal programs, such as "welfare as we know it," are subjected to bipartisan (and anything but colorblind) attacks. The left was capable of dissecting such a shell game, most trenchantly when Stephen Steinberg analyzed it in 1994 as the "retreat from race," and in what will presumably be Christopher Hitchens's last serious book, his 1999 dissection of Clintonism, *No One Left to Lie To*.

But when no political alternatives to quadrennial returns to Democratic candidates who confine their tepid appeals for racial justice to the King holiday and Black churches, or support for Nader campaigns whose leader seemed not so much blind to race as discomfited by its very mention, the retreat from race quickened on the intellectual left. Thus the brilliance of Paul Gilroy is turned to writing *Against Race* and Antonia Darder joins Rudy Torres in producing the triumphal *After Race*. Orlando Patterson holds forth under the title "Race Over," while Loïc Wacquant and the late activist/sociologist Pierre Bourdieu brand analyses of race as an axis of inequality in Brazil as pernicious exports from a United States social-science establishment that is as "cunning" as it is "imperialist."

These works are of course much more, and in some ways much less, than a retreat to Debs's "colorless" ideas. They lack the same focus on, and confidence in, socialist transformation and are often in dialogue less with class struggle than with cultural studies ideas about the importance of "hybridity" and the pitfalls of "essentialism." In most cases they do not promise to re-center class by removing a fixation on race, and when they do, as in Reed's "Class-ifying the Hurricane," they prove unable to deliver on such a promise. They register the increase of immigration, of intermarriage and of cross-racial adoptions, and the need to affix blame (this time on the messengers) in a time when science repeatedly declares the end of race, and white supremacy nevertheless thrives as ideology. Ironically, the very success, largely under United Nations and non-governmental organization auspices, of organizing around race globally has also laid bare the varying national patterns of racialized inequality and the blurred borders between racial, religious, language, and national oppressions.

All of this has rightly made critiques of crude invocations of race as the simple answer to everything more compelling. But while retreats from race are understandable in view of the difficult and changing political tasks that we face, they are no more an answer to how we pursue those tasks when they come from the left than when they come from the right and center. The context in which they emerge, and the stature of voices contributing to them, demand that they be taken seriously. To do so requires us to look at the varieties of left critiques of race-thinking, with the goal of disaggregating them not being simply to show their incompatibility with each other but rather to identify various inspirations to which they respond. The most celebrated advocates of "race is over" and "against race" positions—Gilroy, Patterson, and Bourdieu and Wacquant—do not directly raise the issues of race and class central to this article, but their influence and arguments must be at least briefly discussed if we are to situate the more explicitly class-conscious writings of Darder and Torres and of Reed. In every case, the instability of the positions being invoked suggests all of the excitement, and the problems, of work in progress.

Gilroy's *Against Race* begins with an extraordinarily dense and challenging discussion of the connections between the very idea of "race" and what Gilroy terms "raciology," the nexus of murderous practice, policy, and science born out of seeing race. Race, Gilroy holds, is a "relatively recent and absolutely modern invention" and its scientific credentialing cannot be considered apart from its bloody implication in "evil, brutality and terror." In a new world ostensibly beyond white supremacist science, and one in which Black bodies are marketed as desirable and even superhuman rather than only as degraded, Gilroy sees both new dangers and the possibility for a "novel and ambitious abolitionist project," this time doing away with race itself. "Renouncing 'race'" becomes not only the key to "bring[ing] political culture back to life" but the *ethical* response "appropriate to confronting the wrongs done in the name of raciology. Acknowledging that for "many racialized populations, 'race' and the hard-won, oppositional identities it supports are not to be lightly or prematurely given up," Gilroy proposes a long campaign designed to show that "action against racial hierarchies can proceed more effectively when it has been purged of any lingering respect for the idea of 'race.'" In the book's early stages, a disabusing of racist science and a recognition of the need to see the elisions of gender and to some extent class divisions made by Black nationalist movements seem to have Gilroy rejecting race but endorsing a more mature antiracism.

But, by the book's end, despite asides suggesting that he will not too harshly judge those who hesitate to abandon the politics of anti-racist solidarity in favor of a "heterocultural, postanthropological, and cosmopolitan yet-to-come," Gilroy has dismantled much of the grounds of antiracism. Declaring the "mood" of projects attacking white supremacy to be hopelessly passé as we leave "the century of the color line behind," he also strongly dissents from any firm connection of racism to power or to white supremacy. *Against Race* poses the choice in approaches as one between an outmoded concern for "Africa's antiquity" and an appropriate one for "our planet's future." Gilroy writes, "To be against racism, against white supremacism, was once to be bonded to the future. This no longer seems to be the case" as we "move out of a time in which [race] could have been expected to make sense." The monumental but incomplete and fragile achievements of Black internationalism, so searchingly explored in their contradictions in Gerald Horne's recent *Race War*, are reduced to scattered passages of precocious appreciation for the "planetary." The utopian dimensions that Robin D.G. Kelley shows to be so essential to struggles against white supremacy and capitalism become for Gilroy moments to be captured against the grain, by reading through a lens that can reduce Frantz Fanon to "that prototypical black-European" noteworthy in large measure for his "indiscreetly anti-Marxist spirit."

Like Gilroy, the sometimes-on-the-left Harvard sociologist Orlando Patterson explicitly pronounces Du Bois's remarks on the color line to be well-past their sell-by date. "Race Over" was the headline for Patterson's projections in *The New Republic* in 2000. The article begins from the premise that Du Bois may have been "half-right" regarding the color line in the twentieth century but is certain that any attempt to continue to apply the insight would be "altogether wrong." For Patterson the problems with twenty-first-century race-thinking are now less political and ethical than they are simply demographic. His visions are not very different from endless accounts in the mainstream press that the United States will become a white-minority nation in the not-too-distant future. By 2050, the United States "will have problems aplenty. But no racial problem whatsoever" Patterson tells his readers. By then, "the social virus of race will have gone the way of smallpox." The retreat from race would fall into regional patterns, the details of which call the predictions of racelessness somewhat into question. On the West Coast, "cultural and somatic mixing" would produce a population mainly "Eurasian but with a growing Latin element" but the real engine of change would be in-migration by "an endless stream" of allegedly raceless new US residents who would use new technologies to change appearances. In the Northeast and Midwest, deindustrialized zones of misery would contain the white, African-American and Latino poor, bound together by "social resentment" and a "lumpen-proletarian hip-hop culture," and isolated from the gated communities of the prosperous. In the Southeast, the "Old

Confederacy" race divisions would continue—"race over" would not in fact apply—but somehow this would make no difference in the national picture.

At almost every turn the raceless predictions coexist for Patterson with invocations of old-style race-thinking. "Murderous racial gang fights" remain a fact of 2050 life and new technologies to change race are deployed. But an even more glaring contradiction obtrudes when Patterson adds other sets of prognostications in a 2001 *New York Times* article, "Race by the Numbers," now distancing himself from the view of demographers that whites would become a minority in the United States in the twenty-first century. Arguing that "nearly half of the Hispanic population is white in every social sense," Patterson forecast that "the non-Hispanic white population will . . . possibly even grow as a portion of the population." Patterson may be right that children of non-Hispanic white/Hispanic inter-marriages will identify as (and be identified as) "white," but the jarring contrast between the two articles suggests just how slapdash the race-is-over position remains. Race disappears and whiteness reigns.

Wacquant and Bourdieu's "On the Cunning of Imperialist Reason," published in *Theory, Culture and Society* in 1999 repro-duces with surprising stridency Marx's argument that the ruling ideas of an age are produced by those who dominate, putting it into the service of an attack on the discussions of racial inequality that have recently led to adoption of forms of affirmative action in Brazil. In doing so, they produce yet another separate strain of "against race" argument, finding it hopelessly fixated on the United States. Wacquant and Bourdieu pinpoint the "cultural imperialism" of United States scholars as the source of attempts to flatten varied regimes of race and class oppression, a flattening they see as produc-ing a misreading both of history and of current political possibilities. Focusing on the case of Brazil, Bourdieu and Wacquant contend that United States–inspired, United States–funded and United States–produced research works to impose a "rigid black/white social division" offering the rest of the world a "poisonous" export. Such imperialism insinuates itself, in Bourdieu and Wacquant's view, despite the fact that its arguments are "contrary to the image Brazilians have of their own nation." It does so by trading on a perverse and unspecified combination of antiracist rhetoric and neoliberal financing for scholarship.

However, a series of withering critiques, especially from the Brazilianists Michael Hanchard and John French and from the cultural theorists Ella Shohat and Robert Stam, have dismantled Bourdieu and Wacquant's contention that race is somehow a peculiarly US concept that would have to be exported. The critical responses show that in neither the United States nor Brazil is race regularly deployed for purposes of accusation rather than analysis, and that what Bourdieu and Wacquant call the "neutralization of historical context" is a charge that might be turned back on their own reductive understanding of Brazil. Most importantly, the critics show that the scholars accused of spreading "imperialist reason" and rigid caricatures of the Brazilian social system actually continue a long line of argument *within Brazil* that has consistently featured nuanced debates engaging both United Statesian and Brazilian scholars who well realize that the historical context of displacement of indigenous people, empires, slave-trading and slavery produced a very different, but not incomparable, racial system in Brazil than in the United States. When Stam and Shohat show that the analysis produced by Wacquant and Bourdieu is not devoid of universalistic views of race (and presumed colorblindness) found in French imperialism, the argument that we need a fuller and more complex discussion of race and empire rather than an end to debate is squarely put on the table.

Does Moving Away from Race Move Us toward Class?

The very first words in Darder and Torres's *After Race* attempt to improve on Du Bois's "dictum" regarding the color line: "We echo his statement but with a radical twist. The problem of the twenty-first century is the problem of 'race'—an ideology that has served well to successfully obscure and disguise class interests behind the smokescreens of multiculturalism, diversity, difference, and more recently, whiteness." *After Race* centrally holds that race is a biological myth at long last invalidated by science, but now dangerously recreated because scholars persist in using the term, thereby decisively aiding the rise of culturally based neoracisms and even the recrudescence of biological racism. On this view, the "idea of race" itself, not capitalism, is somehow the "lynchpin of racism."

Like the early sections of Gilroy's *Against Race*, the work of Darder and Torres holds out the hope that retreating from the invocation of race will actually empower a more effective struggle against racialized hierarchies. Indeed, they approve of Barbara Fields's uncharitable contention that "liberal, leftist, or progressive" writers dwell on the "homier and more tractable notion" of race to avoid being "unsettled" by talking about racism. However, as in Gilroy's case, the emphasis on racism is not sustained and neither race nor racism function as what the book calls "categories of analysis"—that is, they cannot be the reasons for people acting as they do, but must themselves be explained.

Insofar as Fields, Darder, Torres and others contend the inattention to class distorts inquiry into all inequalities in the United States, they are exactly right. However, the strategy of banking on the retreat from race to solve that problem is a highly dubious one. It leads to an extremely embattled tone, and to ignoring the most exciting work building on materialist insights. From Cheryl Harris's brilliant studies of whiteness as property, to Eduardo Bonilla-Silva's research on racial systems, to somewhat older South African scholarship on racial capitalism, to Lisa Lowe's important observations on race, universality, and labor at the start of *Immigrant Acts*, much work seeks to revive the class question by bringing racism and class together more systematically, but you would not know it from *After Race*.

Indeed, at critical junctures, the book is so eager to be against race that it departs dramatically from historical materialism and thus cannot much be for class. Darder and Torres praise the liberal sociologist William Julius Wilson, for example, for supposedly demonstrating that "the significance of class has increased and is now far more salient than 'race' in determining the life chances of African Americans." This either/or, class-not-race, position leads *After Race* to ignore the devastating counterarguments Melvin Oliver, Thomas Shapiro, and others have made to Wilson's work and to subordinate to an endnote their own appreciation of the fact that Wilson's work is about as distant from Marxism as possible. That note promises a different approach, focusing "with specificity [on] the dialectic between the means of production and the process of racialization," but so far Darder and Torres have not produced such analysis. Indeed, *After Race* emphasizes theological matters, not slavery, settler colonialism, and the primitive accumulation of capital, in accounting for the origins of racialized groups. Such a view is very much consonant with the book's emphasis on "racisms"—including the tendency to "inferiorize" whites—to the exclusion of any systematic discussion of white supremacy.

This same inattention to white supremacy makes it almost impossible for *After Race* to contribute to pressing discussions of how to build Latino/Black working class unity. The book's puzzling title—clearly race was no more real in 1670 than in 2004—makes sense in terms of the book's structure, one that culminates in chapters on Asian-American and Latino experiences and emphasizes that the "browning of America" will shake old certainties regarding racism. The danger here lies in marking the possibility of abandoning race in terms of the Latino (or "brown"—both categories are insufficiently interrogated) population exceeding that of African Americans. This would leave us passing out of a period of "race," during which blacks predominated, and into a raceless one in which Latinos do. But there is then no sustained analysis of African Americans, of African-American Studies, or of the tradition of Black Marxism, as would seem necessary to calibrate such an argument. Moreover, that African Americans practice "racism" is a consistent refrain of the study, which persistently lays all manner of mischief at the door of the civil rights and Black Power movements. The former, we learn, emphasized a "liberal, rights-centered political agenda [that] undermined the development of a coherent working-class movement in the United States." Here the reflexive move away from seeing racism as having critical explanatory weight at times lets white supremacist trade unionism off the hook and leads to the missing of the centrality of jobs, union organizing, welfare rights, poor people's campaigns, and point-of-production organizing—of class—to the civil rights and Black Power movements. Missing class, it becomes possible to charge that Black Power "seiz[ed] the moment in the name of antiracism and 'black autonomy'," shutting off debate over the consequences of using "the language of 'race' to do battle with racism" and to loosely link a movement animated by anticolonialism, anticapitalism and nationalism to the Nation of Islam's extravagances on "white devils."

While Darder and Torres allow that "racism" is still a problem worth addressing, the recent writings of the radical political scientist Adolph Reed Jr. are done even with all that. Sounding more like Debs than any major left commentator on race and class in recent memory. "Exposing racism," he argues, is "the political equivalent of an appendix: a useless vestige of an earlier evolutionary moment that's usually innocuous but can flare up and become harmful." Reed's two late-2005 articles, "Class-ifying the Hurricane" and "The Real Divide" are in other ways as well the signature pieces so far of the retreat from race. They appear in relatively popular left/liberal venues, *The Nation* and *The Progressive* respectively, and represent attempts by a prominent activist to speak broadly and frankly. Moreover, Reed's scholarship offered significant opposition to liberalism's retreat from race during the Clinton era, especially in his collection *Without Justice for All*. "Class-ifying the Hurricane" appeared while the horrific impact of Katrina in Reed's hometown of New Orleans was fresh in readers' minds, when racist reporting contrasting Black "looters" with white survivors shown doing precisely the same foraging. It noted "manifest racial disparities in vulnerability, treatment, and outcome" of the experience of natural disaster. And then it turned on a dime to excoriate the "abstract, moralizing patter about how and whether race matters." Even so in this first essay Reed's retreat from race could be read as simply a strategic one. "For roughly a generation it seemed responsible to expect that defining inequalities in racial terms would provide some remedial response from the federal government," he wrote. "But for some time race's force in national politics has been as a vehicle for reassuring whites that that 'public' equals some combination of 'black,' 'poor,' and 'loser.'" Katrina lay bare both race and class injustices, but in part because of the growing strength of racism, an effective response to it would have to be strictly "class-ified."

"The Real Divide" repeated, expanded and made more combative the arguments in the *Nation* article. Reed did continue to mention, in a labored construction, that he was "not claiming that systemic inequalities in the United States are not significantly racialized." Indeed "any sane or honest person" would have to acknowledge the overwhelming evidence of "racial disparities [that] largely emerge from a history of discrimination and racial injustice." Nonetheless Reed follows up these generalizations by categorically declaring that "as a political strategy exposing racism is wrongheaded and at best an utter waste of time." It is for Reed a dodge designed to make "upper-status liberals" feel morally superior as they vote for the deeply compromised Democratic Party. In one of the few bits of the article offering ostensible, if misguided, class analysis, exposing racism is said to serve "the material interests of those who would be race relations technicians." As in "Class-ifying the Hurricane" the arguments are partly that racism, being "too imprecise" and too abstract, lacks power as an analytical tool. However, the point Reed develops more is that among whites the very "discussion of race" reinforces "the idea that cutting public spending is justifiably aimed at weaning a lazy black underclass off the dole." The "racism charge," on this view, is easily defeated by Republican appeals to "scurrilous racial stereotypes" and therefore should be jettisoned.

Gilroy's *Against Race* at least acknowledges that a call for giving up on race-based traditions of struggle asks a lot of social movements rooted in communities of color. At law, for example, exposing racism is often the sole strategy available to protect, after a fashion, the rights of the poorest workers in the United States. Reed's view that elite liberalism is the source of movements to expose and combat racism—a view much facilitated by his outspoken opposition to the reparations movements—forestalls consideration of such dynamics, making the retreat from race to be itself something of an abstraction.

Fortunately there is no reason to decide whether to organize or to analyze around either racism or class oppression, one to the exclusion of the other. The case of New Orleans, which moved Reed to present us with such a choice, offers good examples of why we should reject it. Compare, for example, Reed's either/or insistence with the left activist and writer Mike Davis's accounts of post-Katrina New Orleans. Davis raised a series of questions three months into the rebuilding process of New Orleans and perfectly captured the continuing color line:

Why is there so much high-level talk about abandoning the Ninth Ward as uninhabitable when no one is proposing to turn equally inundated Lakeview back into a swamp? Is it because Lakeview is a wealthy white community? And/or is it because the 30,000 reliably Democratic Black votes in the Ninth Ward hold the balance of power in Louisiana politics?

To what extent, Davis wondered, did "ethnic cleansing" and rebuilding coincide? Davis's accounts have also been especially acute on the ways in which elites, including the Black political elite in New Orleans, have played on, and indeed created, Black/Latino tensions during the rebuilding process. How are we to conceptualize those tensions, and to struggle to overcome them, without discussing both race and class, as well as white supremacy?

In recent antiwar demonstrations after Katrina, the most fascinating sign has read: "NO IRAQI HAS EVER LEFT ME TO DIE ON A ROOF." Its words recall haunting post-Katrina images and also sample the celebrated antiwar dictum attributed to Muhammad Ali: "No Vietnamese ever called me 'nigger.'" The latter line was perhaps the quintessential late twentieth-century example of Du Bois's insight, ignored by US-centered readings of his words, regarding how the color line in the United States existed in systems of racialized global inequality. We should allow that the twenty-first-century "NO IRAQI" sign's variant of the earlier slogan is considerably more complex and expansive. Poor whites, and indeed the large numbers of Vietnamese resettled in the Gulf region and abandoned in Katrina's considerable wake, could conceivably march under the "NO IRAQI" sign. In that sense the sign, and the reality of New Orleans, speaks powerfully to the most profound insight in Reed's recent work, namely that the position of poor, mostly Black, New Orleanians suffer from a plight that is "a more extreme version of the precarious position of millions of Americans today, as more and more lose health care, bankruptcy protection, secure employment, affordable housing, civil liberties, and access to education. To combat such misery will require race and class analysis, as well as antiracist and anti-capitalist organization.

As Reed's articles appeared in late 2005, the *New York Times* ran an article titled "For Blacks, A Dream in Decline." It revealed that after a 1980s peak in which one Black worker in four was a union member, now the figure approaches one in seven. In the last year, African-American workers accounted for 55 percent of the loss of 304,000 union members nationally, although they represent only a sixth of all unionized workers. The article quoted William Julius Wilson himself as urgently calling on unions to address the issue. "They haven't done so yet," he added. Union leaders, according to the article, "resist viewing what is happening in racial terms." One prominent labor leader quoted sounded for all of the world like Eugene V. Debs: "We see it as a class issue rather than a race issue." It is both, and the retreat from race and class will get us closer to addressing neither.

CHAPTER 2

Accounting for the Wages of Whiteness:
US Marxism and the Critical History of Race

Nell Irvin Painter's excellent 2010 study *The History of White People* maintains that "critical white studies began with David R. Roediger's *The Wages of Whiteness: The Making of the American Working Class* in 1991 and Noel Ignatiev's *How the Irish Became White* in 1995."[1] I have spent lots of energy over the last twenty years in order to not be the figure Painter points to, and for some very good reasons. However, in this article, I want to acknowledge some kernel of truth in what she holds. The good reasons for disavowing being a founder (or cofounder) of critical whiteness studies are several. To produce such a lineage takes the 1990s moment of publication of works by whites on whiteness as the origin of a "new" area of inquiry, when in fact writers and activists of color had long studied white identities and practices as problems needing to be historicized, analyzed, theorized, and countered. The burden of my long introduction to the edited volume *Black on White: Black Writers on What It Means to Be White*, is to insist on locating the newer studies within a longer stream on whose insights they rely. Moreover, even in the last twenty years, the most telling critiques of whiteness have come from such writers of color as Toni Morrison, Cheryl Harris and, now, Painter.[2]

---

1   Nell Irvin Painter, *The History of White People* (New York: W.W. Norton, 2010), 388.

2   David Roediger, ed., *Black on White: Black Writers on What It Means to Be White* (New York: Schocken, 1998), 1–26; Toni Morrison, *Playing in the Dark: Whiteness and the*

My desire has thus been to acknowledge the critical study of whiteness as a longstanding tradition, pursued mainly by those for whom whiteness has been a problem, including some radical white scholars who now join the argument that an embrace of white identity has led to absences of humanity and of the effective pursuit of class interest among whites. To adopt this broader and more accurate view of the work that had been done seemed to me to most effectively guard against the view that studying whiteness was a fad, akin to passing fancies like "porn studies." Writing an early article on "whiteness studies" in *New York Times Magazine* in 1997, Margaret Talbot distilled this view with particular venom and lack of comprehension. Lamenting that the fad was part of a larger trend toward "books that seem ill equipped to stand the test of time," she chose to only consider white writers on whiteness, and indeed wrote under the title "Getting Credit for Being White."[3]

The particular identification of *The Wages of Whiteness* and *How the Irish Became White* as founding texts have also threatened—in the designs of others, not Painter—that the genealogy of the field thus created would set up attacks on it as an ultra-radical project designed to further revolutionary aims, not scholarly knowledge. That is, Ignatiev and I have occupied high profiles as figures whose books have circulated fairly widely among young activists and whose desire to further the "abolition of whiteness" has been repeatedly stated. The right-wing journalist David Horowitz's hysterical attacks on "whiteness studies" have most insistently played on the theme that such work is not scholarship at all, but indoctrination and propaganda. Horowitz once extravagantly and implausibly tried to locate critical studies of whiteness "in the theoretical writings and politics of mass murderers like Lenin and Mao, and totalitarian dictators like Fidel Castro, Ho Chi Minh, Stalin, Hitler and Mussolini."[4]

Eric Arnesen's three ever-shriller essays on the subject warn similarly against "whiteness studies." They score red-baiting

Literary Imagination (New York: Vintage, 1990); Cheryl Harris, "Whiteness as Property," *Harvard Law Review*, 106 (June 1993), 1709–95.

3 Margaret Talbot, "Getting Credit for Being White," *New York Times Magazine* (November 30, 1997), 116–19.

4 David Horowitz, "Ethnic Studies or Racism," *Frontpagemag.com* (June 1, 1998); Chris Weinkopf, "Whiteness Studies," *Frontpagemag.com* (June 25, 2003).

points—arguing that radical politics drives the manipulated conclusions of writings on whiteness—saving the greatest contempt for my work and especially Ignatiev's as species of "sectarian moralism." Regarding Ignatiev, Arnesen would seem to prefer a purge to debate, writing, "that his [Ignatiev's] political cult-like sensibility should find a respectable place in university history departments is a testament to the academy's perhaps overly generous and ecumenical culture (at least toward matters considered progressive) . . ." On this view, Ignatiev's political activism imparted an indelible mark of "left splinter-sectarianism" to his historical accounts. My own sin is to advance "outlandish" antiracist politics as part of academic writing—to go beyond the "discursive barricades" and to advocate an "'assault on white supremacy' in the real world."[5]

All of this said, I would no longer fully demur from Painter's dating of a new early-1990s beginning for the critical studies of whiteness, as long as it is clear that we are considering the field's specific emergence within the discipline of US history and acknowledge that if Ignatiev and I stood as faces most identified with the boldness and revolutionary commitments of that beginning, we were far from alone in it, or even at its intellectual head. To include a fuller roster of those white writers of the history of whiteness from the 1990s as founders of a new phase in the evolution of this inquiry would thus both add accuracy and lessen the vulnerability of the field to attack, though other important figures equally pursued activist projects and held left commitments intellectually. In particular, Alexander Saxton and Theodore Allen were there at the beginning and with weightier early books than mine and Ignatiev's. Soon Venus Green, Michael Rogin, George Lipsitz, Bruce Nelson, and Karen Brodkin would be publishing important studies.[6] Ignatiev and I

5 Eric Arnesen, "Passion and Politics: Race and the Writing of Working-Class History," *The Journal of the Historical Society*, 6 (September 2006), 323–56; Arnesen, "A Paler Shade of White," *New Republic*, 226 (June 25, 2002), 33–35.

6 Alexander Saxton, *The Rise and Fall of the White Republic: Class Politics and Mass Culture in Nineteenth Century America* (New York: Verso, 2003 [1990]); Theodore Allen, *The Invention of the White Race*, 2 vol. [1: *Racial Oppression and Social Control*; 2: *The Origin of Racial Oppression in Anglo-America*] (New York: Verso, 1994 and 1997); Venus Green, *Race on the Line: Gender, Labor and Technology in the Bell System, 1880–1980* (Durham: Duke University Press, 2001); Michael Rogin, *Blackface, White Noise: Jewish Immigrants in the Hollywood Melting-Pot* (Berkeley: University of California Press, 1996); George Lipsitz,

mainly contributed the most memorable soundbites—the idea of whiteness as a "wage" and the insistence that some immigrants "become white," though even there the phrasings are, as we shall see, very much in the debt of older works by the African-American socialist writers W.E.B. Du Bois and James Baldwin. The presence of this larger group of heterodox, overwhelmingly Marxist, radical historians of whiteness in the 1990s ensured that the slight books Ignatiev and I wrote could not be entirely marginalized and indeed soon received intense discussion across disciplines.

This essay then attempts to situate the 1990s origins of a new, distinctly history-based body of critical studies of US whiteness among a circle of writers with common and disparate left experiences and Marxist ideas, dating back at least to the 1960s and in some cases to the 1930s. The authors of these studies often shared mentors, inspirations, and publishing venues. We knew each other by the twos, threes, and fours, although we never functioned as a group and in fact would have bridled at the idea that a field of "whiteness studies" should exist outside of radical history and ethnic studies. The chapter attempts, then, to describe a milieu, and to recall some of its formation, suggesting the key role of a Marxism grounded in labor activism and in the ideas of C.L.R. James, Baldwin, George Rawick, and above all Du Bois. Even the embrace by some of us of psychoanalysis as a way to shape inquiries emerged from within the left. The achievement of Marxists in recasting study of race through critical histories of whiteness deserves emphasis because the successes of historical materialism in the US have been rare enough over the last two decades. The field's emergence as an historical materialist project, and partly in the specific context of the Black freedom movement, also warrants elaboration because there is some tendency among academic critics to imagine that the critical study of whiteness issues from postmodernism, Freud, and identity politics, even in opposition to Marxism. At its most sloppy, or desirous of scoring supposed points for one kind of Marxism over another, such criticism descended to branding critical whiteness

---

The Possessive Investment in Whiteness (Philadelphia: Temple University Press, 1998); Bruce Nelson, *Divided We Stand: American Workers and the Struggle for Black Equality* (Princeton: Princeton University Press, 2001); Karen Brodkin, *How Jews Became White Folks and What That Says about Race in America* (New Brunswick: Rutgers University Press, 1998).

studies as a "critique of historical materialism" or as an expression of "the anti-materialism so fashionable at present" or even (in a critique of Allen of all writers) as "extreme philosophical idealism."[7] Such critiques have typically credited Arnesen's frankly empiricist and non-Marxist stance early in a review essay and then have later pronounced on which books under consideration are sufficiently materialist and which are not. (It might be said, in mitigation, that Arensen in the space of a few lines was capable of criticizing whiteness scholars for not making a "cleaner" break from Marxism, and then to brand them as "pseudo-Marxists," implying perhaps that he held some unstated commitment to a fully unspecified "real" Marxism. He likewise could deride psychoanalysis and simultaneously claim a perch from which to judge others as practicing "pseudo-psychoanalysis." There was ample room for confusion.[8]) In some cases, there crops up among scholars who have scarcely acknowledged the existence of Marxism in their long careers a sudden interest in defending Marxism against "whiteness studies," one which comes to be directed against those who have long written as Marxists.[9]

Weighty books of history are often responsive to the dangers of the moments in which they appear, but they cannot be called into being in those moments. Much, and not so much, should therefore be made of the fact that the first major studies of working-class white identity and practice were written in reaction to the 1980s regimes of Ronald Reagan and published in or just after the term of George Herbert Walker Bush in the 1990s. These presidencies locate the then-new studies not only in reactionary times, but also in periods in which substantial numbers of white workers, even union members, voted for reaction. For writers, and readers, of critical histories of whiteness, the moment elicited a passionate interest in working-class conservatism and its relationship to race. Thinking and voting as

---

7   Brian Kelly, Introduction to the reprint of Bernard Mandel's *Labor: Free and Slave* (Urbana: University of Illinois Press, 2007), ix–lxix, xxix, and xl ("critique," "anti-materialism," and "idealism").

8   Andrew Hartman, "The Rise and Fall of Whiteness Studies," *Race and Class*, 46 (October 2004), 22–38, 23, 26 and passim; John Munro, "Roots of 'Whiteness,'" *Labour/ Le Travail*, 54 (2004), 175–92.; Arnesen, "Paler Shade of White," 33–35 ("pseudo").

9   Peter Kolchin, "Whiteness Studies: The New History of Race in America," *Journal of American History*, 89 (2002), 156, 159, 166 and passim.

whites, rather than as workers, made the white worker a problem in the present and opened possibilities of making the emergence of the white workers an historical problem as well.

However, the longer trajectories of figures like Saxton and Allen suggest more varied inspirations. Appearing in 1990, Saxton's *The Rise and Fall of the White Republic: Class Politics and Mass Culture in Nineteenth Century America* predated all of the other books under consideration here. *Rise and Fall* was Saxton's fifth book, following three proletarian novels from the 1940s and 50s, and the brilliant *The Indispensable Enemy: Labor and the Anti-Chinese Movement in California*. Coming to the Communist movement in the 1930s, after education at Harvard and University of Chicago, Saxton became an organizer in the railroad and construction industries and served as a paid publicist for the Committee on Maritime Unity, a left effort to unite workers in unions with very different practices where race was concerned. He entered graduate school in history at University of California midlife after losing the opportunity to market fiction, and for a time his requests for a passport, amid early Cold War repression.[10]

Saxton's labor activism frequently centered on race even in the uncommonly tough Jim Crow atmospheres of the railway brotherhoods and the building trades. When he attempted to explore anti-discrimination struggles among railroad workers in his 1948 novel *The Great Midland*, Saxton had to look to the mass production industries to imagine how things might be plotted. As he wrote in reissuing the novel later, he had "never heard of any shop steward on any railroad who defended black workers." At one 1940s point, Saxton agitated for fair employment in the railway crafts and ran into the argument that African Americans should have no representation on fair employment practices committees because they would act out of racial loyalty and self-interest, as whites supposedly did not. "Apparently," Saxton bitingly observed, "white men belong to

---

10   Saxton, *Rise and Fall*, xiii-xviii; Robert Rydell, "Grand Crossings: The Life and Work of Alexander Saxton" *Pacific Historical Review*, 73 (2004), 263–85; Alexander Saxton, *The Great Midland* (Urbana: University of Illinois Press, 1997 [1948]), xv–xxx; Josephine Fowler, "Transcribed Interview with Alexander Saxton," Josephine Fowler Papers, Special Collections, Charles Young Library, University of California, Los Angeles, box 51, folder 2, provides the details on Saxton's life and work.

no race."[11] His attempts to think through how to write about race and class in fiction led in similar directions. An avid student of John Steinbeck's popular successes, he later wrote of the latter's decision to make the workers in *Grapes of Wrath* white refugees from the Oklahoma Dust Bowl, not "Mexican and Mexican-American proletarians" as part of pattern in which "white racism enters [into Steinbeck's work] not generally as affirmation but in the form of silences and omissions."[12] His magnificent first academic book, *The Indispensable Enemy*, dissected the disfigured labor unity eventuating from organization on as white workers and against Asian workers. Saxton's later activism against the Vietnam War and activities in founding Asian American studies joined his labor organizing in shaping his treatment of race in *Rise and Fall of the White Republic*, which emphasized the connections of race to power, and to an ability to create cross-class "white" coalitions at every turn.[13]

Similarly, Theodore Allen drew on a half-century of radical organizing, much of it specifically in industry, in writing his two-volume *The Invention of the White Race* in the 1990s after a series of antecedent articles and pamphlets, mainly with radical presses. Born into a middle-class family in Indianapolis and raised also in West Virginia, Allen was "proletarianized by the Great Depression," as he put it. He tried college for a day, finding it uncongenial to independence of mind. By seventeen he had joined the American Federation of Musicians and was soon a delegate to the central labor body in Huntington, West Virginia and a member of the Communist Party. He came into the Congress of Industrial Organizations mining coal in West Virginia, a state where the United Mine Workers was a racially diverse organization and where the extent of interracial unity very much shaped the prospects of unionism. After an injury took him from the mines, Allen worked mainly in New York City as a factory operative, retail clerk, draftsman, a math teacher at Grace Church School, and later a mail handler, museum worker, and

---

11   Saxton, *The Great Midland*, xvii–xviii.

12   Alexander Saxton, "In Dubious Battle," *Pacific Historical Review*, 73 (2004), 260, n. 20.

13   Rydell, "Grand Crossings," 280 and passim; Alexander Saxton, *The Indispensable Enemy: Labor and the Anti-Chinese Movement in California* (Berkeley: University of California Press, 1971); Saxton, *Rise and Fall*.

librarian at Brooklyn Public Library. Leaving the Communist Party in the late 1950s, he was immediately active in the Provisional Organizing Committee to Reconstitute the Communist Party.[14]

In the 1960s Allen attempted to engage the New Left around the question of its "blindspot" around race and particularly what he saw as the formation of the white race as the real "peculiar institution" in US history. Allen's historical work sought to provide a firm grounding for the position that identification of some workers with the white race constituted the "Achilles heel" of US revolutionary possibilities. So much was this the case and so underdeveloped was thinking on the problem from the left that Allen titled a late 1960s work *Can White Radicals Be Radicalized?* with the word "Workers" included but then struck out in the title, prior to "Radicals." However, in sharp contrast with some others who embraced the term "white-skin privilege," such as the Weatherman tendency inside Students for a Democratic Society (SDS) and then after it, Allen's analysis regarded white workers as capable of being drawn to revolutionary actions. As they learned not be deterred from pursuing their long-term interests by meager and even pitiful short-term and relative advantages, such workers would, on this view, come to see struggles for liberation of other races as central to the movement of a class.[15]

As it was put in the title of a 1967 pamphlet to which Allen contributed, "Understanding and Fighting White Supremacy" became his dual tasks, inseparable and deadly serious. The simultaneous argument for both the overwhelming weight of race in social control throughout US history and the possibility that its weight could shift and change the momentum of struggles decisively made Allen elaborate history, and especially the colonial histories of Ireland and Virginia, very carefully. By the time of his 1975 pamphlet *Class Struggle and the Origin of Racial Slavery: The Invention of the White Race,* Allen had made the interracial Bacon's Rebellion the key event in his accounting of the turn to race as the centerpiece of class control

---

14   Jeffrey Perry, "In Memorium: Theodore W. Allen" (2002), clogic.eserver.org, 1–4; Jonathan Scott, "An Interview with Theodore W. Allen" (1998), clogic.eserver.org, 77–79.

15   Michael Staudenmaier, "Revolutionaries Who Tried to Think: A History of the Sojourner Truth Organization" (unpublished manuscript, 2010), 7–9; Perry, "In Memorium," 4–8; Michael Staudenmaier, "The White Skin Privilege Concept: From Margin to Center in Revolutionary Politics" (unpublished paper, 2007).

by Virginia's elite and in his subtitle he set out the agenda of his research over the next two decades. In his epic two volumes on that invention, the British development of intermediate control strata to enforce colonialism in Ireland provides not only a comparative case to seventeenth-century Virginia but also one whose lessons were inter-imperially deployed in ruling North American places. The effect of concentrating on the two cases is to divorce racial oppression from the timelessness of allegedly natural realities, to make it an historical phenomenon, but a very longstanding and often decisive one.

Allen's collaborator Noel Ignatin would also become a leading figure in writing the critical history of whiteness a quarter century later, by then writing under the name Noel Ignatiev. Ignatin, born in Philadelphia, dropped out of University of Pennsylvania in the early 1960s and for twenty-three years worked in Chicago and elsewhere in the steel, farm equipment, and electrical industries, gaining skills as an electrician and machinist. He met Allen around efforts to reconstitute a communist movement in the 1960s. The two joined forces on a pamphlet addressing white-skin privilege in 1967. Ignatin went from SDS to become a central figure in the Sojourner Truth Organization (STO) from its founding in 1969 through the 1970s. STO distinctively mixed Leninism, workplace- (but not trade union–) based organizing, attraction to the ideas on race, class, and nation of the Trinidadian revolutionary C.L.R. James, efforts at critical solidarity with Black and Puerto Rican revolutionaries, and close study of both US history and historical materialism generally. Active on many fronts, Ignatin particularly wrote on race and the working class, processing experiences within plants in the 1972 speech circulated internally as "Black Worker, White Worker" and published in 1974 as "Black Workers, White Workers." The talk, which described white workers' identity as the result of "sweetheart agreement" between the bosses and them. That agreement left bosses still bosses and workers as workers who had learned to "HUG THE CHAINS OF AN ACTUAL WRETCHEDNESS." The analysis was controversial even inside STO. When *Radical America* published it, editors issued objections in a sort preamble even as they ran the piece.[16]

---

16   Noel Ignatin, "Black Workers, White Workers," *Radical America*, 8 (1974), 40, 47,

Twenty years later Ignatiev's *How the Irish Became White* would wrestle with similar questions of how to balance consent and coercion as they intertwined in making some workers white in the nineteenth-century United States.

Though separated from Ignatiev in age by only a decade, my own experiences were those of a different political generation, joining a New Left late in its evolution in 1969 and coming to be an SDS leader in 1970 in a vibrant chapter on the isolated Northern Illinois University campus at a time when the organization had finished its national existence, but we were not told. My political experience in SDS, the revolutionary socialist Red Rose Bookstore Collective, and the pro-strike and anti-Nazi Chicago organization called Workers Defense featured very much an orthodox Marxist education, leavened by encounters with a declining movement for Black Power, with a rising movement for women's liberation, with surrealism, and with old-time libertarian Marxists gathered in the collective running the Charles H. Kerr Company, the world's oldest socialist publisher. I chaired Kerr's board in parts of the 80s and 90s. That my work is sometimes linked to the post- (and anti-) Marxism of Chantal Mouffe and Ernesto Laclau is thus remarkable in that I actually resisted much use of Antonio Gramsci's increasingly mainstreamed Marxist work as a concession to reformism. Similarly, the emphasis in some of my work on the coinage and usage of "keywords"—for example "boss," "master," and "greaser"—for better and worse came not from deep knowledge of what Arnesen calls "the growing appeal of cultural studies, with its emphasis on . . . word play," but from the British Marxism of Raymond Williams and the Russian Marxism of M.M. Bakhtin.[17]

and 41–60; Michael Staudenmaier, "Unorthodox Leninism: Workplace Organizing and Anti-Imperialist Solidarity in the Sojourner Truth Organization," in Dan Berger, ed., *The Hidden 1970s: Histories of Radicalism*, (New Brunswick, NJ: Rutgers University Press, 2010), 155–76, and "Revolutionaries Who Tried to Think," 11–27 and 31–37.

17   Cf. David Roediger, *The Wages of Whiteness: Race and the Making of the American Working Class* (New York: Verso 2007 [1991]), 17, n. 28 and n. 34, and Eric Arnesen, "Whiteness Studies and the Historians' Imagination," *International Labor and Working Class History*, 60 (October 2001), 4; on Laclau and Mouffe, see Sharon Smith, "Race, Class, and Whiteness Theory," *International Socialist Review*, 46 (March–April, 2006), isreview.org.

Similarly, the attempt in *Wages of Whiteness* to put the choices of antebellum white workers to define themselves as "not slaves" and "not black" in the context of processing the alienation and time discipline attendant on proletarianization, rather than simply in the context of interracial labor competition, was informed decisively by consideration of the work of the British Marxist historian E.P. Thompson.[18] When South African solidarity work became the focus of my activism in the late 80s and 90s, the attendant learning was again principally from Marxists, especially those attempting to open discussions of "racial capitalism," so that among the most cherished responses to *Wages of Whiteness* became for me Jeremy Krikler's attempt to adapt some of its ideas to South African history.[19]

For others, too, interventions in working-class struggles shaped scholarship on whiteness. The leading study of the labor process and the white worker came in Bruce Nelson's 2001 volume *Divided We Stand: American Workers and the Struggle for Black Equality*. Nelson dropped out of Berkeley to become a radical labor activist for most of the 1970s, working on a truck assembly line before pursuing a doctorate. Venus Green, whose magnificent *Race on the Line* remains the most insightful account of how whiteness functioned in a context of labor, skill, and law in one industry, labored and organized in the telephone industry that she studies for a long period before completing a Columbia Ph.D.[20] Karen Brodkin warmed up to writing her *How Jews Became White Folks* by completing a wonderful anthropological account of multiracial struggles of hospital workers, an account she cast as one of solidarity as well as scholarship. George Lipsitz, whose *The Possessive Investment in Whiteness* stands among the most-cited of the seminal works under consideration here, "enrolled in graduate school hoping to learn enough about labor history to understand our failure" after the rout of a radical

---

18   Roediger, *Wages of Whiteness*, 9, 95.

19   Jeremy Krikler, "Lessons from America: The Writings of David Roediger," *Journal of Southern African Studies*, 20 (December 1994), 663–69; Allison Drew and David Binns, "Prospects for Socialism in South Africa: An Interview with Neville Alexander," *Journal of Communist Studies and Transition Politics*, 8 (December 1992), 251–74.

20   Bruce Nelson's website at dartmouth.edu; Green, *Race on the Line*, ix–xi.

collective he joined in the early 1970s to support an oppositional rank-and-file caucus in a Teamsters Local in St. Louis.[21]

Several webs drew us partly together well before the 1990s, beyond the close collaboration of Ignatin and Allen. Lipsitz and I were in St. Louis, and around the same oppositional labor groups, at about the same time in the early 70s and came to know each other through mutual admiration for the St. Louis–based Marxist historian George Rawick, whose 1972 classic *From Sundown to Sunup: The Making of the Black Community* closed with an extended meditation on the origins and costs of whiteness. Rawick, Allen, and Ignatin all wrote widely circulated, often reprinted, and deeply provocative articles on race and class for the sometimes SDS-connected journal *Radical America*, also a major source of work by C.L.R. James, a major direct influence on Ignatin and, through Rawick, on Lipsitz and myself. My most reread source on James was the 1981 special issue of the Sojourner Truth Organization's special issue of *Urgent Tasks* devoted to him. Ignatin, Rawick, and I all wrote in that special issue.

In the late 1970s, when I met Ignatin in Chicago, it was through mutual friendships with members of the Chicago Surrealist Group, especially Penny and Franklin Rosemont, the latter of whom eventually produced a brilliant article on the history and logic of surrealism's critique of whiteness, published in *Race Traitor* under the coeditorship of Ignatiev. Although we disagreed on the role of trade unions at the time, a particular formulation in his *Radical America* reflections on Black and white workers had very much entered my consciousness: "the key problem is not the racism of the employing class, but the racism of the white worker (after all, the boss's racism is natural to him because it serves his class interests)."[22] As much as I now regard the two problems as inextricably linked, the emphasis on

---

21   George Lipsitz, "Conversations with Scholars of American Popular Culture: Featured Guest George Lipsitz," in *Americana: Journal of American Popular Culture 1900 to Present*, (2002), americanpopularculture.com, 4; Lipsitz, *Possessive Investment in Whiteness*; Brodkin, "Studying Whiteness Shouldn't Be Academic," *Borderlands E-Journal*, 3 (2004), borderlands.net.au, 1–3; Karen Brodkin Sacks, *Caring by the Hour: Women, Work, and Organizing at Duke Medical Center* (Urbana: University of Illinois Press, 1988).

22   Franklin Rosemont, "Surrealism: Revolution against Whiteness," *Race Traitor*, 9 (Summer 1998), 19–29; Noel Ignatin, "Black Workers, White Workers," 47.

the white worker's centrality to the racial order was a hard-won insight available in few other places on the left, save those dismissing white workers altogether.

When book-length works on whiteness and the "white blindspot" in US history began to appear, several major works appeared together in one series with the Haymarket list from Verso/New Left Books publishing the work of Saxton, Allen, and myself, under the editing of Mike Davis and Michael Sprinker. The Haymarket series likewise published Vron Ware's *Beyond the Pale* and Fred Pfeil's *White Guys* as early and important interventions in the newly developing field. I was the press's reader for Allen's works, offering little to improve his force and eloquence, but some advice on how to pare the manuscript's daunting length and to divide it into two volumes. When Verso later reissued Saxton's *White Republic*, I wrote the foreword.[23]

The extent and meaning of such connections can be overstated. For example, Allen and I met only once, despite his staying on a first-name basis throughout the writing of his massive critique "On Roediger's *Wages of Whiteness*." Nor, of course, did a common commitment to Marxism imply agreement on particulars, with the tone and content of that same Allen essay providing a good example, right down to Ted's rejection of the very term "whiteness."[24] (These, however, were political arguments in which it should be said that Allen's tone was far more balanced and comradely than glosses on his position have been.) The common choice by Ignatiev, Allen, and myself of the experiences of the Irish as keys to white racial formation makes sense in terms of Marx's and Engels's own emphases on the Irish as central to how the British working class was divided and ruled, but our various accounts of the Irish spin in very different directions, separated by centuries in time and an ocean in space.[25] In the balance of

---

23   Saxton, *Rise and Fall*.

24   Cf. Theodore Allen, "On Roediger's *Wages of Whiteness*" (2002), clogic.eserver.org, 1–27, and Gregory Meyerson, "Marxism, Psychoanalysis, and Labor Competition," *Cultural Logic* (1997), clogic.eserver.org.

25   Noel Ignatin, "White Blindspot," in Noel Ignatin and Ted Allen, eds., *Understanding and Fighting White Supremacy* (Chicago: Sojourner Truth Organization, 1967), sojournertruth.net, 9; Noel Ignatiev, *How the Irish Became White* (New York: Routledge, 1995), passim; David Roediger, *Wages of Whiteness*, 133–63; Theodore Allen,

this article, some of the differences among the early US writers of critical histories of whiteness will become clear, especially concerning the use of psychoanalysis. These were, however, difference among Marxists, not, as is sometimes argued, differences between Marxism and cultural studies. As Ignatiev puts it in characterizing of his work, mine, Saxton's, and Allen's, "what these works have in common . . . is that they take class struggle as their starting point"—class struggle, as we shall see, as theorized especially in a moment of high and grounded appreciation of the work of Black Marxists.[26]

In a high compliment marred only by his desire to be dismissive and offensive, the Princeton historian Sean Wilentz has called the critical study of whiteness "black nationalism by another means."[27] Some of the writers above might demur from the specific terminology, feeling a need to distinguish between narrow and revolutionary nationalisms or even to note the narrowness in all nationalism. However termed, in a broad sense the impact of African-American struggles and thought, especially in the moment of Black Power, shaped the critical study of whiteness decisively. Suddenly, there was a "white left" named as such and even developing self awareness and self critique. There was, after the mid-60s articulations of Black Power, after the statements of the Student Non-Violent Coordinating Committee on the need for white radicals to organize among whites and against white supremacy, and above all after tremendous motion by Black industrial workers in Detroit and elsewhere, a new possibility opened for a pamphlet like Allen's late-60s intervention *Can White Radicals Be Radicalized?* to be written and read. There was, as Ignatiev memorably put it in the early 70s, a "civil war in the mind" of some white workers as they reacted to the appeals of the energy and success of Black workers' struggles.[28]

The realization, as Ignatiev later wrote, that "as a matter of survival, the direct victims of white privilege have always studied it," became especially powerful in this context of glimmers of white left

---

Invention of the White Race, I: 52–158.

26   Noel Ignatiev, "Whiteness and Class Struggle," *Historical Materialism*, 11 (2003), 227–35.

27   Wilentz as quoted in Margaret Talbot, "Getting Credit for Being White," 119.

28   Noel Ignatin, "Black Workers, White Workers," 42.

self-awareness and of a too-often ignored continuing common work among Black and white radicals during the Black Power period.[29] He first, and I later, found especially much in the example and writing of James, whose longstanding insistence that struggles for African-American liberation were not separate from or subsidiary to the question of class became an important argument for the need to encourage white workers to support Black liberation as their struggle.[30] The approach to the connection of immigration and whiteness, and to the senses in which some despised and poor European immigrants "became white" in the United States, very much grew from the essays of James Baldwin. Most of these came to be collected in his *The Price of the Ticket*, the title of which connects whiteness, migration, and misery in the United States. But in terms of offering a "plot" for the racialized history of immigration, it was Baldwin's short, direct, and popular 1984 piece "On Being 'White' and Other Lies . . ." in the African-American fashion magazine *Essence* that gave us the decisive formulation: "White men—from Norway, for example, where they were *Norwegians*—became white: by slaughtering the cattle, poisoning the wells, torching the houses, massacring Native Americans, raping Black women." However much this dramatic rendering required more—for example, more of the sense and practice of race of the Irish in Ireland and the British empire before coming, it distilled a truth that opened tremendous intellectual space in immigration history. Ignatiev, who made me aware of the *Essence* article, most ably claimed that space in his *How the Irish Became White*.[31]

Such connections among African-American thought, Black Power, and the critical history of whiteness focused especially on multiple and longstanding apprehensions of the great African-American thinker and militant W.E.B. Du Bois. Du Bois's *Black*

---

29   Ignatiev, "Whiteness and Class Struggle," 228.

30   Scott McLemee, ed., *C.L.R. James on the "Negro Question"* (Jackson: University of Mississippi Press, 1996), passim.

31   James Baldwin, *The Price of the Ticket: Collected Nonfiction, 1848–1985* (New York: St. Martin's/Marek, 1985), esp. xix, 409–14, 425––33, and 667–75; David Roediger, ed., *Black on White*, 177–78 ("Norwegians"); Noel Ignatiev, "'Whiteness' and American Character: An Essay," *Konch*, 1 (Winter 1990), 136–39; Ignatiev, *How the Irish Became White*.

Reconstruction in America gave subsequent writers both the terminology and the model with which to undertake their tasks. Thus
Ignatin's and Allen's use of the term "white blindspot," both in their
1969 pamphlet and afterwards, modifies a line from that Du Bois
volume. In titling his article on race and shop-floor dynamics "Black
Worker, White Worker," Ignatin used the first two chapter titles
from Du Bois's masterpiece, the first work to problematize the "white
worker"; the very idea of the "wages of whiteness" came from *Black
Reconstruction*'s memorable phrase regarding the "public and psychological wage" afforded to poor white Southerners after the Civil War,
wages making them privileged and keeping them poor and in line.
Indeed, Ignatiev wrote in a 2003 essay in *Historical Materialism*,
"Among scholars it was W.E.B. Du Bois who first called attention to
the problem of the white worker."[32]

Within the Communist Party, and the web of relations to African-
American organizations it maintained, Saxton and Allen encoun-
tered Du Bois's ideas in a way unavailable within the white academic
mainstream, especially during the post–World War Two period in
which anti-communist repression sought to target and marginalize
Du Bois. Saxton, as it happened, shared both a hometown (Great
Barrington, Massachusetts) and a university (Harvard) with Du
Bois. And yet, as Saxton later wrote, neither place taught him about
Du Bois. "What I learned about Du Bois," he wrote, "I learned from
the Communist Party," whose literature representative sold Saxton
Black Reconstruction at a time when it was largely ignored. Similarly,
and despite the fact that the Communists ridiculously promoted
James Allen's *Reconstruction* as a more politically sound text than
Black Reconstruction, Theodore Allen's long experience in the Party
left him knowing enough of the latter work to make it the basis of
his rewriting of US history from the mid 1960s onward.[33] As the

---

32 Ignatiev, "White Blindspot," 243–51; Noel Ignatiev, "'The American
Blindspot': Reconstruction According to Eric Foner and W.E.B. Du Bois," *Labour/Le
Travail*, 31 (Spring 1993), 243 (on Du Bois on the "American Blindspot") and passim;
Perry, "In Memorium," 4; Roediger, *Wages of Whiteness*, 12; W.E.B. Du Bois, *Black
Reconstruction in America* (New York: Free Press, 1988 [1935]), 3–31 and 700–01
("public and psychological wage"); Ignatiev, "Whiteness and Class Struggle," 227
("first called attention").

33 Saxton, *The Great Midland*, xxiv; Ignatiev, "The American Blindspot," 250.

radical labor leader and historian Jeff Perry, Theodore Allen's literary executor, noted in a memorial after the latter's death, *Black Reconstruction* informed the design of Allen's historical writings from the start, namely mid-1960s attempts to overcome "the white blindspot" in a study of the Civil War, Populism, and the Great Depression. In reacting to what he rightly saw as unjust neglect of *Invention of the White Race* by scholars late in his life, Allen took comfort in the view that the dynamic called to mind "the 'white-centric' attitude that greeted the appearance of Du Bois' *Black Reconstruction*, the classic class-struggle interpretation of the history of the post-Civil War South." It was Allen who introduced *Black Reconstruction* to Ignatin.[34]

My own experiences in studying with the great African-American expert on Du Bois and on Black nationalism and class Sterling Stuckey likewise made for constant readings and re-readings of *Black Reconstruction*. Indeed, more broadly, when I collected the writings for the edited volume *Black on White: Black Writers on What It Means to Be White*, fully two-thirds of the selections were from classic readings in African-American history I had done with Stuckey. While it is most often pointed out that Du Bois's *Black Reconstruction* inspired the title of *Wages of Whiteness*, it structured the book multiply and even entirely.

It was the ability to be able to see profound motion and tragically persistent patterns regarding race—to place the self-activity of the Black worker and the whiteness of the white worker at the very center of US history—that made Du Bois so indispensable. When, for example, Ignatiev undertook an extended comparison of Du Bois's work on Reconstruction with the more-publicized accounts provided by Eric Foner, he insisted that the idea of a "general strike of the slaves"—so critical in Du Bois's view of war and emancipation and so attenuated in Foner—made the two works qualitatively different. At stake was the centrality of self-emancipation of slaves and the knowledge that this motion created the possibility that white workers might seek something more than being "not slaves."

---

34 Perry, "In Memorium," 4 ("blindspot"); Jonathan Scott and Gregory Meyerson, "An Interview with Theodore W. Allen" (1998), clogic.eserver.org, 1–2 ("white-centric"); Ignatiev, "The American Blindspot," 243, n. 1.

From the first line onward, Du Bois insisted that *Black Reconstruction* was "drama" and later that it was "tragedy" as well. Du Bois portrayed Black workers as at the center of everything, as "the real modern labor problem." Emancipation brought an "upward moving of white labor," but reassertions of white supremacy followed. In one of countless formulations that show Du Bois linking the origins of race with capitalism, but not adopting the farfetched view that white supremacy could not in turn be itself a decisive factor in class rule, he wrote that the "color caste founded and retained by capitalism" was during and after Reconstruction "adopted, forwarded and approved by white labor." In the post–Civil War South and the world, "when white laborers were convinced that the degradation of Negro Labor was more fundamental than the uplift of white labor, the end was in sight."[35]

In trying to explain why white labor acquiesced (and more) in such tragedies, all the while able to "discern in [them] no part of our labor movement," Du Bois produced the passage that came to give *Wages of Whiteness* its title.[36] The passage begins with an acknowledgement that the group under consideration, white Southern laborers during Reconstruction, "received a low wage," as they would have to in a devastated and defeated region. However, they "were compensated in part by a sort of public and psychological wage . . . because they were white." "Public deference and titles of courtesy" accrued to them, as did admission to parks and the best schools. Police "were drawn from their ranks," and legal structures, "dependent on their votes," kept them out of jail. The franchise had "small effect upon the economic situation," but much on perceptions of dignity, Du Bois adds, elaborating a litany of matters involving both policy and psychology. It has been objected that treating "the wages of whiteness" in significant measure as psychological seems to dismiss the material benefits also forthcoming, with Ignatiev allowing that I perhaps took the material dimensions for granted. This is true enough, but it also applies to Du Bois's attempts in the original to

---

35   Ignatiev, "The American Blindspot," 244 and passim; Du Bois, *Black Reconstruction in America,* 3 and 727 ("drama" and "tragedy"), 16 ("modern labor problem"), 30 ("upward moving" and "color caste"), and 347 ("degradation").

36   Du Bois, *Black Reconstruction in America,* 727.

show how a system worked when resources of rulers were so meager that little buying off of anyone was possible. My own task was also to describe a situation—the antebellum North—in which the small Black population meant that a labor market could not be shaped wholesale by racial competition and segmentation, and ideological, psychological, political, and cultural appeals to whites mattered much more than immediate economic self-interest. Ignatiev is quite right that this was not always and everywhere the case.[37]

In any case, the main criticism from outside of Marxism was of a much different order, and by its very extremity perhaps helped Ignatiev and me to see how close our positions were on a larger political spectrum. Arnesen, after a desultory attempt to develop and contextualize Du Bois's ideas on the "public and psychological wage," suddenly shifted gears in a featured *International Labor and Working Class History* essay to make Du Bois the problem. At first seeming—the writing exceptionally unclear—to accuse "whiteness studies" of adopting a superficial, decontextualized reading of Du Bois, he then accuses Du Bois himself of embodying a foolish "Marxism-lite." It then turns out that the "lite-ness" consists of adhering to the idea that workers have interests in common, not really one of the frothier notions of Marxism.[38]

Whatever else divided our views, it seems certain that Saxton, Allen, Ignatiev, and myself took for granted that Du Bois had made anything but a "lite" intervention into Marxism. Indeed, Paul Richards's 1970 article in *Radical America*, "W.E.B. Du Bois and American Social History: The Evolution of a Marxist" described Black Reconstruction as we all would have, not simply as Marxist but as central to any development of an "American Marxism." So ingrained was this assumption that my own placement of Du Bois after a section on the deficiencies of much Marxist writing was undoubtedly insufficiently great for this reason. Never imagining that Du Bois would be seen as a "post-Marxist," let alone as

37 Du Bois, *Black Reconstruction in America*, 700–01; Ignatiev, "Whiteness and Class Struggle," 230–31; David Roediger, *Wages of Whiteness*, 6–12; Allen, "On Roediger's *Wages of Whiteness*," 7.

38 Arnesen, "Whiteness and the Historians' Imagination," 9–11, esp. 10 ("lite"); Paul Richards, "W.E.B. Du Bois and American Social History: The Evolution of a Marxist," *Radical America*, 4 (1970), 62 and 56–61.

"Marxism-lite," I took for granted that *Black Reconstruction* developed, rather than departed from (or debased), Marxist theory. That position made sense among the milieu writing early critical histories of whiteness, but led regrettably to confusion among a broader audience and as time passed.[39]

Deriding any serious consideration of psychoanalytical insights has emerged as a point of overwrought unity between rightward-drifting critics like Arnesen and left ones like Gregory Meyerson.[40] But even here the debates ought to acknowledge that the use of the ideas of Freud and other psychoanalytical writers in *Wages of Whiteness* came out of Marxism and Black revolutionary traditions. A story regarding the great Marxist and psychoanalytical political scientist Michael Rogin perhaps provides a useful point of entry. When *Wages of Whiteness* appeared, even with the example of Saxton's *Rise and Fall of the White Republic* at hand, I worried that my work was beyond all boundaries of acceptability, even intelligibility, and would be roundly attacked. Before reviews much appeared, Rogin sent me a draft of his essay on the book, slated to appear in *Radical History Review*. I did not know him at the time, only his extraordinary scholarship. The generous and long review essay he wrote reassured me about the book's reception—indeed it put the book's arguments more clearly and adventuresomely than I had. But there was one problem: throughout the piece, in total dozens of times—the draft misspelled my name as "Roedinger." After hesitating, I contacted him with thanks and with the hope that corrections might be made. They were, but the real payoff was Rogin's response to me. He excitedly said that the error should be read as a tribute, an attempt to smuggle in an "n" so that all letters in his name would be in mine as well, making him a "father" of the book. The response underlined what I already knew, that Rogin took psychoanalysis more seriously than I. But it also sent me back to Rogin's *Fathers and Children: Andrew Jackson and the Subjugation of the American Indian*,

---

39   Richards, "W.E.B. Du Bois and American Social History," 62 and 56–61; Hartman, "The Rise and Fall of Whiteness Studies," 34 ("post-Marxist").

40   Arnesen, "Whiteness and the Historians' Imagination," 21–23; Meyerson, "Marxism, Psychoanalysis, and Labor Competition," passim; Frank Towers, "Projecting Whiteness: Race and the Unconscious in the History of Nineteenth Century American Workers," *Journal of American Culture*, 21 (Summer 1998), 47–57.

which I had remembered mainly for its "psychohistory," but which also tellingly deployed Marxist categories of accumulation and which featured a long first section, amounting to a third of the book, titled "White." In that sense, Rogin was rightly claiming, at the level of methods (including historical materialism) and content, to have been a "father" of critical histories of whiteness. When Saxton was a graduate student at Berkeley, Rogin, who later became a leading student of whiteness and immigration, was one of his mentors.[41]

While, like many New Left students, I read attempts to bring Marx and Freud together—Herbert Marcuse, Norman O. Brown, Juliet Mitchell, Eli Zaretsky, Wilhelm Reich, and above all Frantz Fanon—the specific possibility of applying insights from these works to race in US history came through appreciation of the closing chapters of George Rawick's *From Sundown to Sunup: The Making of the Black Community*. There Rawick departed from his classic history of slavery to probe modern racism more broadly, especially in its early phases after Europe's "discovery" of the Americas and expanded slave trade with Africa. During this transition to capitalism, Rawick argued, the various repressions of desire required to fashion societies and personalities devoted to the accumulation of capital exacted tremendous human costs. Especially among slave-traders and colonial slaveholders, white racism came to be developed, indeed invented, hard by such repressions. The Africans met and commoditized as part of the development of plantation economies came to be seen as embodiments not only of owned labor, but also of the desires that elites had only recently, and only partially, repressed. In organizing their own disappointments and desires, elites imagined Black workers as both degraded and as possessed of ties to nature, eroticism, and pre-capitalist work rhythms that held appeal even as they were deplored. In Rawick's memorable phrasing, "The Englishman," in such interactions, "met

41 Iain Boal, "In Memoriam [to Michael Rogin]" forensicgenesis.org, esp. on Rogin's ties to radical labor movements; Laura Mulvey, "Professor Michael Rogin," *Independent* (December 14, 2001), independent.co.uk; Michael Rogin, "Black Masks, White Skin: Consciousness of Class and American National Culture," *Radical History Review*, 54 (Fall 1992), 141–52; Michael Rogin, *Fathers and Children: Andrew Jackson and the Subjugation of the American Indian* (New York: Knopf, 1975), xxxiv, 2–3, 19–113, and 165–205; Rogin, *Blackface, White Noise*; Rydell, "Grand Crossings," 279.

the West African as a reformed sinner meets a comrade of his previous debaucheries," all the while creating "a pornography of his
former life." Rawick, who as my friend and mentor taught me much
about Marxism in the 70s and 80s, relied at key points on Marcuse,
Fanon, Freud, and especially on the Austrian-born Marxist associate of Freud, Wilhelm Reich. Reich's Nazi-era work attempted to
understand the "mass psychology of fascism," as based on character
structures wedded to both internalizing and dealing out misery.
Rawick called Reich's *Character Analysis* "that great underground
classic of modern thought" and held that his own analysis of white
supremacist and master-class ideology "could not have been written
without [Reich's] monumental attempt to relate Marx and Freud."
Rawick, a friend in the 1950s of Reich's socialist associate, the
psychoanalyst Erich Fromm, risked much in so deeply calling on
psychoanalysis. C.L.R. James, for whom Rawick served as personal
assistant in the 60s, found *From Sundown to Sunup* to be "the best
thing I have read on slavery," predicting it "will make history."
However, even James sharply registered displeasure with its Freudian
closing chapters. Nonetheless such risks were incurred from within
Marxism.[42]

My perhaps-too-simple analysis in *Wages of Whiteness* took
Rawick's work on race, slavery, and early capitalism into the
realm of Northern white working-class formation in the antebellum period. As proletarianization brought new losses of access to
the commons and new forms of time discipline and social regi-
mentation to far greater numbers of people, workers processed
loss by projecting onto Black workers what they still desired in
terms of imagined absence of alienation, even as they bridled at
being treated as slaves, or as "white niggers."[43] There were likewise other inspirations beyond Rawick, as I had begun close

---

42   George Rawick, *Listening to Revolt: Selected Writings of George Rawick.* (Chicago:
Charles H. Kerr Company, 2010), xlii (James's reaction); 102 ("reformed sinner"), 180,
n. 9 (on debts to Reich), and 31, 66, 162, and 93-119, generally; see also John Abromeit,
"Whiteness as a Form of Bourgeois Anthropology: Historical Materialism in the Work of
David Roediger, Max Horkheimer and Erich Fromm," *Radical Philosophy Review*, 16
(2013), 325–43.

43   David Roediger, "Notes on Working Class Racism," *New Politics*, 7 (1989), 61–67
explores specific debts to Rawick; Roediger, *Wages of Whiteness*, 66–84.

association with the surrealist movement where commitments to Marx and Freud coexisted. Especially through friendly debates with the surrealist writers Paul Garon and Franklin Rosemont, I increasingly learned about the older writings on racism of the important organizer of a global network of Marxist psychoanalysts, Otto Fenichel, and of Sándor Ferenczi, as well as the more recent work of Joel Kovel.[44]

As importantly still, there has come to be a sense that psychoanalysis was there at the beginning with Du Bois's choice to discuss a specifically "psychological wage" as central to white identity. The useful recent scholarship on Du Bois and psychoanalysis at times gravitates too easily towards connections between "double consciousness" and Freud's ideas. However, since Du Bois had not read Freud when he wrote about "double consciousness" in *The Souls of Black Folk* in 1903, such affinities had to exist at a high level of abstraction regarding ideas emerging among "intellectual contemporaries."[45] As Du Bois had it in his 1940 autobiography *Dusk of Dawn* it was in about 1930 that "the meaning and implications of the new psychology had begun slowly to penetrate my thought. My own study of psychology . . . had pre-dated the Freudian era, but it prepared me for it. I now began to realize that in the fight against race prejudice, we were not facing simply the rational, conscious determination of white folk to oppress us; we were facing the age-long complexes sunk now largely to unconscious habit and irrational urge . . ."[46] In 1935, midway between that realization and *Dusk of Dawn*, Du Bois published *Black Reconstruction*, which could thus hardly have used the phrase "psychological wage" lightly. There is a sense then in which the critic Andrew Hartman, though fully unsympathetic to

---

44 David Roediger, *Colored White: Transcending the Racial Past* (Berkeley: University of California Press, 2002), 40 and 252, n. 36. On Fenichel, see Russell Jacoby, *The Repression of Psychoanalysis: Otto Fenichel and the Political Freudians* (New York: Basic Books, 1983).

45 Peter Coviello, "Intimacy and Affliction: Du Bois, Race and Psychoanalysis," *MLQ: Modern Language Quarterly*, 64 (2003), 2 and 3–37; Christina Zwarg, "Du Bois on Trauma: Psychoanalysis, and the Would-Be Black Savant," *Cultural Critique*, 51 (2002), 1–39. All of the material on Du Bois and psychoanalysis benefitted from research by Donovan Roediger.

46 W.E.B. Du Bois, *Dusk of Dawn* (Piscataway, NJ: Transaction Publishers, 2009 [1940]), 295–96; Shannon Sullivan, "On *Revealing Whiteness*: A Reply to Critics," *Journal of Speculative Philosophy*, 21 (2007), 231–32.

the Freudian approach, is onto something in his overstatement that "Roediger furthers Du Bois's psychoanalysis," though I certainly did not know enough about Du Bois and Freud to see this dimension when I first wrote.[47]

As in the case of James's reaction to Rawick, some of the early writers of critical histories of whiteness deplored the bits of psychoanalysis in *Wages of Whiteness*. Allen in particular found "resort to the language of psychoanalysis" unfortunate, but he to a surprising extent joined the fray, praising much in the work of Kovel and Fanon, though on somewhat narrow bases, including the improbable view that Fanon "proceeded from Marxist economic determinist premises." Saxton's firm judgment was that "difficulties seem exceptionally severe for psychohistory because of its assumption that *real* causes are psychic ones that can be approached only through metaphorical interpretation." This stance so impresses Hartman that his review essay hinges its pronouncement that Saxton is the best historian of whiteness—I agree—on it. It so impresses Eric Arnesen that he exempts Saxton from even having to be considered within the benighted study of whiteness. However, Saxton's categorical pronouncements come as he explains why psychoanalysis cannot explain the origins of white supremacy, again a position with which I agree. Shortly thereafter, he discusses John Quincy Adams's views on *Othello* in a very different way and explains, "I am of course bringing forward an argument previously rejected, to the effect that white European Americans constructed metaphors linking African blackness to shameful actions and to the dark passions of sexuality." He continued, "While I consider this [psychohistorical] argument unpersuasive as an explanation for the initiation of African slavery, it seems to work plausibly well when placed in a dependent relationship to prior ideological productions"—also a position with which I agree.[48]

Ignatiev meanwhile found that *Wages of Whiteness* "errs" by losing track of "attendant material advantage" without which there could

---

47 Hartman, "Rise and Fall of Whiteness Studies," 35.

48 Saxton, *Rise and Fall*, xvi, 13 ("exceptionally severe"), and 89 ("previously rejected"); Hartman, "The Rise and Fall of Whiteness Studies," 35–36; Arnesen, "Whiteness and the Historians' Imagination," 27, n. 4, and 31, n. 83.

hardly be sustained "psychological value of the white skin." However, he added, "I do not know enough about psychoanalysis to venture a judgment on how much it can explain by itself." Rogin, Rawick, and Rosemont, on the other hand very much championed the use of psychoanalysis, though not by itself. Like so much else, this is a question on which Marxists differ, though not as starkly as some retrospective accounts of early critical white histories imply.[49]

A closing clarification of just what is claimed in this article is apposite: the argument is that the Marxist left generated the most influential early historical studies of whiteness in the US past. The claim is not that by virtue of their historical materialist origins that those works are therefore correct or complete. Indeed many of the gaps in my work particularly might better be traced to their origins in the specific debates and movements I have outlined above. The relative inattention to gender, which Allen remarked on near the end of his life, is one example. I have attempted with mixed success in later works to remedy this blindspot, which weakened *Wages of Whiteness*, but to date more by adding rather than fundamentally rethinking the whole ensemble of social relations. We would have been better poised, perhaps, if we had followed James Baldwin's relationship to psychoanalysis, with its rich dimensions of sexuality and gender as well as race, as well as Du Bois's invocation of psychology. Similarly, as my exchange with Rogin suggested, the classic Marxist debates are much more at home discussing the relation of whiteness to slavery than to settler colonialism, another problem only beginning to be addressed in my own work.[50] Likewise it seems possible that a particular desire to unearth the story of how white workers forwarded racism left the relationship of whiteness to capital and to management relatively underdeveloped.[51] But however deep these

49   Ignatiev, "Whiteness and Class Struggle," 230–31.

50   Robyn Wiegman, "Whiteness Studies and the Paradox of Particularity," *boundary 2*, 26 (Autumn 1999), 115–50; Scott and Meyerson, "An Interview with Theodore W. Allen," 3–5; Roediger, *Colored White*, 103–37, and Roediger, *How Race Survived US History*, 12–29, 51–63, and 127–28; Jean-Paul Rocchi, "Dying Metaphors and Deadly Fantasies: Freud, Baldwin and Race as Intimacy," *Human Architecture: Journal of the Sociology of Self-Knowledge*, 7 (March 2009), 159–77.

51   Elizabeth Esch and David Roediger, "'One Symptom of Originality': Race and the Management of Labour in United States History," *Historical Materialism*, 17 (December 2009), 3–43.

deficiencies, which might make us as Marxists think about the possibility that we do have much to learn from other bodies of theory, it remains the case that both the errors and the considerable strengths in early critical histories of whiteness grew out of Marxism, in specific political moments.

CHAPTER 3

A White Intellectual among Thinking Black Intellectuals: George Rawick and the Settings of Genius

I was in the crowd for perhaps the last public talk by my friend George Rawick, given at University of Missouri at St. Louis in 1988. Serious health problems, which would soon take his life, weighed on the meandering lecture. In the question-and-answer period, the anthropologist Enoch Page focused matters and engaged George around the then-new Spike Lee film *School Daze*, and the ways it commented on intra-racial class conflict. When the questions turned to color prejudice in the black community—a topic so productive of keen interest and easy conclusions that "everybody's prejudiced" among some white students—George was fully transformed. Now lecturing forcefully, he did not speak for suppressing discussion of the issue, but for framing it. Such prejudices had wicked force, and material foundation, during and after slavery, he observed. But from the mixing of various African ethnicities into an African-American people to the care of mixed race children during the Jim Crow era, he asked, did not the uncommon ability of Black communities to incorporate difference, even across the color line, constitute the main story, especially if the white community was the object of comparison?[1]

---

1 For a little more on my own relationship with Rawick, much more detail on his biography, and the texts of his most important writings, see George P. Rawick, *Listening to*

I heard in the way that a very ill Rawick warmed to that particular topic an index of his political and historical commitments, but also one fully leavened by his autobiography. He and I, a quarter century apart in age, bonded during the fifteen years prior to his death not only over thinking about history and revolutionary commitments together but also because we both intensely felt ourselves the beneficiaries of the openness of Black communities, movements, and intellectuals. At a post–Black Power time when white left common sense had it that Black nationalism had driven white radicals from the interracial beloved community of civil rights, he was frequently a spokesperson for Facing Reality, a group led by C.L.R. James, perhaps the senior Black radical intellectual most admired by young Black Power advocates. I was mentored and embraced as a young student and writer by the great Black left-nationalist historian Sterling Stuckey, despite my headlong and headstrong retreats from African-American topics. Indeed, I was later shocked to learn that Stuckey was seen by some liberal writers as wanting to erect racial boundaries in the beloved community of scholars studying African-American history, as my experience was just the opposite. When Rawick and I met in restaurants and coffee shops and ultimately in nursing homes and hospitals in St. Louis, we shared, often unspoken, a sense of great good fortune that thinking Black intellectuals had helped us find voices. This article makes no claims that we shared an experience exactly, and still less that Rawick's very idiosyncratic life typified anything about infinitely varied white intellectuals and an equally heterogeneous Black intellectual tradition. Instead it is the peculiar and unfinished nature of collaboration in Rawick's case that makes his story revealing of the ways in which white intellectuals variously have entered Black intellectual life.

Rawick described his mid-1950s political transformation away from the certainties of the "white left"—the very term would have been a new one among white radicals at the time if it were used at all—with a startling simplicity that telescoped truths and, as we shall see, somewhat outran reality at times. Rawick told me in a published

Revolt: The Selected Writings of George P. Rawick, David Roediger with Martin Smith, eds. (Chicago: Charles H. Kerr, 2010), with afterwords by Enoch Page, Ferruccio Gambino and George Lipsitz. Thanks to Martin Smith and to the late Franklin Rosemont for assistance with this article.

interview from 1989 that an anonymous Black thinker turned him around:

> The Young Socialist League had a meeting. Bayard Rustin had been to Montgomery where he met Martin Luther King and had run some workshops on nonviolence. After the meeting a black worker asked me what we wanted them to do. I asked him what he wanted to do . . . We were interrupted and then he wandered off. I realized that I had no program. He went away without any answer . . . I had recently been at an NAACP [National Association for the Advancement of Colored People] meeting and was put down for having a program. There were ten other white radicals who had come to present programs; all were variants of "Join Us" coupled with some abstractions . . . I found that "Join Us!" provoked a deep silence.

In that silence, Rawick also discovered a commitment to oral history and other forms of investigation of the central role of the unheralded, and especially of slaves, in history and in struggle.[2]

In accounting for how he later came to write the pathbreaking history of slavery *From Sundown to Sunup: The Making of the Black Community* and to edit, under the title *The American Slave: A Composite Autobiography*, upwards of 10,000 pages of published narratives by (extra)ordinary ex-slaves, Rawick credited a particular and celebrated Black intellectual, recalling:

> In 1964 in London, C.L.R. James told me, I want you to give a lecture here, in [James's] living room, on American history. After the lecture he asked, "What do we know about the slaves' reaction to slavery?" I told him not a hell of a lot. He asked, "Is there any material we have?" I told him what little I knew of the slave narratives. That began the process of my collecting and publishing *The American Slave*.[3]

---

2   "Black Freedom and the WPA Slave Narratives: Dave Roediger Interviews George Rawick" in Don Fitz and Dave Roediger, eds., *Within the Shell of the Old: Essays on Workers' Self-Organization* (Chicago: Charles H. Kerr Company, 1990), 9–10.

3   Ibid.

Placing himself physically, politically and eventually professionally among thinking Black intellectuals, Rawick became one of the most important intellectuals bridging the old left and the new, as well as perhaps the US thinker most able to envision how a history of the whole working class might be written.

From 1964, when he finished and signed the long manifesto/article "The American Negro Movement" until the mid 1970s when his health began to seriously fail, Rawick was arguably the most influential student of the US working class, although he is almost never counted among the founders of the "new labor history" that emerged in that period. He published the most important historical articles in *Radical America*, the Students for a Democratic Society–associated journal, and impacted greatly such radical scholars as Peter Linebaugh, Franklin Rosemont, Noel Ignatiev, Enoch Page, Robin D.G. Kelley, Rosemary Feurer, Huw Beynon, Margaret Washington, Bruno Cartosio, George Lipsitz, Nando Fasce, Ferruccio Gambino, and Peter Rachleff. His influence on Eugene Genovese, then the leading US Marxist historian of slavery, led to major changes in the latter's presentation of slave resistance, if not to all that Rawick might have wanted. Eric Foner at the time found *Sundown to Sunup* superior to any other recent history of slave culture and equally astute on the history of racism. Genovese termed it "the most valuable work I know by a white man on slave life in the United States." August Meier and Elliott Rudwick's 1986 study *Black History and the Historical Profession* counted Rawick as the first historian to place the slave community at the center of his analysis.[4] There were two crowning glories. First was the incredible appearance of more than forty volumes of slave recollections, done without massive grants

    4   Eric Foner, as quoted in Greenwood Press publicity materials on the book, at greenwood.com. Genovese's review, "Getting to Know the Slaves," from the *New York Review of Books* (September 21, 1972) is, with a wealth of further reviews, clipped in the George Rawick Papers (hereafter cited as GRP), Western Historical Manuscript Collections, Jefferson Library, University of Missouri at Saint Louis, box 3, folder 15. Further reviews are in GRP, box 4, folders 17 and 20; see also August Meier and Elliott Rudwick, *Black History and the Historical Profession, 1915-1980* (Urbana: University of Illinois Press, 1986), 255, and John Hope Franklin, "Afro-American History: State of the Art," *Journal of American History*, 75 (June, 1988), 168. Alex Lichtenstein's otherwise useful, "In Retrospect: George Rawick's *From Sundown to Sunup* and the Dialectic of Marxian Slave Studies," *Reviews in American History*, 24 (1996), 723, understates the book's impact.

(though with important help from Ken Lawrence, Jan Hillegas, and others) and, through much of his career, without a tenured job. The second involved a remarkable, for his time and still, ability to write about the history of slavery and that of industrial workers together, indeed an impressive inability to write about them apart or even to read the daily papers without thinking of slave resistance.

Rawick's essays concentrating centrally on slavery, and those focusing on the industrial working class, reflected brilliant insights into the ways in which race and class worked, and worked together, in US history. His 1969 *Radical America* article "Working Class Self-Activity" popularized the term used in its title in and beyond the United States. It pinpointed how the mass industrial unions of the 1930s—organizations whose successes Rawick brilliantly situated transnationally alongside the degradation of other working classes in the 30s by fascism, Nazism, and Stalinism—came to be: "The unions did not organize the strikes; the working class in the strikes and through the strikes organized the unions."[5] Even *Sundown to Sunup* leaves, though it does not really completely leave, the every-night life of slaves in its two brilliant materialist and psychoanalytical final chapters, concentrating there on capitalism and on the white racism that shaped the slave's existence. The Italian writer Ferruccio Gambino has best taken the measure of these chapters, writing of how they showed that "the taming of the sexual impulse according to a new work schedule and fatigue, the dictatorship of the season-less clock, [and] the postponement of gratification as a virtue *per se* led whites to justify [racial] superiority."[6]

Rawick's most significant insight—if he wrote nothing else these words alone would establish him as a critically important contributor to the history of slavery—came when he intervened in 1968 in stalled, ill-premised debates over whether more slaves were rebellious "Nat Turner" types or quiescent, damaged "Sambo" figures. After expressing indebtedness to the passages on slavery and contradiction in Hegel's *Phenomenology of Mind*, Rawick held, "The slave struggles

5 George P. Rawick, "Working Class Self-Activity," *Radical America*, 3 (March, 1969), 23–31.

6 Ferruccio Gambino, "In Memory of George P. Rawick: Sizing Up the Magnitude of Dismantling Racism," *1999 Zeischrift für Soziolgeschichte des 20. und 21 Jahrhunderts 17*, (2002 [1991]), 109–10.

with the master by struggling with his [own] internal dilemmas . . . unless the slave is simultaneously Sambo and revolutionary, Sambo and Nat Turner, he can be neither Sambo nor Nat Turner."[7] Near the end of *Sundown to Sunup*, Rawick stood the traditional left anxiety about race struggles diverting workers from perceiving class interests squarely on its head: "The pressure of Blacks for equality intensifies all social conflicts in the US."[8] While almost everyone at the time would have read his "The American Negro Movement" as highly unorthodox "Negro history," Rawick saw it a down payment on the broader history of "the making of the American working class" as well. His emphasis, like that of his friend Vincent Harding, the great African-American theologian and historian, and of Stuckey, fell always on how African-American history and self-activity changed how we view the whole history of the United States, a history Black people created, partook of, and stood in a position to indict.[9] In that sense all of his most telling insights, including those not "about race," stemmed from immersion in African-American thought and revolt.

Indeed, it is tempting to ask whether Rawick, a white, very sporadically observant Jewish American, ought to be placed among the significant Black intellectuals of the late twentieth-century United States. This article does not ask that question, sharing as it does Rawick's own appreciation for the difficulties of transcending race—even as he sometimes moved spectacularly across racial lines— in a highly unequal racial order. But the article does hope to consider

---

7   George P. Rawick, "The Historical Roots of Black Liberation," *Radical America*, 2 (July–August 1968), 1–13; see also George P. Rawick, "Some Notes on a Social Analysis of Slavery: A Critique and Assessment of *The Slave Community*" in Al-Tony Gilmore, ed. *Revisiting Blassingame's The Slave Community: The Scholars Respond* (Westport, CT: Greenwood Press, 1978), 21–22 n. 6 on Hegel.

8   Rawick, *Sundown*, 159

9   Rawick, "The American Negro Movement," *International Socialism*, 16 (Spring 1964), 16–24, online at marxists.org; "Paul Buhle Interviews George Rawick" [hereafter "OHAL interview"], Oral History of the American Left, housed at Tamiment Institute of Bobst Library at New York University. (The interview took place on October 4, 1984; the first of its two audiotapes is lost, but a master recording is available to researchers.); Meier and Rudwick, *Black History and the Historical Profession*, 206–11. Rawick insisted on the 1964 article as a basis for the whole "history of the American working class" even in his C.V., filed in the Rawick Papers, box 1, folder 1. See also George P. Rawick to Dear Vince[nt Harding] (May 20, 1974), Rawick Papers, box 6, folder 46.

how Rawick as a particular, even peculiar, figure entered a distinct part of the world of thinking Black intellectuals and strugglers. That Rawick most intensely participated in that world during the middle and late 1960s, at a time when standard accounts posit that Black Power sent or perhaps banished whites, and particularly Jews, from interracialism, and that he did so in concert with leading Black nationalists, makes his story particularly worth retelling. Among its lessons are that the shared elaboration of ideas and freedom dreams cut against any hard lines keeping white activists apart from Black thought and struggle, and that transnational dimensions of Black social movements could in particular engage a white intellectual. Another lesson is that a grounded appreciation of the ways in which "Black" functioned as a political category of resistance formed in specific historical contexts actually left, as Stuckey emphasizes, the nationalist tradition often quite open to alliances with whites.[10] Finally, Rawick's case suggests that entering the world of radical Black intellectuals was no panacea promising a settled wisdom or success in what James called the pursuit of happiness. Rawick entered no utopia but rather a new terrain with new tensions—though within Facing Reality those tensions almost never hinged directly on race.

A White Leftist: Young Rawick, Red Miseries, and Brushes against Race

In the first thirty years of his life, Rawick hardly seemed bound for intellectual and political adventures within Black intellectual traditions, although race touched his life at almost all decisive turns. He grew up in a Brooklyn, New York community of first- and second-generation Jewish Americans. In his personal papers his Bar Mitzvah announcement sits hard by a youth award from the American Legion. His family's home abutted the headquarters of the Lubavitcher movement and he was raised by orthodox and observant Jews. In a family of "radical rabbis and failed businessmen," one

---

10 Sterling Stuckey, *Slave Culture: Nationalist Theory and the Foundations of Black America* (Oxford: Oxford University Press, 1987).

grandfather was both a socialist and a rabbi. Rawick took after-school classes preparing him for rabbinical training and showed a political bent. At Erasmus Hall, the high-achieving Brooklyn high school he attended, his school years overlapped with those of opera star Beverly Sills and boxing kingpin Bob Arum as well as Selma Weinstein, already drawn to the Trotskyist left, and eventually to become Selma James, C.L.R.'s wife. The world was first learning the new word "racism" as Rawick went through school and it initially applied to the systematic terror Hitler directed against Jews. As letters from relatives under Nazi rule stopped coming and his family feared the worst, Rawick moved briefly to communist politics. A friend signed his high school yearbook "To a fellow Pinko." He joined the Communist Party–influenced American Youth for Democracy before graduating, in either 1944 or 1945.[11]

Rawick wanted out of Jewish Brooklyn. Professing a desire "to the United States to go to college," he chose Oberlin in Ohio, which he soon regarded as "the world center of hypocrisy, racism, anti-Semitism, and premature McCarthyite intimidation of its leftist students and faculty." Oberlin nonetheless pointed Rawick towards civil rights activism. He came to disdain the institution for its betrayal of its great abolitionist heritage by keeping down the local Black community, which Rawick portrayed as a colony in the "company town" set up by the college. He became a candidate-member of the Communist Party (CP) in the branch in Lorain, Ohio, a city with a significant Black working class—as well as Toni Morrison's heavy industrial hometown. But Rawick found little room for maneuver, creativity, or happiness in his own short stay in the orbit of the CP. The CP venture in which Rawick most participated, support for Henry Wallace's Progressive Party presidential campaign in 1948, impressed him not for its real anti-racist accomplishments but for its dire defeat.

---

11   "OHAL Interview;" Joe Pollack, "Teacher, Activist, Friend," *St. Louis Post-Dispatch* (July 22, 1990), Rawick Papers, box 1, folder 1; Gambino, "In Memory of George P. Rawick," 104–05, and his afterword to Roediger with Smith, eds., *Listening to Revolt*, 136–47; Joe Pollack's email to author (December 29, 2008); Rawick, "I Dissent" in Paul Buhle, ed., *History and the New Left: Madison, Wisconsin, 1950–1970* (Philadelphia: Temple University Press, 1990), 54; Rawick's high school year book, *The Arch* (June 1947) is in Rawick Papers, box 1, folder 2, which also holds the Bar Mitzvah announcement.

He recalled that the campaign managed to revive "snatches of the melody" from the CP initiatives of the 30s but proved to be the point when "the political energies of the Popular Front . . . reached their final spasm." He worked briefly for Vito Marcantonio, the CP-supported congressman perhaps most representing left interracialism in politics, but at Marcantonio's Washington, DC office, far from his Harlem political base.[12]

Accounts of Rawick's expulsion from the Communist youth movement vary, but most follow his Oral History of the American Left interview in recording the charge as "chauvinism," or more fully and ridiculously, alleged support for "anti-semitism, male chauvinism, and Jim Crow." The latter two charges rested on an accusation that Rawick had declined to dance—he explained that he did not know how to dance—with an African-American comrade at a meeting of a party-influenced group in Cleveland. One of the party youth leaders approving the expulsion was the young Robert Fogel, later an anything-but-radical economist and historian of slavery and a Nobel laureate, who also aided the expulsion of Genovese though that case was separate from Rawick's.[13]

Rawick processed his misadventures around the CP in early articles—one in *South Atlantic Quarterly*—on student movements and on Communist rigidities.[14] Politically he moved in the early 1950s to the Independent Socialist League (ISL), a small but very active collection of radicals led by Max Shachtman, who critiqued the Soviet Union as a no-longer-revolutionary "bureaucratic collectivist" state. Descended

---

12 The fullest oral history with Rawick, punctuated well by a meowing cat, is by an unnamed Italian visitor and was done on September 11, 1987. It is in the Rawick Papers, box 7, folder 45, tapes 45–46. Despite Rawick's health at the time, the patience of the interviewer, unfortunately unidentified, elicited remarkable responses, including that on the quote on the decision to attend Oberlin. Hereafter the 1987 oral history is cited as "1987 Interview." See also "OHAL Interview;" Rawick, "I Dissent," 54–55 and Pollack, "Teacher, Activist, Friend."

13 "Gene Genovese to Dave Roediger" (November 18, 2008) in possession of the author; Lichtenstein, "In Retrospect," 715; "OHAL Interview." See also Kent Worcester's *C.L.R. James: A Political Biography* (Albany: State University of New York Press, 1995), 227.

14 George Rawick, "The American Student: A Profile," *Dissent*, 1 (Autumn 1954), 393; George Rawick, "From Faith to Dogma: The Communist Party Line, 1928–1939," *South Atlantic Quarterly*, 53 (April 1954), 193–202.

from Trotskyism, the ISL made sense as a reaction against what Rawick was coming to call Stalinism, and as a platform from which a young graduate student could rapidly and impressively learn Marxist theory, journalistic writing, and how to speak forcefully in public. In short order he became a frequent contributor to, and then editor of, the youth and cultural magazine *Anvil*. His articles similarly proliferated in the ISL's *Labor Action* and *New International*, sometimes under the pseudonyms George Post or George Rawlings. He rubbed elbows with such figures as the labor and pacifist leader A.J. Muste, the popular psychologist Erich Fromm, the novelist Harvey Swados, and the sociologist C. Wright Mills, whose words in *Anvil* he claimed at times to have ghost-written from notes.[15]

Nonetheless, the ISL also involved Rawick in deep unhappiness. As he wrote in a short piece for a 1981 symposium on surrealism, he increasingly felt as the 50s wore on that he lived in a left that "was not red—it was grey." All was too serious. The "Grand Scientists" of Marxism "were all very serious." They had "to be P*R*O*P*E*R*L*Y T*R*A*I*N*E*D by other Grand Scientists," men who prized planning "just like capitalists, only more so." He chafed at a socialism that promised little that was grander than "more long tons of steel"— one in which comrades "bored each other to tears (no one else listened)" as they forgot that Marxism was "not political economy but rather the critique of political economy." The New York intellectuals, as the Jewish anti-Stalinist left centered in that city styled itself, came to be seen by Rawick as part of "a pretty disgusting world" hostile to popular culture and popular politics. Nevertheless, Rawick "was part of it . . . had aspirations toward it," and was capable of flaying himself because he "never made it" in ways that those who moved out of ISL to lead sectarian groups of their own or to

---

15   The relationship with Mills best conveys the dynamics involved, in which confidence born of sectarian politics served Rawick both well and poorly. See esp. "C. Wright Mills to Dear Mr. Rawick" (February 9, 1957), Rawick Papers, box 7, folder 44; "Rawick to Dear Dr. Curti" (February 28, 1955) in Merle Curti Papers, Special Collections, State Historical Society of Wisconsin box 34, folder 24. "1987 Interview" and "OHAL Interview;" George Rawick, "The Sociology of C. Wright Mills" (unpublished typescript, also undated), Rawick Papers, box 3, folder 13; Mills, "The Complacent Young Men," *Anvil*, 18 (Winter 1958), 13ff, reprinted in Irving Louis Horowitz, ed., *Power, Politics, and People: The Collected Essays of C. Wright Mills* (New York: Oxford University Press, 1963), 387–94; George Rawick, "The Powerful," *Anvil*, 16 (Winter 1957), 7.

provide leadership to the more and less hawkish wings of the Democratic Party might have seemed to. He was, he said, "insufficiently cynical" to be a successful sectarian New York intellectual, but he was cynical enough to want to be one.[16]

Where popular culture was concerned, Rawick also decidedly counted himself retrospectively as part of the problem. He belonged in a group that cultivated "a certain puritanical quality [being] only interested in 'serious' things." Seeking to be "divorced from the ordinary," Rawick tried to "systematically cut [himself] off from [his] family" in Brooklyn. A kid who was "totally unaware of comics," a young adult who "never liked movies," and a sports fan whose interests stayed confined to the Brooklyn Dodgers, who themselves moved forthwith to Los Angeles, Rawick fit perfectly.[17] He specifically distanced himself also from the "beat generation" of cultural dissent in the 50s, identifying them, distinctly negatively, with "narcotics, liquor, be-bop, and sexual promiscuity," until warming to the beat poet Lawrence Ferlinghetti late in the 50s because the latter so supported left projects.[18] Politically, the Shachtmanite tendency to fear the Soviet Union at least as much as it desired radical change in the United States led, Rawick came to think, to a calculus predicated not on judging how far workers might be prepared to go but rather how far struggles could go without aiding the Soviets. "When the main enemy was not at home," Rawick eventually concluded, "there could be no revolutionary perspective."[19]

At the time that Rawick encountered the anonymous Black worker after Rustin's speech on Montgomery, he was being pulled in many directions. "We were trying," Rawick later said of the 1950s, "to find new paths away from the Old Left." He by then knew Rustin, as well as the Chicago African-American street poet Joffre Stewart, from

---

16   George Rawick, "Symposium on Surrealism," *Cultural Correspondence*, 12–14 (Summer 1981), 69, and "1987 Interview"; Alan M. Wald, *The New York Intellectuals: The Rise and Decline of the Anti-Stalinist Left from the 1930s to the 1980s* (Chapel Hill: University of North Carolina Press, 1987) provides context and a far more sympathetic view of the New York intellectuals.

17   "1987 Interview" and "OHAL Interview."

18   "1987 Interview" and "OHAL Interview." Cf. "Rawick to Dear Dr. Curti" (January 8, 1956), Curti Papers, box 34, folder 24, and "Rawick to Dear Merle" (December 10, 1959 and August 4, 1960) in Curti Papers, box 34, folder 24.

19   "OHAL Interview."

anti–Korean War activism. Indeed, to his death Rawick delighted in telling a story illustrating Rustin's style and fearlessness. While he was out drinking with Rustin during the Korean War and Red Scare, eavesdroppers took offense at what they heard as "commie" bar talk. Rustin rose up and dramatically intoned, "Sir, I am a Negro, a pacifist and a homosexual. What more do you require of me?"[20] Rawick realized early on that the maturing freedom struggle held great promise, with his earliest editorial contributions to *Anvil*, and many of his own articles, covering civil rights. But Shachtmanism itself brought Rawick few contacts with Black activists, and fewer still with Black ISL members. Predecessors of the ISL tendency had generated significant debates on race and socialist theory in large part because for a time C.L.R. James and Shachtman had cohabited in the same formation, even as they expressed differences regarding the former's support of the right of self-determination among Blacks and the latter's insistence on a class-centered integrationism. But by the time Rawick joined, James and his followers had moved on and the assumption that Black people needed a program developed by the white revolutionary left was little challenged.[21]

Nor did Rawick's academic life provide him with either a deep knowledge of Black life and history, or a secure position from which to listen to the struggles of others, positions that would have left him less surprised by the post-Montgomery world. His embattled career as a doctoral student at University of Wisconsin had him thinking deeply of race, but mostly via the subtle and not-so-subtle experiences of anti-Semitism directed against himself. He entered the history program with two fellow students who also would become leading radical scholars of the 60s, 70s, and 80s, Herbert Gutman and Warren Susman, with the three being, he recalled, the first

---

20   See Joffre Stewart, "The Home to May Day," in David R. Roediger and Franklin Rosemont, eds., *Haymarket Scrapbook* (Chicago: Charles H. Kerr Company, 1986), 241; "OHAL Interview." On Rustin and Shactmanism, see John D'Emilio, *Lost Prophet: The Life and Times of Bayard Rustin* (Chicago: University of Chicago Press, 2004), 252 and 277–78. The great Rustin story recounted here was one Rawick frequently repeated to me.

21   See Christopher Phelps's introduction to Max Shachtman, *Race and Revolution* (New York: Verso, 2003); George Rawick, "The Negro Fights for Freedom," *Anvil*, 17 (Fall 1957), 3–5; George Post [Rawick], "CP's New Line Woos the Negroes," *Labor Action* (May 21, 1956), 2.

cohort of openly Jewish graduate students in the department's history. Both Gutman and Susman died even before Rawick, a fact he often put down in part to what all had to swallow from the "group of old fossils" running the department. In Paul Buhle's edited volume of mostly luminous reminiscences of Madison by radical historians *History and the New Left*, Rawick called his short contribution "I Dissent." It led off with "I, for one, never found the Holy Land to be located in the Department of History of the University of Wisconsin–Madison, 1951–1957, particularly not in American history."[22]

Although he learned much about listening to the voices of the voiceless from Merle Curti's democratic sensibilities and pioneering social history methods, Madison was hardly a place to study race. After a year there lacking financial aid, he transferred briefly to Cleveland's Western Reserve University, studying there with the noted historian of slavery Harvey Wish, in the same graduate program that was training Bernard Mandel, the pioneering historian of labor and race and a white writer who later proclaimed that by virtue of his study, politics, and interracial private life he had become Black.[23] But Rawick returned to Madison after a year and dissertated on youth movements and the state in the New Deal, an opportunity to revisit the history of the CP, though in a work finding its greatest life in brief sections discussing racism and militarization in welfare programs and anticipating New Left analyses of the New Deal as a state capitalist initiative. A remarkable section in the chapter on "The CCC [Civilian Conservation Corps] and the Negro" described armed self-defense by Black CCC workers in Monroe, North Carolina—where Robert Williams would soon make such self-defense famous.[24]

---

22   Rawick, "I Dissent," 54–55, "OHAL Interview," and reminiscences of my own conversations with Rawick.

23   Rawick, "I Dissent," 54–56; on Western Reserve University and Mandel, see Brian Kelly's introduction to the reissued Bernard Mandel, *Labor, Free and Slave: Workingmen and the Anti-Slavery Movement in the United States* (Urbana: University of Illinois Press, 2007), esp. xiii–xiv.

24   George P. Rawick, "The New Deal and Youth: The Civilian Conservation Corps, the National Youth Administration, and the American Youth Congress," (unpublished Ph.D. diss., University of Wisconsin, 1957), 158–59 and 137–70; Philip Altbach, *Student Politics in America: A Historical Analysis* (Edison, NJ: Transaction Books, 1997), 106, n. 28; George Rawick, "A New Look at the New Deal: Rhetoric and Reform Joined to Trustification," *The New International* (Spring–Summer 1958), 104, 107, 108, and 111.

Thus, while exposed to the moral example of the Black freedom movement, Rawick took his inspiration from a distance. As the 50s ended he published the pamphlet *Socialism as Problem and Ideal*, which offered an annotated bibliography based on a study group he had run. By turns embarrassing—praising Sidney Hook as the best exposition of Marxism—and adventuresome—as in its bows to Fromm, to the Italian novelist Ignazio Silone, to Mills, and to libertarian socialists like George Woodcock and Daniel Guérin—it reached not at all toward African-American liberation or decolonization. Thus Rawick was not, and could not have been, transformed overnight by a conversation after a Rustin talk, but that conversation was certainly central to his eventual transformation. Himself a leading scholar of oral history methodology, Rawick used his own reminiscences to convey a broad truth about Black thinkers and his transformation rather than to narrate specific details, which inevitably were far messier.[25]

In the late 1950s—that is, well after he would have heard Rustin's lecture—Rawick had enthusiastically and uncritically assigned Stanley Elkins's *Slavery* to students at University of Chicago, where Elkins also taught. Indeed, the two had become friends around Rawick giving a talk on campus that broached comparisons between US slavery and Nazi concentration camps, a thesis animating *Slavery*, before the two men knew each other's work. Rawick at first took *Slavery*, which brought the Rawick family's highly personal history with Nazi terror together with the study of US history, as centrally an indictment of Hitler-like American racism and as an apt commentary on the success of totalizing systems in ending not only resistance but also the very will to resist. For a time he registered no objection to Elkins's view that the repressive system produced docile "Sambo" personality types. Only in 1961 would Rawick write to Merle Curti that Elkins' book was "brilliant, perverse, wrong-headed, and wrong," prompting Curti to remind Rawick of earlier positive assessments. Rawick's listening, in concert with Black intellectuals, to

---

25 George Rawick, *Socialism as Problem and Ideal* (New York: Young People's Socialist League, 1960?). On oral history, see George Rawick, "Some Notes on the Development of Life Histories of Working Class People in the United States," unpublished paper in the possession of David Roediger (March 1979).

voices in the slave narratives became a way to fully interrogate Elkins's views only later.[26]

Coming around Thinking Black Intellectuals

During prestigious, brief postings at Harvard, Cornell, and Chicago, Rawick produced little academic writing, even as his activist commitments also receded. As he later put it, he was handicapped by being a rebel against the arid anti-radicalism he encountered at the upper reaches of academia, but more importantly by being a Marxist who did not believe in the agency of the working class. While the latter was perhaps a not uncommon plight, in Rawick's case it was a disabling one, especially insofar as revising a study of the New Deal was concerned. While glad to be shed of what he saw as the conformist world of elite universities, he was left with trouble getting work anywhere until a 1960 appointment, secured with the help of the great Marxist economist Andre Gunder Frank, at Detroit's Wayne State University in the experimental Monteith College. His tenure there, and at nearby Oakland University, put him into contact with Facing Reality's Martin Glaberman, a Detroit auto worker, poet, sociologist, and Facing Reality stalwart. Rawick gradually entered the world of Facing Reality, a group with C.L.R. James at its center, in 1960 and 1961, around common projects including socialist study classes.[27]

Although soon active in the Congress of Racial Equality (CORE) in Detroit, he revealingly described his initial attraction to Facing Reality as based on a classical Trotskyist debate—he liked the "purity" of the group's "state capitalist" analysis of the class nature of the Soviet Union over Shachtman's emphasis on rule by a bureaucratic class—not on

26 On Elkins and Rawick, see "Rawick to Dear Dr. Curti" (April 21, 1959 and February 24, 1960) in Curti Papers, box 34, folder 24, "OHAL Interview," and "Rawick to Dear Merle" (April 22, 1961) in Curti Papers, box 34, folder 24. See Meier and Rudwick, *Black History and the Historical Profession*, 254–56, a useful account marred by a misreading of Facing Reality's, and Rawick's, position on Black nationalism.

27 "OHAL Interview" and "1987 Interview." On Glaberman, see esp. Martin Glaberman, *Punching Out and Other Writings*, Staughton Lynd, ed. (Chicago: Charles H. Kerr Company, 2002).

questions regarding Black autonomy. The group's book-length 1958 manifesto *Facing Reality* spelled out new libertarian alternatives to vanguardist modes of operation in a way that seemed to dramatically offer ways out of the Old Left, but only gradually did Rawick spell out these politics and their connections to race and to listening to the actual words and dreams of slaves. Gradually, though, the study groups came to include not only such young white leaders of Students for a Democratic Society as Tom Hayden, Al Haber, and Bernadine Dohrn but also militants who would spearhead the Detroit Revolutionary Union Movement (DRUM), and the League of Revolutionary Black Workers, including Ken Cockrel, Luke Tripp and John Watson. Both Wayne State and Oakland differed greatly from the elite universities in serving working class students and Rawick had chances to listen to organic intellectuals that he had not had in the 50s.[28]

In 1963 and 1964 and again in 1967 and 1968, Rawick traveled to London to work as James' personal assistant, a job that descended to small details—in one handwritten note in the archives, Rawick reminded himself and others that "Nello," as intimates called James, found Southern Comfort too sweet and preferred other spirits—but also soared to great excitement. Rawick introduced a 1978 edition of James's classic study of Herman Melville, *Mariners, Renegades, and Castaways*, reflecting on the "great privilege" of working closely with James in the 60s, and Kent Worcester's biography of James uses Rawick's warm reminiscences as a counterweight to the jaundiced, thinly fictionalized account of James and his London circle offered by the celebrated writer V.S. Naipaul. There was great reason to feel privileged and transformed. Rawick was present, for example, when James first met the great British social historian and self-avowed romantic E.P. Thompson. Finding in Facing Reality "a libertarian view, Marx, and the best of romanticism," Rawick's attraction to Thompson's views sped his shedding of the pragmatist Marxism of Hook. What came to strike Rawick was less the purity of James's historical materialism than that he was "the least doctrinaire and sectarian Marxist I know."[29]

---

28   "OHAL Interview;" Worcester, *James*, 143.

29   George Rawick, "Introduction" to C.L.R. James, *Mariners, Renegades, and Castaways* (Detroit: Bewick Editions, 1978), ix–xvi; the Southern Comfort note is on a scrap in the Rawick Papers; "Rawick to Dear Merle" (December 20, 1963), in Curti Papers, box 34, folder 24; for "least doctrinaire" see "OHAL Interview"; see also Rawick, "The English Working Class," *International Socialism*, 23 (Winter 1965/66), 23–25.

One particular recollection underlines the way in which it was both James (as speaker and listener) and his milieu that so impressed Rawick, who wrote that he

> witnessed with amazement the great intensity and variety of his political and literary activities. Through his house passed hundreds of West Indian, American African and English intellectuals, students, workers, and political people. He somehow had time for a seemingly endless stream of people [including] not only leading intellectual figures and ... ordinary people whose questions he answered with concern and from whom he consciously learned. I shall never forget his lifelong habit of interrogating people as to the histories of their lives in the most minute details. It was from this practice, as well as constant reading, that James derived much of his understanding of modern society. Indeed many of his works were coauthored with his comrades as part of a practice based upon the understanding that political work must be collective, involving in writing trained intellectuals as well as non-intellectuals.[30]

The circles around James in these years, and often enough passing through his house, included an amazing assemblage of African, African-American, and West Indian intellectuals, including Naipaul, George Lamming, Andrew Salkey, Vincent Harding, Aimé Cesaire, Orlando Patterson, Stuart Hall, Robert Hill, Richard Small, Joan French, Walter Rodney, Norman Girvan, and Kwame Ture, as well as important white writers on race, gender, and class, including Selma James, Rawick, and William Gorman. Ironically James's Staverton Road lodgings were more consistently the site where Rawick participated in daily give-and-take with Black intellectuals than the increasingly African-American city of Detroit, where Facing Reality influenced far more young Black activists than it managed to recruit.[31]

---

30   Rawick, "Introduction," xv and ix–xvi.

31   Ibid., and Worcester, *James*, 173–77; see also George Rawick, "Personal Notes," *Urgent Tasks*, 12 (Summer 1981), 118–21; Rupert Lewis, *Walter Rodney's Intellectual and Political Thought* (Detroit: Wayne State University Press, 1998), 37; Santiago Colás, "Silence and Dialectics: Speculations on C.L.R. James and Latin America," in Grant Farred, ed., *Rethinking C.L.R. James* (Cambridge, MA: Blackwell, 1995), 143–46.

It was in such regular collective activity that Rawick entered a world of Black intellectuals and began to study race and slavery. He got to see how such a collaborative process worked soon after first arriving in London. James and others in Facing Reality were working on completing a programmatic statement on the United States and the "Negro Question," mostly drafted by Glaberman. The task was made more difficult and urgent when John F. Kennedy's assassination occurred, changing "everything," after early drafts of the document had been completed. In the freewheeling discussion of revisions that then proceeded, Rawick and his young wife Dianne Luchtan participated alongside veterans of the group. He transcribed the discussion in a long, typed summary that perfectly illustrates how Facing Reality wrote collectively and individually, with listening to each other central to the process. The transcript of the discussion also emphasizes the critical role of the writing of history in clarifying political tasks, a position that would soon ease the tensions between academic and agitational work for Rawick.[32]

The ideas in this discussion document became the basis for Rawick's seminal 1964 "The American Negro Movement" article, suggesting how quickly he became a focus of Facing Reality's efforts to understand race and how eagerly he pursued James's query regarding what slaves thought. Near the end of the article, Rawick included a passage that showed he had moved far beyond Elkins's views and presaged where his intellectual life would go: "If anyone doubts human vitality and the human ability to withstand persecution and grow . . . read the personal testimony of hundreds of former slaves gathered in the ten thousand manuscript pages of the Slave Narrative Collection of the Federal Writers Project, in which the American government, in the 1930s, provided funds for interviewing . . . ex-slaves." James was, Rawick held, able to tell what he and others were ready to write. At the foundational moment of Black Power, it was writing on the historical basis of Black resistance and self-organization that he urged from Rawick.[33]

---

32 "Discussion of M.G. [Martin Glaberman] Draft of Document on the Negro Question" (December 29, 1963, notes taken by Rawick), Rawick Papers, box 3, folder 15. For another excellent entry to Facing Reality's life, see C.L.R. James and Martin Glaberman, "Letters" *Urgent Tasks*, 12 (Summer 1981), 76–80.

33 Rawick, "American Negro Movement," "OHAL Interview."

At times the collective hammering out of such writing rather defied notions of authorship. With James, the author of the greatest book ever on slavery and revolt, *The Black Jacobins* (1938), returning to those subjects in the 1960s, and with Facing Reality comrade William Gorman continuing his important writings on race, there was some question about who wrote what. In Rawick's view, expressed to Paul Buhle who interviewed him in 1984, any questions of plagiarism confused academic standards with those of revolutionary projects hinging on collectivity: ideas did not have owners. He granted that it looked, in passages of his own writings and those of James in the celebrated essay "The Atlantic Slave Trade and Slavery: Some Interpretations of Their Significance in the Development of the United States and The Western World," published in *Amistad* in 1970, like somebody was copying off of somebody. But he remembered that Gorman actually put together the final version of the *Amistad* piece and that everybody drew on ideas it would have been impossible to have without James.[34]

Other kinds of productive cross talk in the group also had consequences. Selma James's feminism, eventually including a leading role in Wages for Housework campaigns, came to greatly influence Rawick's views on slavery, highlighting the roles of gender, sexuality, and social reproduction. Thus he was among the professional historians most able to appreciate Angela Davis's seminal writing on women and slavery and structured some of his critique (and autocritique) of studies of slave "personality types" and resistance. In particular Rawick came to question the reflexive assumption that the male slave, whether Nat Turner or Sambo, should be at the center of debates and narratives.[35]

34 "OHAL Interview" and "1987 Interview." The James article in question, with the role of William Gorman also at play, was C.L.R. James, "The Atlantic Slave Trade and Slavery: Some Interpretations of Their Significance in the Development of the United States and The Western World," in John A. Williams and Charles F. Harris, eds., *Amistad*, 1 (New York: Vintage Books, 1970), 119–64. See also "W'm [William Gorman] to My Dear G [George Rawick]" (undated), box 5, folder 28.

35 "Dear Ferruccio [Gambino] from George [Rawick]" (February 22, 1983) Rawick Papers, box 6, older 34; "OHAL Interview"; on Davis, see Rawick, "Some Notes on a Social Analysis of Slavery," 22; for further material on Selma James, the personal and the political, see esp. Rawick Papers, box 5, folder 23 and "Selma to My Dear George" (February 7, 1975), Rawick Papers, box 7, folder 49.

Whether such impulses toward sharing and debates were characteristics of the moment, of Facing Reality's style, of "the left," and/or
of "Black" intellectual production raises interesting questions.
Rawick, I think, would in many ways have been more ready than
James to argue for an African, and African-American, creative
style—rooted, of course, in history and not in "race"—based on
borrowing, improving, debating, and sharing. Indeed, he made just
such an argument, regarding everything from family forms to music,
in the "last lecture" which this article begins by discussing. He
would, I think, have appreciated, as a talking back to empire, Walter
Rodney's deeply meaningful flourish in the beginning of *How Europe
Underdeveloped Africa* (1973), when Rodney turned the academic
convention of thanking those who had helped him to write, but
acknowledging that personal responsibility for mistakes rested with
him, squarely on its head: "That," Rodney wrote, "is sheer bourgeois
subjectivism. Responsibility in matters of these sorts is always collective, especially with regard to remedying the shortcomings."[36]
Rawick, in intellectual practice, was privileged not just to be around
C.L.R. James but also a collectivity that was both revolutionary and
Black.

Such collective production did not preclude taking off in distinc-
tive directions. By 1969, Rawick had completed a draft of his history
of slavery, answering James's question on the slave's view of slavery
by introducing the first nineteen volumes of Federal Writer's Project
slave narratives with an elegant slim draft volume that was particularly astute regarding connections to Africa, on the slave family, and
on the place of slavery and racism in the history of capitalism. James
responded to the draft by writing to Glaberman "to inform you offi-
cially that this is the best thing I have read on slavery in general and
in particular in the United States," predicting that it "will make
history." James's lavish praise came despite suspicions that the closing chapters were too Freudian (or perhaps Fanonian) or read too
much as if they belonged in a second book. Rawick stuck by his
controversial closing chapters, and the use of psychoanalytical
insights in writing history generally, invoking at times the dissenting

---

36 Walter Rodney, *How Europe Underdeveloped Africa* (London: Bogle-L'Ouverture
Publications, and Dar es Salaam: Tanzanian Publishing House, 1973), preface.

Marxist/Freudian work of Wilhelm Reich as key to understanding the workings of the master class in the slave South.[37]

Over time and through practice, Rawick deeply changed, entering both Black and western worlds more fully. Hunger for both news of rebellious Detroit and a new view of slavery helped to make Rawick's 1967 speaking tour of Germany and Italy an incredible success. He spoke on C. Wright Mills, on capitalist restructuring in the 1930s, but above all on Black revolt, in Padua, Berlin, Florence, Frankfurt, Milan, and elsewhere. At the height of the Black Power insurgency, he represented Facing Reality's views on African-American revolt. He spoke, as Gambino put it, "to thousands of students in occupied universities . . . breaking the spell of a Cold War image, fed by official US propaganda, the image of a US white intelligentsia intimidated into permanent silence."[38] Intellectually, changes to Rawick were profound and multivalent. By the late 60s, steeped in Facing Reality's passionate embrace of dialectics, Rawick would credit Hegelian inspirations as his own. The close attention of the group, and especially of James, to popular film, television, and sport as keys to understanding social relations and desires differed much at first from Rawick's own tastes, but by the 1970s he had softened a little on movies, cherished relationships with St. Louis Cardinal football players who were his neighbors, and even watched television. In 1977 he would review the blockbuster television miniseries *Roots* for the *St. Louis Globe-Democrat*, the city's reactionary morning daily.[39]

---

37 "Nello/C.L.R. James to My Dear Marty [Glaberman]" (November 6, 1969), Rawick Papers, box 5, folder 28; On Rawick, dialectics, and psychohistory, see his "Historical Roots of Black Liberation," 7. My own debts to Rawick are noted in Roediger, "Notes on Working Class Racism: A Tribute to George Rawick," in Roediger and Fitz, eds., *Shell of the Old*, 11–17.

38 George Rawick, "Report for *Speak Out* on George Rawick's Tour of Italy and Germany" (unpublished account, 1967), Rawick Papers, box 4, folder 20; cf. Gambino. "In Memory," 104–05; "1987 Interview"; and Rawick, "Anni Trenti: Lotte Operaie USA," in S. Bologna, G. Rawick, M. Gobbini, A. Negri, L. Ferrari Bravo, F. Gambino, *Operai e Stato: Lotte Operaie e Riforma dello Stato Capitalstico tra Rivoluzione d'Octobre e New Deal* (Milan: Feltrinelli, 1972), 47–53 and 147–56. See also Rawick Papers, box 6, folders 34 and 38 on Italy.

39 George Rawick, "Roots of Millions," *St. Louis Globe-Democrat* (February 5, 1977). Rawick also reviewed Gutman's *The Black Family in Slavery and Freedom* (December 25–26, 1976) and several other books in the *Globe-Democrat*; see also Lipsitz's afterword to Roediger with Smith, eds.; Rawick, *Listening to Revolt*, 153–63.

However, such privileges, transformations, and triumphs could hardly solve everything, personally or politically. Within Facing Reality itself things went far less than well. In the swirling world of 1967 and 1968 in Detroit, Europe, and Southeast Asia, the opportunities for greatly expanded influence by the group seemed palpable. But the few dozen members and supporters were best poised to offer classes and produce publications, especially the increasingly well-mounted and terrific *Speak Out*, which owed much of its success to Rawick and Luchtan.

The tensions between the Facing Reality project of being a sounding board for workers' thoughts and actions and providing a revolutionary leadership surfaced perhaps more in such a period of euphoria than in those of seeming stasis. The question of why the group did not "get anything out of" its intense activities in, and penetrating insights on, Detroit concealed perhaps a deeper question about what it should have wanted to get. Rawick's view, that it too often had little to offer to Black militants beyond saying, at bottom, "Do what you're doing. It's great," identified the problem, but not a solution. At the international level, the meetings and endless transatlantic correspondence in 1967 to produce a manifesto on the world situation—titled *The Gathering Forces* and modeled on the *Facing Reality* publication of a decade before—proved difficult. In the latter case, the use of forms of workers' democracy in the Hungarian Revolution of 1956 framed discussions of factory labor in Detroit aptly, but by 1967 the centers of world revolution were disparate and at times far afield from the factory city where the group was most rooted.[40]

All of these political problems granted, the tensions leading to the dissolution of Facing Reality were fundamentally personal in many

---

40   For debates over the format and purpose of *Speak Out*, see Rawick Papers, box 5, folders 27 and 28, esp. "Martin [Glaberman] to Dear George [Rawick] and Dianne [Luchtan]" (June 23, 1967). Among Rawick's contributions were outstanding pieces on Detroit, esp. "Race and Class in Auto," *Speak Out*, 2 (1969–70); for his analysis of the 1967 Black rebellion in Detroit for a British readership, see George Rawick, "The Flames of Black Revolution," *Labour Worker* (Great Britain), 75 (September 1967), 4–5. See also "OHAL Interview;" Worcester, *James*, 174–77 and 186. Rawick's letters to Glaberman (August 1 and 25, 1967), Rawick Papers, box 5, folder 27, is a wonderful example of the many letters reflecting the collaboration and conflict, personal and political, that went into *Gathering Forces*.

ways. Rawick, who quit the group a year before its breakup, argued against "killing each other" while finding political reasons to stay together in a group that could no longer function. He counted the ease with which C.L.R. James could take up the role of "guru" as part of the problem, although it must be said that James also resisted such a role impressively at times. Poverty, the coming of old age, and new opportunities to teach in the United States left James making tragic and sometimes contradictory material and psychological demands on the group. Most seriously, although Facing Reality had extremely advanced politics on women's liberation, it could not transcend patriarchy in a single small group, one whose leading members were often married to each other. Marital tensions and splits assumed political forms. Or perhaps, in Selma James's marriage to C.L.R., these issues were both personal and political, reflecting patterns of work and reward that Selma also analyzed in larger worlds of production and social reproduction. Rawick's own marriage would break up in 1968, leading to his terribly honest line, "I can understand why women find it hard to live with me. I find it hard to live with me," as well as more specific reflections and self-criticisms. When the group did vote to disband, Glaberman recorded Rawick, technically out of Facing Reality, as a "Yes" vote, angering C.L.R. James because it made the tally against continuing more lopsided, the group by then dwindled to an extent where a single vote seemed to matter. Interestingly, as James mounted arguments for continuing as a group, he focused more and more on the importance of Facing Reality's intellectual production, especially Rawick's work on slavery.[41]

Through it all, no set of issues dividing the group was framed in terms of the race of those offering sometimes bitterly contending

---

41 "OHAL Interview," and George Lipsitz to David Roediger, email (January 22, 2009); for a very self-critical letter on his own marriage "Rawick to Dear Dianne," Rawick Papers, box 7, folder 4; "Nello [C.L.R. James] to My Dear Marty [Glaberman]" (November 6, 1969), Rawick Papers, box 5, folder 28. For Glaberman's account, and C.L.R. James's 1968 defense of continuing as a small organization, see Martin Glaberman, ed., *Marxism for Our Times: C.L.R. James on Revolutionary Organization* (Jackson: University of Mississippi Press, 1999), xxii–xxiv and 182–83 respectively. The disputes within Facing Reality near its end are best followed in the Rawick Papers, esp. box 5, folders 27 and 28. See esp. "George [Rawick] to Dear Marty [Glaberman]" (August 1 and October 9, 10, 17, and 25, 1967), Rawick Papers, box 5, folder 27.

positions. Perhaps the tragic, pervasive gendered personal divides within the group, along with palpable divides between those on the ground in Detroit and those in London during and after the 1967 rebellions, provided such clear lines of division as to make appeals to race suffer by comparison. But likewise it is possible that long inter-racial experience within a group noteworthy, at least in London, for its remarkable aggregation of Black intellectuals made for a situation in which some of the most searching analyses of white racism and strongest advocacy of Black self-activity centrally included fortunate white intellectuals as well. This hardly made Rawick imagine that he had transcended race more broadly. He recalled that when he was expelled from Detroit CORE, as the organization moved from being a mostly white group to advocating Black Power, that he was most pleased with the transformation, right down to his own removal. But other experiences of racial lines hurt more. He wrote, for exam-ple, of a desire to share work on slavery with Stuckey as running afoul not only of past political differences but also of the US color line, which at times left him hesitant to approach Black scholars.[42]

Sick as he was, Rawick stayed in a world of thinking Black intel-lectuals in the two decades of his life remaining after he left Facing Reality. He managed, at least on some level, to cooperate with both C.L.R. James and Selma James. He provided US leadership for the international academic campaign for an inquiry in the wake of Walter Rodney's assassination in Guyana in 1980.[43] Above all, he reached and heard students at University of Missouri at St. Louis and in electric classes of African-American women students in East St. Louis. We have audiotapes of scores of his classes thanks to recordings made by an Italian associate, Livio Manfrin. Irene Manfrin, Livio's daughter, has transcribed many of the lectures for her doctoral work in Italy. In them remarkable observations, and great stories, on US history continually gave way to Rawick posing big questions—under such wonderful titles as "Don't Wait for the

---

42   "George P. Rawick to Dear Julius Lester" (May 1, 1971), Rawick Papers, box 6, folder 46; "OHAL Interview." On differences between the Detroit comrades and those in London regarding interpreting the 1967 Detroit rebellion, see "Marty [Glaberman] to Dear George [Rawick]" (September 28, 1967), Rawick Papers, box 5, folder 27.

43   "OHAL Interview" and, on the Walter Rodney campaign, Rawick Papers, box 6, folder 42.

White People" and "It Is Difficult to Have a Chance"—and then falling silent. Working-class students, white and especially African American, disagreed with him and each other. His classic response was that he could certainly understand the conclusion—for example that change only comes with violence—but wondered if there were also other responses. At a time when so many white scholars cast themselves as victims of the allegedly silencing impact of Black Power, he worked across color lines, listening when a young auto worker expressed dreams to be his own boss and then again years later when the same worker described building a radical caucus at Ford's nearby Hazelwood, Missouri plant. In part, long experience working in interracial settings structured such successes. So, too, did a longstanding political agreement with radical Black Power's impulses, which gave him a voice, and a capacity to refrain from always using it.[44] Finally, in class and out, Rawick's listening was animated by a conviction that workers want a humane society, and therefore a new society, and that Black workers' attempts to figure things out, however variously, contradictorily, and imperfectly, have to be one of our starting points. In those important senses, he was a white product of, a beneficiary of, and producer of generations of thinking among Black intellectuals.

---

44 The three transcribed lectures from Rawick's Fall 1979 Black History class that Irene Manfrin kindly sent to me all illustrate these points on teaching, especially "That's a Very Optimistic Book." See also "OHAL Interview," "1987 Interview," and "Dear Ferruccio [Gambino] from George [Rawick]" (February 22, 1983), Rawick Papers, box 6, folder 34. For Irene Manfrin's work see "The Development of George Rawick's Thought about Modern Slavery" ("L'evoluzione del pensiero di George Rawick in tema di schiavitù moderna") from University of Padua, Political Science (2007). See also Enoch Page's afterword to Listening to Revolt, 148–52.

PART TWO

HISTORIES: THE PAST AND PRESENT OF RACE AND CLASS

CHAPTER 4

Removing Indians, Managing Slaves, and Justifying Slavery: The Case for Intersectionality

I n the introductory chapter on "The Planter" during slavery that framed his matchless *Black Reconstruction in America*, W.E.B. Du Bois made the lies and truths that masters told to each other and to the world about their knowledge of the managing of Africans the key to their wealth, power, and limitations. While planters necessarily "insisted on the efficiency of Negro labor for ordinary toil" and on its "essential equality of physical condition with the labor of Europe," the South's "pedantic periodicals" screamed that "higher intelligence" was impossible for "Negro labor." Such a stance justified, and bespoke, the managerial authority that masters studiously assumed. Grand claims of racial knowledge born of management experience ramified tragically. What began in the South proved "singularly disastrous for modern civilization in science and religion, in art and government." To the "watching world" a racism designed to supervise what Du Bois called "slave industry" seemed to be "the carefully thought-out result of experience and reason," even as planters contradictorily obsessed over facing "sullen labor" determined to do as little work as possible.[1]

The proslavery Georgia-born historian U.B. Phillips posited the absence of writings by slave masters on managing labor in his epic

---

1 W.E.B. Du Bois, *Black Reconstruction in American, 1860–1880* (New York: Free Press, 1988 [1935]).

1918 study *American Negro Slavery*. Phillips began a chapter titled "Plantation Management": "Typical planters though facile in conversation seldom resorted to their pens. Few of them put their standards into writing except in the form of instructions to their stewards and overseers." He informed readers that these writings amounted to little more than "counsels of perfection, drafted in widely separated periods [and] localities, and varying much in detail."[2] In recently attempting to open up the consideration of race and the management of labor in US history, Elizabeth Esch and I found much more than Phillips thought was available. We surveyed a literature on slave management in which masters spoke to themselves and to the world volubly regarding fostering the industry of slaves. The literature is so massive that it leaves no doubt that developing a managerial ideology was a central concern of many planters. In the sixty-nine examined annual volumes of *Farmer's Register*, *Southern Planter*, *Southern Cultivator*, *American Cotton Planter*, and *De Bow's Review*, "management of slaves" came up for substantial discussion sixty-five times and "management of negroes" ninety times.[3] Of course very often related issues were discussed in less direct language as plantation management was debated. Indeed these journals ought to be considered the first systematic management publications in the United States.

Research in these sources has led to an extended account of how plantation labor was chosen and bossed in the production of staple crops.[4] For present purposes I want to discuss instead two further dimensions of the research, which help to account for Du Bois's observation regarding the centrality of management to the image and the self-image of masters. The first concerns how the management of slaves was embedded in discourses concerning the management of

---

2   Ulrich Bonnell Phillips, *American Negro Slavery: A Survey of the Supply, Employment and Control of Negro Labor as Determined by the Plantation Regime* (New York: D. Appleton and Company, 1918), 261.

3   Thanks to Zachary Sell who did much of the digital searching here. The volumes included were *Farmer's Register* (1833–1843) [hereafter *FR*], *Southern Planter* (1841–1866) [hereafter *SP*], *De Bow's Review* (1850–1864) [hereafter *DR*], *Southern Cultivator* (1843–1866) [hereafter *SC*] and *American Cotton Planter* (1853, 1854, 1855, and 1857) [hereafter *ACP*].

4   David R. Roediger and Elizabeth Esch, *The Production of Difference: Race and the Management of Labor in US History* (New York: Oxford University Press, 2012), 19–61.

land so that even as the North and the South gradually parted company on the justifiability of slavery, planters benefitted from a broadly shared acceptance of settler colonialism. The claims to know how to manage "negroes" better than Africans could manage themselves were part and parcel of claims to be able to manage land better than the removed Indians who had lived on that land. Secondly, the literature on the management of slaves foregrounded the reproduction of slaves, on which claims of great success could be grounded, alongside claims of managing production that were necessarily more modest. Broaching reproduction potentially raised the question of slave breeding, opening masters to abolitionist attacks. But the fact that masters managed to tremendously increase the slave population and its value justified slavery in the view of the planter class as somehow good for Africans and as economically viable as a system. Thus the defense of slavery in the eyes of masters themselves, and from the charges of critics, was deeply "intersectional," as Black feminist theorists put matters.[5] Never simply a matter of claiming excellence in managing slave labor in the fields on class (and race) lines, the defense of slavery turned as well on the intersectional convergence of slavery, settler colonialism, and women's reproductive labor.

Dispossessing Indians, Husbanding Land, Managing Negroes

While holding Africans as slaves informed Southern management as a set of ideas and practices, such management had many broader meanings, some of them intimately linking land use to settler-colonial dispossessions of Indians. In 1840, *Farmer's Register* approvingly reprinted the 1818 edition of *Arator*, John Taylor of Caroline's series of agricultural essays, as a contribution to discussions of plantation management. Introducing management of Africans after a long analysis of "managing" fertilizers, Taylor apologized:

> Perhaps this subject ought to have preceded that of manuring, as it is idle even to think of a good system of agriculture in any point

---

5   Patricia Hill Collins, *Black Feminist Thought: Knowledge, Consciousness, and the Politics of Empowerment* (New York: Routledge, 2000 [1990]).

of view, if the labor on which it depends is convulsed by infusions the most inimical to its utility; and if those who direct it, are to live in a constant dread of its loss, and a doubt of their own safety.[6]

Within a few lines, the subject changed to military management, specifically during the Haitian Revolution. Soon Indian corn, cider, and sheep came up as objects whose management interested Taylor and the *Register*. Weymouth Jordan's study of the antebellum journal *American Cotton Planter* finds a similar panoply of concerns running through its pages: "It crusaded for railroads, manufacturing, direct trade with Europe, diversification of crops, horizontal plowing, crop rotation, use of fertilizers [and] Negro management." An early corre-spondent further laid out agricultural reform as "planting more corn, potatoes, peas; sowing more wheat, oats, rye; raising more mules, horses, hogs, cattle; and have better milch cows."[7]

The subject of managing black labor soon developed into a central concern of the journals with characteristic and fruitful complica-tions. After hundreds of references over previous years referring to "management" as the efficient care of bees, cows, soil, silk-worms, sheep, hay, and other things non-human, *Farmer's Register* reprinted an article from the *Carolina Planter* in which Dr. R.W. Gibbes, gingerly backed into the subject of the "management of slaves" as one: "too much neglected, but one of infinite magnitude, and preg-nant with evil . . . I mean a proper regard to, and management of, slaves."[8]

Such strains in early writings on slave management complicate the claim that antebellum Southerners originated modern manage-ment solely through the race management of Africans. "Management"

---

6 John Taylor of Caroline, "Labor," from his *Arator*, as reprinted in *FR*, 13 (December 31, 1840), esp. 728 and 730

7 Weymouth Jordan, "Noah Cloud and the *American Cotton Planter*," *Agricultural History*, 31 (October 1957) 45; see also "J.H. Zimmerman to *ACP*," *ACP*, 3 (February 1855), 57; "Plantation Book," *Southern Planter*, 12 (August, 1852), 251.

8 H.C. "On the Management of Negroes," *FR*, 1 (February 1834), 564–65; Dr. R.W. Gibbes, "Proper Regard to, and Management of, Slaves," *FR*, 13 (July 31, 1840), 426–27; Ulrich Bonnell Phillips, "The Slave Labor Problem in the Charleston District," *Political Science Quarterly*, 22 (September 1907), 419 and 422.

clearly meant many different things in the proliferation of Southern writings using the term. Through the 1830s, the term was decidedly more likely to apply to managing land and crops than to enslaved labor, and this tendency did not disappear at the height of managerial writings in the 1840s and 1850s. The leading modern collection of Edmund Ruffin's writings aptly carries the title *Nature's Management.*[9] In describing his own system of management and what he did for slaves, one planter-expert wrote of acting on the conviction "that man is as much duty bound to improve and cultivate his fellow-men as . . . to cultivate and improve the ground."[10] When management of labor was broached, experts tended to discuss black workers in conjunction with managing and improving land and animals. Within the longer and wider view of US history, such placing of alleged white managerial genius vis-à-vis slaves alongside a general ability to husband and develop nature sets proslavery arguments within the context of settler colonialism's dispossession of indigenous people. The antebellum South, and especially the Southwest, was not only the site of slavery but also of brutal dispossession, dislocation, and decimation of Indians. Some of the same political forces later calling for abolition of slavery also vigorously protested the removal of Southern Cherokees, Creeks, and Choctaws to trans-Mississippi territories in the 1830s.[11]

The same ideological imperative to defend Southern slavery applied also to justifying Indian removal. Justifications of dispossession connected expansion to the ability of white settlers to manage nature's gifts, including slaves. In C.C. Clay's 1853 homage to Alabama in the *American Cotton Planter*, frontier and plantation merged:

> Alabama . . . may truly triumph over her compeers as most worthy to bear the banner of Agriculture . . . she is a child in years, but yesterday reclaimed from the Indian, whose footprints are still visible in her virgin forests, how marvelous her past progress! How

---

9 Edmund Ruffin, *Nature's Management: Writings on Landscape and Reform, 1822–1859*, Jack Temple Kirby, ed. (Athens: University of Georgia Press, 2000), xvii–xviii.

10 Unsigned, "Laborers for the South," *SC*, 16 (August 1858), 235.

11 Alisse Portnoy, *Their Right to Speak: Women's Activism in the Indian and Slave Debates*, (Cambridge: Harvard University Press, 2005).

incalculable her future attainments! And yet, the plenitude of her riches, the magnitude of her power, and the brightness of her glory, are attributable to a single production of her soil—the cotton plant![12]

The Indians, the Southern intellectual George Fitzhugh argued in a proslavery tract, were "*ferae naturæ*" as "wild as those who met Columbus on the beach." In a riposte to anti-removal forces, he added "[the Indian] is doomed to extermination, and those who most sympathize with his fate would be the first to shoot him if they lived on the frontier." In a particularly fractured 1853 account, William S. Price wrote, "The Indians have had ample opportunity for improvement in the ... moral government of civilization; the protection of our government is and has been thrown around them ... sums of money have been appropriated to their use ... without any valuable consideration ... from them in return." Aid to Indians, Price significantly added, came out of "the properly directed labor of the African heathen," but "the result of all these efforts is that they [Indians] are Indians yet, and are likely to continue such."[13]

If, as Alexander Saxton has posited, "white racism is essentially a theory of history," the offerings of proslavery theorists continually found ways to bring African and Indian histories together and to keep them apart. Writers fabricated mega-histories naturalizing and aggrandizing supposed white abilities to manage nature, humans, and human property. Fitzhugh began with the Bible to ground Indian "extermination" and African slavery. The former group would vanish "like the races of Canaan," but Africans might survive since "God did not direct his chosen people to exterminate all races; such as were fit for slaves they were ordered to make slaves of." Fitzhugh brought history's long arc to the present: "Despite the mawkish

12 "Address of the Hon. C.C. Clay," *ACP*, 3 (July 1855), 195.
13 George Fitzhugh, *Sociology for the South, or the Failure of Free Society* (Richmond: A. Morris, Publisher, 1854), 286–87; "William S. Price to Freeman Hunt, Editor of the *Merchants' Magazine*: Moral Benefits of Slavery," *ACP*, 1 (June 1853), 172–74. On the profound connections of proslavery thought to colonization and civilizationist racism, see also Brian Schoen, *The Fragile Fabric of Union: Cotton, Federal Politics, and the Global Origins of the Civil War* (Baltimore: Johns Hopkins University Press, 2009), 163–66.

sensibility of the age, practical men are . . . pursuing the same course; they slay the Indians hip and thigh, as in the days of Moses and Joshua, and enslave the negroes."[14] Price connected proslavery arguments to supposed white abilities to husband nature and to civilize Africans strikingly. "Now if it is the . . . desire and ambition of civilized man to bring the things of the earth to a state of usefulness," he held, "how much more is it his duty to bring persons bearing his own physical (and probably mental) image purported to have descended from the same common stock, who are by millions roaming the earth's surface, as wild as beasts of the forest, without any . . . usefulness, a terror to civilized men."[15] Enslaving Africans was on this view the nurturant flip side of the white managerial genius that killed off Indians.

Managing Reproduction: Claiming Paternalism and Success

Managerial literature frequently regarded the slave as a product as well as a producer. Noteworthy for its innovations enabling subscribers to systematically study individual labor in cotton picking, *Affleck's Southern Rural Almanac and Plantation and Garden Calendar for 1854* nonetheless held, "As the business of cotton growing is now conducted, a planter's almost sole wealth consists in negroes." Historians of accountancy credit Thomas Affleck, the almanac's editor, with pioneering "depreciation techniques for human property."[16] Affleck insisted that "*a fine crop* consists first in an increase in the number, and a marked improvement in the condition

---

14   Alexander Saxton, *The Rise and Fall of the White Republic: Class Politics and Mass Culture in Nineteenth Century America* (New York: Verso, 2003 [1990]), 390; Fitzhugh, *Sociology for the South*, 286–87.

15   William Price, "Commercial Benefits of Slavery," *ACP*, 1 (December 1853), 355; see also David A. Chang, *The Color of the Land: Race, Nation, and the Politics of Landownership in Oklahoma, 1832–1929* (Chapel Hill: University of North Carolina Press, 2010), 23.

16   *Affleck's Southern Rural Almanac and Plantation and Garden Calendar for 1854* (Washington, MS: Affleck's Southern Nurseries, October 1853), 15 ("December"); Richard Fleischman and Thomas Tyson, "Accounting in Service to Racism: Monetizing Slave Property in the Antebellum South," *Critical Perspectives on Accounting*, 15 (April 2004), 376–99.

and value of the negroes."[17] In 1855 the Louisiana overseer S.B. Raby took solace that "any deficiencies in the cane crop" would be more than compensated for by births that increased "our crop of negroes," exemplifying what the historian of sugar and slavery Richard Follett nicely calls the "coldly rational ethos of demographic management." South Carolina's Plowden C.J. Weston emphasized to overseers that they would be judged "First—by the general well-being of the negroes . . . the small amount of punishment; the excess of births over deaths; the small number of persons in hospitals, and the health of children."[18] The Carolina physician W. Fletcher Holmes reasoned that since for upcountry planters "the principal value of the negro . . . is his increase," medicine had a particular role to play in the accumulation of wealth.[19]

Such concern for slave health, reproduction, and value caused many articles on the "management of negroes" to begin with an emphasis on adequate provisioning that imparts a paternalist and even munificent tone. On the one hand the "first obligation" was to provide "suitable food and clothing." Presupposing hard work and the need for the young to grow strong, expert masters urged the providing of ample meal and meat and sometimes advised readers to provide "nutritious" (and cheap) vegetables such as "cabbage, kale, or mustard for greens . . . squashes, Irish potatoes [and] in fall and winter sweet potatoes, turnips, pumpkins, and peas." Others warned

---

17   William Kauffman Scarborough, *The Overseer: Plantation Management in the Old South* (Baton Rouge: Louisiana State University Press, 1966), 70 quoting Affleck; Ulrich Bonnell Phillips, *American Negro Slavery: A Survey of the Supply, Employment and Control of Negro Labor as Determined by the Plantation Regime* (New York: D. Appleton and Company, 1918), 261–62.

18   Richard Follett, *The Sugar Masters: Planters and Slaves in Louisiana's Cane World, 1820–1860* (Baton Rouge: Louisiana State University Press, 2005), 69 (Raby and "demographic management"). The Weston text is included in John Spencer Bassett, *The Southern Plantation Overseer, As Revealed in His Letters* (Northampton: Smith College, 1925), 31, and discussed in Charles Joyner, *Down by the Riverside: A South Carolina Slave Community* (Urbana: University of Illinois Press, 1984), 51.

19   Sharla M. Fett, *Working Cures: Healing, Health, and Power on Southern Slave Plantations* (Chapel Hill: University of North Carolina Press, 2002), 15, 27 (Holmes), and 18. See also Amy Dru Stanley, "Slave Breeding: An Antebellum Argument over Commodity Relations, Love, and Personhood," unpublished paper presented at *Slavery's Capitalism: A New History of American Economic Development*, Brown University and Harvard University (April 7–9, 2011).

that vegetables ought not be the excuse for "stinting" on other dietary staples. The importance of a good breakfast, in order to have the slave "remain diligently at work," struck a distinctly modern note. James Towns told *Southern Cultivator* readers that the "management of negroes" had to be done "with an eye to their health, their comfort, and their happiness [in] the master's interest."[20]

Often masters cast the tensions that led to high turnover among overseers in terms of the supposed inability of the latter group to take seriously the need to cultivate a "crop of negroes" as well as the crops in the ground. "Overseers are not interested in raising children, or meat [or] in improving land" ran a much-echoed lament in the *American Cotton Planter*. Despite the fact that overseers' pay did not typically include a share of the agricultural commodities produced, they continued to be accused of one-sidedly focusing on maximizing such production. An Alabama report on the "Management of Slaves" complained of overseers, "As they have no property in our slaves, they lack the check of self-interest." Advice literature, overwhelmingly written by masters, provided constant reminders to overseers not to punish "negroes" in anger or with passion, risking lasting damage to the master's property. The *American Cotton Planter*'s discussion of the "duties of overseers," for example, stressed, "Never display yourself before [slaves] in a passion; and even if inflicting the severest punishment, do so in a mild, cool manner," using the whip "slowly and deliberately." Indeed so persistent were these tropes and so slight was the material basis for overseers to behave in such counterproductive ways, that it seems possible that hired managers picked up on the fact that planters themselves, whatever their protestations, would fire overseers more quickly when the crop suffered than when the slaves did and perhaps projected their own lack of control in inflicting punishment onto those below.[21]

20 Agricola, "Management of Negroes," *SC*, 13 (June 1855), 171; N.D. Guerry, "Management of Negroes—Duties of Masters," *SC*, 28 (June 1860), 176; Robert Collins, "Essay on the Management of Slaves," *DR*, 7 (January–February 1862), 155; James M. Towns, "Management of Negroes," *SC*, 9 (June 1851), 87.

21 "MWP to *American Cotton Planter*: Plantation Economy," *ACP*, 1 (December 1853), 377; A Subscriber, "Overseers," *ACP*, 2 (May 1854), 150; John A. Calhoun and others, "Management of Slaves," *SC*, 4 (August 1846), 113; Jacob Metzer, "Rational

Paternalist management insisted on connecting slaves and animals. In an 1855 contribution to *De Bow's Review* on the "Management of Slaves," John A. Calhoun argued that if "it is a matter which pertains to the interest of northern agricultural societies to attend well to the improvement of their lands, and the improvement and comfort of their stock . . . how much more important it is for us to turn our attention to the best means of governing our slaves."[22] Even as the master-manager's self-interested paternalism had a distinctly modern and therapeutic tone, it consistently and logically cohabited with the most pernicious aspects of proslavery ideology and practice. The soft discourse of concern, sincerely delivered if shallowly rooted, could blunt abolitionist critiques. However, concern with improving the value of "the negro" connected as well to the harshest incarnations of white supremacy, grounded in comparisons of slaves to livestock, with both made to be raised, improved, and bred. Care by the master was necessary, that exemplar of planter paternalism George Fitzhugh wrote, because "not a single negro was ever reclaimed from his savage state till he was caught, tied, tamed, and domesticated like the wild ox or the wild horse."[23]

The planter J.W. Pitts strikingly put a softer paternalism and the animality of Africans side-by-side. "The surest and best method of managing negroes," he held, "is to love them." His reasoning continued, "We know, from a thousand experiments, that if we love our horse . . . he will become gentle, docile, and obedient." The "same effect" worked the same magic "upon sheep, cattle, dogs, the lion, the elephant, bird [and, improbably enough] fish." It should, Pitts

---

Management, Modern Business Practices, and the Economies of Scale in Ante-Bellum Southern Plantations," *Explorations in Economic History*, 12 (April 1975), 125–27; Eugene D. Genovese, *Roll, Jordan, Roll: The World the Slaves Made* (New York: Pantheon, 1974), 13–14; Unsigned, "The Duties of an Overseer," *ACP*, (December 1854), 355; Editor, "Anonymous Communications," *ACP*, 3 (September 1855), 274. Cf. Farmer and Planter, "The Duties of an Overseer," *SP*, 17 (July 1857), 414, for evidence of internalizing the need for slave welfare and reproduction by one who had worked "in the harness" as an overseer."

22   John A. Calhoun and others, "Management of Slaves," *DR*, 18 (June 1855), 713. Cf. Unsigned, "Management of Slaves and & c.," *FR*, 5 (May 1, 1838), 32–33.

23   George Fitzhugh, *Sociology for the South, or the Failure of Free Society* (Richmond: A. Morris, Publisher, 1854), 287.

reasoned, also work with servants. Towns described the payoff of his managerial liberality as follows: "a negro shows when he is well-fed as readily as a horse; and mine look slick and greasy, and they work lively and are cheerful and happy."[24] The traveler and writer Frederick Law Olmsted learned of the practice under which a planter sent "rascally" slaves away from home and loved ones "for the alleviation of their complaint." One would, he was told, similarly get rid of a horse seen as troublesome. Such brutality comported well with paternalism's use of sale, rather than the whip, as its moment of force to secure obedience. When managers talked and wrote about "negroes" and "hogs" together, they did not abandon paternalism.[25]

Of course making paternalism work was not the only point of such animalizing comparisons. Thus the *Southern Cultivator* praised the new owner of a failing plantation for one day shooting many sickly livestock in order to demonstrate his ruthlessness to workers, while promising to kill 150 underperforming slaves the next day. The master then staged a contrived consultation with an overseer who "persuaded" him to spare the slaves, agreeing to let them live for an eighteen-month probationary period, a strategy that allegedly produced great improvements in productivity. But even this drama was not seen by the author of the account as incompatible with informed, modern paternalist management. He assured readers that such a feigned stay of execution designed to produce "a new spirit of industry" among the slaves did not constitute effective brutality since it rested on managerial knowledge that "the Creator seems to have planted in the negro an innate principle of protection against the abuse of arbitrary power." [26]

Paternalist management intersected most tragically with the animalizing of slaves in the realm of reproduction. The *American Cotton Planter* featured an ad appealing to the desire of masters for

---

24   John W. Pitts, "Best Method of Managing Negroes," *SC*, 18 (October 1860), 325; Towns, "Management of Negroes," 87.

25   Frederick Law Olmsted, *The Cotton Kingdom: A Traveler's Observations on Cotton and Slavery in the American Slave States, 1853–1861* (New York: Da Capo Press, 1996 [1861]), 248; Ulrich Bonnell Phillips and James David Glunt, eds., *Florida Plantation Records from the Papers of George Noble Jones* (St. Louis: Missouri Historical Society, 1927), 154–55.

26   Unsigned, "Revolutionizing a Plantation," *SC*, 16 (November 1858), 346.

the slave woman who could "breed like a cat." Although advertisements for slave sales frequently referred to reproduction, propriety and politics kept direct consideration of methods of breeding largely out of public discourse. What was broadcast, as historian U.B. Phillips unapologetically chronicled, was that masters particularly extended their paternalistic "care of negroes" to "breeding wenches." Accounts glorying in the adaptability of "Guinea's" inhabitants for labor in the slave states specifically referred to reproductive labor as well as to agricultural production; African women as a group were said to be "naturally fit" for both roles.[27]

Attempts to balance reproductive and agricultural labor illustrated how partial, cruel, and sanctimonious paternalism was bound to be. The memories of ex-slaves featured atrocities against pregnant women and mothers of newly born children. Planters only sometimes granted such women a short respite from field labor, allowed them to work in more nearby parts of the fields, avoided their exposure to "low damp tide lands," or placed them together with other women in a special "sucklers' gang." If, as Follett argues, "slave women faced a master class who attempted to manipulate their sexual lives to optimize reproduction," such manipulation was often wrapped up with both paternalism and terror. Pregnancy could best be encouraged and coerced, since promiscuity and infecundity were seen as connected, through the policing of slave women's sex lives and their reproduction. The rules on P.C. Weston's rice estate in 1856, for example, granted all of every Saturday off for any slave woman "with six children alive at any one time."[28]

---

27   Phillips, *American Negro Slavery*, 261–62; Stephanie M.H. Camp, *Closer to Freedom: Enslaved Women and Everyday Resistance in the Plantation South* (Chapel Hill: University of North Carolina Press, 2004), 63; Pamela D. Bridgewater, "Ain't I a Slave: Slavery, Reproductive Abuse and Reparations," *UCLA Women's Law Journal*, 14 (2005), 122, n. 166 ("cat") and 89–162. On advertisements as a public discourse in which capacity for reproductive was prominently mentioned, see Gerald Norde, "From Genesis to Phoenix: The Breeding of Slaves during the Domestic Slave Era, 1837–1863, and Its Consequences" (Unpublished Ph.D. diss., University of Delaware, 1985), esp. 109.

28   Fred Moten, *In the Break: The Aesthetics of the Black Radical Tradition* (Minneapolis: University of Minnesota Press, 2003), 16 and 1–24; Joyner, *Down by the Riverside*, 45; Scarborough, *The Overseer*, 70; Fett, *Working Cures*, 176; Follett, *The Sugar Masters*, 69; John Hebron Moore, *The Emergence of the Cotton Kingdom in the Old Southwest, Mississippi, 1770–1860* (Baton Rouge: Louisiana State University Press, 1988), 84; Elizabeth

Masters acted with sound, if awful, managerial logic, Abraham Lincoln told an 1860 audience that the value of US slaves was two billion dollars. He may have underestimated by a billion dollars or more, in a year when the value of the cotton crop was just over 200 million dollars. Indeed from 1810 forward women's reproductive labor probably produced more value than was realized through production, though the value of slaves of course ultimately depended on profitable production.[29] The "increase" continually increased, making what the legal scholar Adrienne Davis has called the "sexual economy of American slavery" seem to be the greatest success story in plantation management until emancipation happily undermined the story and the wealth of planters.[30]

For a long time, the master class managed to convince itself and enough Northern allies that its modern, market-driven paternalism made it not so different and deadly a system that its representatives ought not lead the nation politically. Belief in white settler colonialism's role in maximizing the profits drawn from "husbanded" land was shared North and South, giving defense of slavery plausibility and purpose. Indeed the two advantages of the slave South—wealth bred of slave reproduction and the shared national practice of Indian removal—arguably worked too well. The tremendous natural

Fox-Genovese, *Within the Plantation Household: Black and White Women of the Old South* (Chapel Hill: University of North Carolina Press, 1988), 187–90; on sucklers' gangs, see Phillips, *American Negro Slavery*, 264; John R. Commons and others, *A Documentary History of American Industrial Society*, 10v. (New York: Russell & Russell, 1958 [1909]), 1:122; Bridgewater, "Ain't I a Slave: Slavery," 122, n. 168 ("dozen") and 89–162. Marie Jenkins Schwartz, *Birthing a Slave: Motherhood and Medicine in the Antebellum South* (Cambridge: Harvard University Press, 2006), esp. 17–20, 189–91, and 224–25.

29 James L. Huston, *Calculating the Value of the Union: Slavery, Property Rights, and the Economic Origins of the Civil War* (Chapel Hill: University of North Carolina Press, 2003), esp. 116 (Lincoln), 28–32 and 292, n. 7; Douglass C. North, *The Economic Growth of the United States, 1790–1860* (Englewood Cliffs, NJ: Prentice Hall, 1961), 233; Gavin Wright, *Slavery and American Economic Development* (Baton Rouge: Louisiana State University Press, 2006), 67; Roger L. Ransom, "The Economics of the Civil War," *EH.net Encyclopedia*, Robert Whaples, ed. (August 24, 2001), eh.net.

30 Adrienne Davis, "'Don't Let Nobody Bother Yo' Principle': The Sexual Economy of American Slavery," in Sharon Harley and the Black Women and Work Collective, eds., *Sister Circle: Black Women and Work* (New Brunswick: Rutgers University Press, 2002), 103–27; see also Zillah Eisentein, *Against Empire: Feminisms, Racism, and the West* (London: Zed Press, 2004), 85–91.

increase of the slave population made the slave South a threat to pre-empt so much free (that is, Indian) land in the West that coalitions of settlers North and South collapsed under strain. Neither the argument for the beneficent implications of the natural increase in slave property nor that for the prepossessing ability of plantation agriculture to improve the land could sustain planter appeals for settler unity with Northern farmers and industrialists wanting to husband the same resources.

CHAPTER 5

"One Symptom of Originality": Race and the Management of Labor in US History
Coauthored with Elizabeth Esch

An industrial army of workmen, under the command of a capital-ist, requires, like a real army, officers [managers], and sergeants [foremen, overlookers], who, while the work is being done, command in the name of the capitalist. The work of supervision becomes their established and exclusive function.

—Karl Marx

John R. Commons, the staid liberal reformer who founded academic labor history in the United States, and Ernest Riebe, the funny, fighting cartoonist of the Industrial Workers of the World (IWW), doubtless had very little in common politi-cally. Commons supported American Federation of Labor–style unionism, worrying when its limited social goals strayed beyond collective bargaining. Riebe offered IWW publications the adven-tures of Mr. Block, the clueless, conformist anti-hero whose misad-ventures showed just how much misplaced faith in the beneficence of capitalists, politicians, and police that workers would have to shed to make a revolution. And yet Riebe and Commons shared an understanding of the relationship between race and the manage-ment of labor, one that seemed crystal clear to them as early twentieth-century observers of American workplaces, but that is quite lost to historians today. In 1907 Commons's *Races and Immigrants in*

Figure One.
Ernest Riebe, "Mr. Block: He Meets Others" from Riebe's *Twenty-Four Cartoons of Mr. Block* (Minneapolis: Block Supply Company, 1913).

America argued, well after Frederick Winslow Taylor had marketed scientific management, that US management had shown just one "symptom of originality," namely "playing one race against the other." Six years later Louisiana lumberjacks struggling for a union would laugh bitterly over a Mr. Block comic wonderfully named "He Meets Others."

In the strip, a well-dressed manager circulates from one racialized group of workers to another—Anglo-Saxon, Irish, German, Italian, Chinese, Polish, and Black. Drawn to resemble Mr. Block, these various others are played against one another by the manager. Threatening and cajoling them to greater competition and productivity through appeals to masculinity, to fear, and to racial and national divisions, by the last frame the manager is reclining peacefully, having succeeded in getting the various workers to work frantically while swapping racial slurs.[1]

Managers, so central to the racial functioning of the workplace in the narratives offered by Commons and Riebe, scarcely appear in accounts of the history of white supremacy and class in US history. Managers, we argue, were never outside of the US racial system. Further, the degree to which management understood itself as possessing scientific knowledge links it to, rather than distinguishes it from, the organization of work under slavery. For us, the separation of slavery from the mainstream of both labor and economic history leads to impoverished accounts that suppose there was no

1   The epigraph is from Marx's *Capital: A Critique of Political Economy*, 3 vols., (Chicago: Charles H. Kerr, 1906), vol. 1: 364. John R. Commons, *Races and Immigrants in America* (New York: The MacMillan Co., 1907), 150; Chris Nyland, "Taylorism, John R. Commons, and the Hoxie Report," *Journal of Economic Issues*, 30 (December 1996), 985–1016, provides an account of Commons's relations to scientific management and to Frederick Winslow Taylor himself around the issues of trade unionism and restriction of output. See also Yngve Ramstad and James L. Starkey, "The Racial Theories of John R. Commons," *Research in the History of Economic Thought and Methodology*, 13 (1995), 1–75. The cartoon is included in Ernest Riebe, *Mr. Block: Twenty-Four IWW Cartoons*, Franklin Rosemont, ed. (Chicago: Charles H. Kerr Publishing, 1984). For the context of the cartoon, see David R. Roediger, *Towards the Abolition of Whiteness: Essays on Race, Politics, and Working Class History* (London and New York: Verso, 1994), esp. 143–45, and Michael Cohen, "'Cartooning Capitalism': Radical Cartooning and the Making of American Popular Radicalism in the Early Twentieth Century," *International Review of Social History*, 52 (2007), 35–58. Research assistance form Martin Smith and Zach Sell was indispensable in completing this article.

sustained literature on the management of labor until the 1880s. Yet the outpouring of studies on managing slaves, and even on managing slaves "scientifically" in the antebellum years, reveals how deeply entwined racial and managerial knowledge had already become. However unexplored, links between race and management are profound. Commons's striking connection of the cutting edge of management with the bloody history of race contrasts sharply with the bloodless efficiency of stop watches and assembly lines that dominate our thinking, and that often focused the hopes of progressive reformers like Commons himself.[2]

Labor historians have participated in the failure to see the ways race shaped the managerial personality, which functioned in the workplace as the daily representative of capital. In perhaps the two most influential studies of the innovations and peculiarities of US management by Marxists, race is either little present, as in the case of Harry Braverman's important work, or transcended by capital, as in that of Antonio Gramsci. The provocative and neglected sections on management in C.L.R. James's *American Civilization* are silent regarding race. The most searching critique building on Marxism, but seeking to transcend the tendency of Marxist scholars to divorce labor from the specific bodies and histories of those performing it, remains the opening chapter of Lowe's *Immigrant Acts*. Lowe shows the stakes involved in a theoretical challenge to abstractions practiced in the name of materialism and even at times of interracialism. She powerfully demonstrates why Marxism is indispensable, and why too much of Marxist scholarship is slow to apprehend the "specific history of the United States" where race, capital, and class are concerned.[3]

---

2   On the dating of the origins of management discourse, see Daniel Nelson, *Managers and Workers: Origins of the Twentieth-Century Factory System in the United States, 1880–1920* (Madison: University of Wisconsin Press, 1996), 50. Cf. James O. Breeden, ed., *Advice among Masters: The Ideal in Slave Management in the Old South*), 811–24.

3   Lisa Lowe, *Immigrant Acts: On Asian American Cultural Politics* (Chapel Hill: Duke University Press, 1996); Harry Braverman, *Labor and Monopoly Capital: The Degradation of Work in the Twentieth Century* (New York: Monthly Review Press, 1975); Antonio Gramcsi, "Americanism and Fordism," *Selections from the Prison Notebooks* (New York: International, 1971), 279–318. Cf. James, *American Civilization*, Anna Grimshaw and Keith Hart, eds. (Cambridge, MA and Oxford, UK: Blackwell, 1993), 173–79 (on Ford) and 181–85. The interesting Australian revisionist defenses of Taylorism as

Lowe argues that Marxism has too often stopped at allowing for race-making processes like the slave trade and the seizing of native lands only in an early period of primitive accumulation, though race-making continued to matter greatly in the history of capitalism. She insists that in the world's most developed capitalist nation the connection of race and exploitation persisted and ramified, driving the accumulation of capital and shaping subsequent strategies of rule. "In the history of the United States," Lowe writes, "capital has maximized its profits not through rendering labor 'abstract' but precisely through the social productions of 'difference,' . . . marked by race, nation, geographical origins, and gender."[4] It will not do, of course, to simply turn things over and make management all about race. But Commons was right that race hovered over and permeated the processes through which US labor was chosen and bossed. "Race management" came into being far before scientific management, and the two for a time coexisted as complementary rather than alternative strategies to extract production and profit.

The Canadian economist Michael Lebowitz and the Bengali historian Dipesh Chakrabarty have produced especially important, and uncannily similar, work underscoring Lowe's argument. Both find enough missing, or "underdeveloped" in Marx that they respectfully propose additions. Chakrabarty's 2000 essay "Universalism and the Logic of Capital" provides a long, meandering, and thrilling jaunt through not only Marx's use of the term "abstract labor" but also through how Marx understood labor in the transition to capitalism and the process of abstraction historically. The emphasis in

---

"radical," and as cooperating with unions in a "challenge to capitalist property rights" in ways allegedly compatible with Marxism also ignore questions of race and management. See Nyland, "Taylorism, John R. Commons and the Hoxie Report," 986 and 1013, and D.J. Kelly, "Marxist Manager Amidst the Progressives: Walter N. Polakov and the Taylor Society," Faculty Papers, University of Wollongong (2004). Ironically, Marx's own remarks on capital as a "personality" opposing and extracting labor point in a direction like that charted by Lowe in that such capitalist and managerial personalities clearly embodied and perceived race. See Karl Marx, *Pre-Capitalist Economic Formations* (New York: International Publishers, 2000), 118.

4 Lowe, *Immigrant Acts*, 27–28. Nyland's article describes incompatibilities of approaches between Commons and the Taylorists, which contextualizes the former's minimizing of scientific management's place as an important US intervention, but the important direct clashes of Commons with Taylor came during and after 1914.

Marx was clearly not just on capital's role in getting past "national barriers and prejudices" (without being able to "*really* overcome" them). Instead it was more broadly on removing the local, the individual, and above all the "useful" character of labor thoroughly enough that the capitalist could idealize purchasing labor not of a person, or even as an object, "but as activity, . . . as the living source of value" reduced to abstraction. "As against capital," Marx concluded, "labor is the merely abstract form, the mere possibility of value-positing activity, which exists only as a capacity, as a resource in the bodiliness of the worker." This "life-process" of capital realizes itself in constantly overcoming labor's resistance, but never finally doing so, as it needs the confrontation with such resistance to expand its ability to imagine abstraction and to extract the most value from this capacity.[5]

In this move, or reminder of Marx's move, Chakrabarty opens the possibility of seeing the perpetually and necessarily incomplete universality engendered by capital as part of the system's very logic. Chakrabarty asks us to think of Marx as seeing the worker arriving at a factory gate with a "History 1" consciousness—a sense of the past that is "internal to the structure of being of capital." The very presence of the worker at the morning whistle "represents a historical separation between his/her capacity to labor and the necessary tools of production [and] shows that he or she embodies a history that has realized this logical precondition of capital." Marx insists on this History 1 reality and foregrounds it, Chakrabarty holds, in a way necessary to see abstract labor as a universal. History 1 constitutes no dream land for capital, no terrain for simply maximizing profit. It unfolds in the context of acceptance of a normal workday, eight hours in Chakrabarty's example, with conditions set by the existing "contract of law—the wage contract." Abstraction, not optimal exploitation, makes History 1's logic internal to capital. Marx meanwhile leaves "underdeveloped" what Chakrabarty calls the

---

5   Dipesh Chakrabarty, "Universalism and Belonging in the Logic of Capital," 652–76, quotes from 663, 667, 669, and 670. Cf. Marx, *Grundrisse: Foundations of the Critique of Political Economy*, trans. Martin Nicolaus (Harmondsworth, UK: Penguin, 1973), 296–98; on abstract labor see also Moishe Postone, *Time, Labor, and Social Domination: A Reinterpretation of Marx's Critical Theory* (Cambridge: Cambridge University Press, 1993), esp. 123–85.

"History 2" consciousness also carried to work by the worker. As Chakrabarty puts it in continuing to describe the laborer approaching the factory, "my fictional person also embodies other kinds of pasts. These [History 2] pasts . . . do not belong to the life process of capital. They enable the human bearer of labor power to enact other ways of being in the world, other than, that is, being the bearer of labor power." Everything from "bodily habits," to "unselfconscious collective practices" goes into making History 2.[6] This supplementing of Marx allows us to see how a Little Mexico arises amid the universal labor of globalized Beardstown. But it perhaps stops short of helping us in asking why capital there wants both cheap labor and heterogeneous, variously vulnerable labor. The rethinking stops short of placing racial and national division *within* as well as outside of the History 1 logic of capital.

Lebowitz goes considerably further towards thinking about such a possibility. Though working much more avowedly from within a Marxist political tradition than Chakrabarty, Lebowitz finds in Marx a gap not only underdeveloped but missing entirely from the central sections of *Capital*. In lecturing in 2005 on his receipt of the prestigious Isaac and Tamara Deutscher Memorial Prize for Marxist scholarship, he argued that what is missing in Marx's most celebrated accounts of capital's relation to labor is another unnamed variable, which he termed the "x-factor." Lebowitz insisted on locating x as "part of the essence of capital, indeed, an essential aspect of the logic of capital," and defined x as "the tendency to divide workers." Lebowitz allowed that x was something Marx "recognised well," for example in discussions of antagonisms between Irish and English workers. Indeed, Marx elevated those antagonisms to being "the secret . . . by which the capitalist class maintains its power," adding,

6 Chakrabarty, "Universalism and Belonging," all quotes from 671 but the last, from 672. Cf. Postone, *Time, Labor and Social Domination*, 12–13, 321 and 356, for similar formulations, sometimes phrased so as to suggest that it is recent change in capitalism and social movements that necessitates opening towards "non-class-based social identities" (12) like race, ethnicity, and gender, or accepting that Marxism will be "increasingly anachronistic" (12) and wanting it as an "emancipatory critical theory" (13); Vasant Kaiwar, "On Dipesh Chakrabarty's *Provincializing Europe: Postcolonial Thought and Historical Difference* and Ranajit Guha's "Dominance without Hegemony: History and Power in Colonial India," *Historical Materialism*, 12 (2004), 191–93.

"that [capitalist] class is fully aware of it." But Lebowitz was firm and frank in holding that divisions among the working class, specifically "racism and sexism," do "not appear as part of the essence of capital in Marx's *Capital.*" He then learnedly explained why. Capital's tendencies towards the "centralising, uniting and organising of the working class" exist on this view in tension with "the importance to capital of dividing workers." So much is this the case that even as capital seeks productivity, which Lebowitz calls "q," it includes the x-factor in its calculus. "What matters," he concluded, "is not productivity but the relationship between productivity and the degree of separation (q/x)." Thus where working class universalism is concerned, "capital encourages the development of the collective worker in itself, but has no interest in the emergence of the collective worker for itself," but rather the opposite.[7]

Lebowitz's x-factor takes us so far down the road to penetrating the dramas of Mr. Block's "He Meets Others" comic that the caveat, or perhaps addition, we enter must seem small. In casting attacks by capital on "workers' unity" as driven by the imperative to maximize relative surplus value, not productivity per se, his analysis lingers on the possibility that "capital's drive for surplus-value can lead to specific alterations in the mode of production that lower productivity as such—as long as they divide workers."[8] Such a possibility certainly exists—the introduction of a new group, or "race," of workers into the Louisiana piney woods historically might lead to hate strikes against their arrival, or fights, or quitting by other groups. However, this way of posing matters without considering also the possibility that in some jobs the daily grinding out of productivity is not only consonant with, but also dependent on, playing races against each other, potentially consigns racism too narrowly to the long-term strategies of capital in defensively forestalling resistance and not enough to short-term efforts to quicken the pace of work.

If anything, Commons's formulation underplays the broad connections between racial knowledge and management in two

---

7   Michael A. Lebowitz, "The Politics of Assumption, The Assumption of Politics," *Historical Materialism*, 14 (2006), 29–47, all quotes from 39, save the last two, at 38 and 40. For the Marx passage on Ireland, see "Marx to Sigfrid Meyer and August Vogt in New York" (April 9, 1870), marxists.org.

8   Lebowitz, "Politics of Assumption," quotes from 39 and 40.

ways. While racial competition functioned as one important moment and motive in linking management and race, the idea of a hierarchically understood process of "racial development" undergirded slavery, settler expansion, and industrial capitalist growth, making the ability to manage other races a distinctly "white" contribution to civilization.[9] This article offers modest suggestions for how the project of considering such a large and understudied topic might be undertaken.

We begin with the relationships of settler colonialism and especially slavery to the management of work. A second section details the ways late nineteenth- and early twentieth-century imperialism sent into the world not only capital and soldiers, but also American mining engineers and other managers whose claims to expertise turned on their supposed knowledge of race and racial development and their experience with exploiting racial divisions among workers. Finally, we return to Commons, considering how race management and scientific management coexisted well into the twentieth century domestically, with the most enlightened managers countenancing and furthering the playing of races against each other.

Settlement, Slavery, and the White Managerial Impulse

In connecting management and race, Commons bespoke long-standing, even foundational, American traditions. As members of both a white settler and a slaveholding society, Americans developed a sense of themselves as white by casting their race as uniquely fit to manage land and labor and by judging how other races might come and go in the service of that project. Dispossession of Indians, and the "changes in the land" that it entailed and celebrated, found much justification in the supposed inability of indigenous people to "husband," or manage, the resources at their command.[10] Early

---

9 Cheryl Harris, "Whiteness as Property," *Harvard Law Review*, 106 (1993), 1709–95.

10 William Cronon, *Changes in the Land: Indians, Colonists, and the Ecology of New England* (New York: Hill and Wang, 1983), and Carolyn Merchant, *Ecological Revolution: Nature, Gender, and Science in New England* (Chapel Hill: University of North Carolina Press, 1989).

American management decisions centered on what sort (and quickly on what "race") of coerced labor was most economical, skilled, durable, efficient and tractable. After a period in which Indian slavery seemed a possibility, the last century of the colonial period featured cycles of favoring white indentured servants or African slaves. Management-by-ethnicity led slave traders and owners to attempt to discern in Africans putative propensities to survive and to resist, making such matters measurable and marketable according to the "tribe" of those imported. Similarly, in the fur trade judging the abilities and fostering the willingness of specific Indian tribes and individuals to organize and defend the gathering and transport of vast quantities of furs, defined management.[11]

It was clearly in the nineteenth century when "race management" became formalized into the thoroughly modern practices and discourses that Commons had in mind. The factory and plantation coexisted as the most spectacular sites for management of labor in the Americas with, if anything, the latter providing models for the former. As Robin Blackburn has written, "By gathering the workers under one roof, and subordinating them to one discipline, the new industrial employers were . . . adapting the plantation model."[12] The words "overseer," naming the manager surveilling and speeding up the labor of slaves, and "supervisor," naming the manager performing just the same roles in industry, have the same literal meaning. Similarly, the word "factories" had named the West African staging areas gathering laboring bodies for the slave trade, and then for the production of cotton making possible the textile "factories" of England and of New England[13]

Antebellum US politics, as well as economics, turned on the relative merits of free versus slave labor. Such discussions easily devolved into considerations of the (dis)abilities of African-American labor, in

---

11   Martha C. Knack, *Native Americans and Wage Labor: Ethnohistorical Perspectives* (Norman: University of Oklahoma Press, 1996), and John Morris, "Capitalism into the Wilderness: Mountain Men and the Expansion of Capitalism into the Northern Rockies, 1807–1843" (Ph.D. diss., University of Missouri, 1993).

12   Robin Blackburn, *The Making of New World Slavery: From the Baroque to the Modern 1492–1800* (London: Verso Books, 1998), 565.

13   Walter Rodney, *How Europe Underdeveloped Africa* (Washington, DC: Howard University Press, 1981).

the fields and especially in manufacturing, as against those of "white" labor or of the "Irish race." Far from simply arraying the industrial North versus the agrarian South, the ideological conflicts over these matters saw capitalists in the two regions study and debate not only the relative merits of slavery and free labor, but also the productivity of "black" versus "white" workers. In the 1850s, 20 percent of all manufacturing capital was invested in the South, and the slaveholders most inclined toward proslavery Southern nationalism often led the highly theorized and quantified charge for more such investments. A Lowell weaver imported to oversee production in a Carolina mill, for example, reported that "there is full as much work done by the blacks" who also were supposedly "much more attentive to the looms" than Northern white workers. When white skilled workers protested to the federal government over their replacement by slaves in the Norfolk Dry Dock in 1830, management's response showed how thoroughly difference could be quantified and how easily distinctions between slave and free slipped to become those between Black and white. Stones "hammered by White Men" cost precisely $4.05 more than those "hammered by blacks" in one sample. Ironmasters calculated and reached similar conclusions, despite worries that slaves perhaps wasted more pig iron and charcoal in the production process. Even as the Civil War raged, the Richmond *Examiner* found time for disquisitions on race management, broaching the possibility that the South could rectify its mistake in employing Black labor too overwhelmingly in agriculture. It argued that a refurbished system of bondage based on an "elaborate . . . subdivision of labor," could respond to both the "advanced intelligence" and the "thievish propensities" of slaves, and therefore constituted the key to "the management of the race."[14]

Calculations leading to the replacement of free Black workers in service and seaports in the North by desperately poor Irish immigrants hinged on the extent that such desperation made the Irish

14   Robert Starobin, *Industrial Slavery in the Old South* (New York: Oxford University Press, 1971), 11–14; Linda Upham-Bornstein, "Men of Families: The Intersection of Labor Conflict and Race in the Norfolk Dry Dock Affair, 1829–1831," *Labor*, 4 (Spring 2007), 65; for the iron industry, see Charles Dew, *Bond of Iron: Master and Slave at Buffalo Forge* (New York: Norton, 1994), esp. 107; *Scientific American*, New Series, 9 (December 19, 1863), 386, contains the Richmond quotation in an unsigned note.

willing to underbid African Americans in terms of wages. But the transition from one group to the other, and the threat that other reversals could occur, also featured broad discussions of whether the African or the Irish "race" was more tractable and efficient. When, for example, the wealthy New York City hater of Irish Americans George Templeton Strong maintained that the Irish had "prehensile paws," not hands, his judgment came in the context of extracting labor from immigrant workers at his home and quickly led to comparisons: "Southern Cuffee seems of a higher social grade than Northern Paddy."[15] The antebellum replacement of white American-born "helps" in domestic labor with "servants" of the Irish "race" likewise involved scrutiny and comparison, as did the turn from native-born to Irish women in Northern textile mills.[16]

The potential for the so-called development of Africans as workers and as a race was a central preoccupation of slaveholders, as a voluminous managerial literature made clear. In the major journals, published work at least as frequently focused on the "management of [N]egroes" as on the "management of slaves." When the title referred to slaves, the practical issues like housing rations, supervision, discipline, and diet, bulked larger. When the subject was proclaimed to be managing "[N]egroes," broad pronouncements on racial difference more consistently appeared as part of the calculus of how to run an efficient, productive plantation or farm. But the differences were far from absolute as business knowledge and racial knowledge were thoroughly mixed, and the major plantation

---

15   Noel Ignatiev, *How the Irish Became White* (New York: Routledge, 1998); David R. Roediger, *The Wages of Whiteness: Race and the Making of the American Working Class*, (New York and London: Verso, 1991); Jonathan Glickstein, *Concepts of Free Labor in Antebellum America* (New Haven: Yale University Press, 1991) and Starobin, *Industrial Slavery in the Old South*. For Strong, see Dale T. Knobel, *Paddy and the Republic: Ethnicity and Nationality in Antebellum America* (Middletown, CT: Wesleyan University Press, 1986), 82–99 and George Templeton Strong, *The Diary of George Templeton Strong: The Civil War, 1860–1865*, Allan Nevins and Milton Halsey Thomas, eds. (New York: Columbia University Press, 1952), 342 and 345.

16   Thomas Dublin, *Women at Work: The Transformation of Work and Community in Lowell, Massachusetts, 1826–1860* (New York: Columbia University Press, 1981); Mary Cain, "Race, Republicanism and Domestic Service in the Antebellum United States," *Left History*, 12 (Fall–Winter 2007), 64–83; Eugene D. Genovese, *Roll, Jordan, Roll: The World the Slaves Made* (New York: Pantheon, 1974), 24.

management journals often took the "makeup" of Africans into account. At its most bizarre extreme, masters imagined a serendipitous "innate" characteristic of Africans that utterly deflected abolitionist charges regarding mistreatment of slaves. They were a people, so this theory argued, "whose ethnical element, like the mule, restricts the limits of arbitrary power over [them]." White owners' both abused enslaved people and discoursed on not resorting to "hard treatment" of the slave because they professed to know that abuse "only tends to make him . . . unmanageable."[17]

The assumption that a race, as well as a group of individuals, was being managed sometimes shaped the very ways that productivity was organized and measured among slaves. A lively recent debate among historians of accountancy presses this set of issues usefully. Richard Fleischman and Thomas Tyson argue that racism at times contributed to the decision of plantation managers to eschew compiling individual production data, concentrating instead on gangs, in a discussion focusing on Hawaiian sugar production as well as in antebellum Louisiana. The crude distinction between "full hands" and "half hands" by Louisiana masters suggests some attempt to balance individual and group productivity, though in parts of the South the ideal was to manage individual slaves in a quantifiable

---

17 Samuel Cartwright, "Dr. Cartwright on the Caucasians and the Africans," *De Bow's Review and Industrial Resources, Statistics, etc., Devoted to Commerce* [hereafter *DR*], 1 (July 1858), 46–47 and 52 ("like the mule"); Dr. Samuel Cartwright, "How to Save the Republic," *De Bow's Review of the Southern and Western States*, 11 (August 1851), 186–87 ("a female or a baby") [Note that *De Bow's Review* slightly changed titles over the years but we cite all as *DR* below.] Cf. Robert Collins, "Essay on the Management of Slaves," *Southern Cultivator* [hereafter *SC*], 12 (July 1854), 205–06; Agricola, "Management of Slaves," *SC*, 13 (June 1855), 171–74; John A. Calhoun, "Management of Slaves," *DR, 18* (June 1855), 713; Collins, "Management of Slaves," *DR*, 17 (October 1854), 421–23 ("innate principle of protection"); A Small Farmer, "Management of Negroes," *DR*, 11 (October 1851), 369–72; A.T. Goodloe, "Management of Negroes," *SC*, 18 (April 1860), 130–31; A.T. Goodloe, "Management of Negroes—Again," *SC*, 18 (August 1860), 279–80; A.T. Goodloe, "Management of Negroes—Caution!" *SC*, 18 (October 1860), 305; N.D. Guerry, "Management of Negroes—Duties of Masters," *SC*, 28 (June 1860), 176–77; Robert Collins, "Essay on the Management of Slaves," *DR*, 7 (January–February 1862), 154–57; James M. Towns, "Management of Negroes," *SC*, 9 (June 1851), 87–88; Arkansas River, "Dickson's Planting—Overseers—Negroes, Etc.," *SC*, 18 (October 1860), 304–05; J.W. Pitts, "Best Method of Managing Negroes," *SC*, 18 (October 1860), 325–26; Hurricane, "The Negro and His Management," *SC*, 17 (September 1860), 276–77; A Tennesseean, "Management of Negroes—Bathing Feet," *SC*, 11 (October 1853), 302.

system of tasks. In any case, the formation of workers into a gang that, as many planter-managers boasted, "could be driven," was explicitly seen in racial terms. "You could never depend on white men," the refrain went, "and you couldn't drive them any; they wouldn't stand it."[18] Walter Johnson has shown that race management reached even into the understanding of the value of so-called mixed-race slaves. Lighter-skinned women, for reasons situated at the intersection of European standards of beauty and the practice of sexual exploitation by masters, were more highly priced than darker-skinned "African" women. But among slaves who were men, a light skin generally decreased value as managerial "common sense" dictated that mixed-race slaves could withstand hot and back-breaking labor in sugar production less well, and that they were more likely to be unmanageable workers prone to running away.[19]

The most celebrated "scientific" proslavery thought to emerge from the Deep South came squarely out of the imperatives of management and for the justification of the system in the face of

18 Geoff Burrows, "The Interface of Race and Accounting: A Comment and an Extension" and Fleishman and Tyson, "Interface of Race and Accounting: A Reply to Burrows," *Accounting History* (May 2002), 7-32; Willie Lee Rose, ed., *A Documentary History of Slavery in North America* (Athens: University of Georgia Press, 1999), 337-44; Breeden, ed., *Advice among Masters*, 69-74. See also Genovese, *Roll, Jordan, Roll*, 61, 310, 361 and 371; Ira Berlin, *Generations of Captivity: A History of African-American Slaves* (Cambridge: Belknap Press, 2004), 132, 149, 178 and 212; Joseph Reidy, "Obligation and Right: Patterns of Labor, Subsistence, and Exchange in the Cotton Belt of Georgia" and Steven F. Miller, "Plantation Labor Organization and Slave Life on the Cotton Frontier: The Alabama-Mississippi Black Belt, 1815–1840," both in Ira Berlin and Philip D. Morgan, eds., *Cultivation and Culture: Labor and the Shaping of Slave Life in the Americas* (Charlottesville: University of Virginia Press, 1993), 140–41 and 164–65 as well as 15 of the editors' introduction to the volume. On race and driving, see Robert William Fogel and Stanley Engerman, *Time on the Cross: The Economics of American Slavery* (New York: Norton, 1989 [1974]), 204–05, including the quotation; Frederick Law Olmsted, *A Journey in the Seaboard Slave States: With Remarks on Their Economy* (New York: Dix and Edwards, 1856), 204–06, and Olmsted, *The Cotton Kingdom: A Traveller's Observations on Cotton and Slavery in the American Slave States, 1853–1861* (New York: Da Capo Press, 1996 [1861]), 153 and 452. See also Mark M. Smith, *Mastered by the Clock: Time, Slavery, and Freedom in the American South* (Chapel Hill: University of North Carolina Press, 1997), esp. 133–50 for dramas eventuating when masters attempted to use clock time to impose work discipline on slaves holding to "African" conceptions of time.

19 Walter Johnson, *Soul by Soul: Life in the Antebellum Slave Market* (Cambridge: Harvard University Press, 1999), 142–62.

abolitionist attacks. On the latter score, the idea that Southern masters "knew," and therefore could develop, the Negro, loomed large. In describing his own system of management and what he did for slaves, one planter-expert wrote of acting on the conviction "that man is as much duty bound to improve and cultivate his fellow-men as he is to cultivate and improve the ground." Paternalism and Christianity figured in his arguments, but so, too, did claims to a managerial knowledge serving racial development. Since race management in the antebellum plantation South was often about this promise of racial development, it meshed perfectly with the reality that planters profited from growth in the value of their slaves, not just in the value of crops. Managing in ways designed to produce unscarred slaves developed these enslaved people both as the assets of owners and as a race of Africans. The claim of a superior knowledge of Africans necessary for plantation management and race development based itself on the mastering of slaves in production.[20]

The practice of race management linked race and work early and powerfully. By the 1830s the kinds of danger, filth, overwork, and subservience that could be particularly demanded of African-American workers, free and slave, had spawned a linguistic Americanism, with "nigger work" enduringly entering the language. Similarly, to work hard came to be termed "niggering it" alongside usages like "slave like a nigger." Still others derided whites working in cotton and sugar cultivation as those "who make [N]egroes of themselves." Specific jobs were connected to the race management practices directed against the vulnerable workers doing them. When poor, often immigrant, whites so needed those jobs that they displaced or joined black workers in doing them, they heard the terms "white nigger" or increasingly "Irish nigger." Occupational dangers were also managed around race and slave status, though in contradictory ways. Frederick Law Olmsted famously recorded an instance in which Irish workers were preferred on a very dangerous

---

20 Unsigned, "Laborers for the South," *SC*, 16 (August 1858), 235; Samuel Cartwright, "Diseases and Peculiarities of the Negro Race," *DR*, 1 (September 1851), 331–35. Also see "Dr. Cartwright on the Serpent, the Ape and the Negro," *DR*, 31, (December 1861), 507–16, and Dr. S. Cartwright, "Negro Freedom an Impossibility under Nature's Laws," *DR*, 30 (May–June 1861), 648–59.

draining job even though the Virginia planter employing them thought "a [N]egro could do twice as much work, in a day, as an Irishman." The planter reasoned that an Irish worker's death, unlike a slave's, did not cost capital. However, Illinois excluded the Shawneetown salt mines from its ban on slavery because slave miners were seen as more racially suited for the perilous work in them. Race management was deadly business for those exploited by it.[21]

The physician, slaveholder, and University of Louisiana professor Dr. Samuel Cartwright famously identified two major African pathologies while writing in the Southern regional, agricultural, and management journal De Bow's Review in 1851. The first condition, the "disease causing negroes to run away," was termed "drapetomania" by Cartwright, who called the second "dysaesthesia aethiopica," an illness whose "diagnostic" was an inefficient, seemingly "half-asleep" performance on the job. These symptoms and their cures— "preventively . . . whipping the devil" out of potential drapetomaniacs, and avoiding any possibility of "negro liberty" to avoid dysaesthesia—make it impossible for us to take Cartwright's science seriously, but antebellum experts suffered few such qualms. His seemingly bizarre combination of emphases on the status of the conditions he invented as individual maladies, if socially produced, and as parts of a complex of inherited "racial" inferiorities, capture a pattern running through race management. At bottom, the enterprise hinged on both a firm sense of biologically determined white supremacy and on the malleability that made managing possible, and in Cartwright's view, necessary. He argued, from the Bible and from science, that Africans literally possessed an inherited racial "instinct," housed in the feet and knees, to genuflect before whites. Without productive

---

21   Roediger, *Wages of Whiteness*, 144–45 and 180; Mandel, *Labor: Free and Slave*, 63; Cartwright as quoted in Eugene D. Genovese, *The Political Economy of Slavery: Studies in the Economy and Society of the Slave South* (New York: Vintage, 1967), 47; Starobin, *Industrial Slavery in the Old South*, 215 (on Shawneetown, where the mechanism involved a wage, paid to slaves from other states, who, with their master's permission hired themselves out for a term and then returned to slavery, with the bulk of the wage going to the master); Olmsted, *Journey in the Seaboard Slave States*, 90–91; see also Ulrich Bonnell Phillips, *American Negro Slavery: A Survey of the Supply, Employment and Control of Negro Labor as Determined by the Plantation Regime* (New York: D. Appleton and Company, 1940 [1918]), 301–03 and U.B. Phillips, *Life and Labor in the Old South* (Boston: Little, Brown, 1929), 186–87.

management the loss of this instinct produced disease and disaster. Also "innate" was a "love to act as body servant or lacquey," a tendency to "glory in a close, hot atmosphere, " an "ethnical" proclivity to desire being punished by whips rather than other devices, and an "ethnological peculiarity" ensuring that "any deserved punishment, inflicted with a switch, cowhide or whip, puts them into a good humor." Cartwright slid from seeing the conditions he described as curable, preventable "diseases" afflicting only a minority of slaves to suggesting a more constitutional and obdurate problem by terming the maladies "peculiarities of the negro." Cartwright made management the cure for "Negro peculiarities." He insisted that "the seat of negro consumption is not in the lungs, stomach, liver, or any organ of the body, but in the mind, and its cause is generally mismanagement or bad government on the part of the master."[22]

Cartwright specified two distinct ways in which his supposed knowledge was a race manager's wisdom. He first chided Northern scientists for being blind to matters so clear to masters and overseers who were in daily contact with slaves, claiming that free Blacks in the North displayed dysaesthesic symptoms almost universally, but that their supposedly "masterless" status made both diagnosis and cure impossible outside the South. However, he then confined real knowledge to the slaveholding class, underlining the conclusion of some advice literature on slave management by insisting that the master's racial knowledge excelled that of overseers. The latter, he complained, wrongly dismissed slave misbehaviour as "rascality" rather than scientifically seeing it as disease and inferiority.[23]

---

22   Samuel A. Cartwright, "Ethnology of the Negro or Prognathous Race: A Lecture Given November 30, 1857, Before the New Orleans Academy of Science" (n.d.), Samuel A. Cartwright and Family Papers, Printed Pamphlets, Special Collections, Louisiana State University Library, 6, 9, and 14. For a sharp awareness that crops, plantation order, slaves as assets and race development were all being produced by plantation management, see Guerry, "Management of Negroes—Duties of Masters," 176–77. On consumption, see Cartwright, "The Diseases of Negroes—Pulmonary Congestions, Pneumonia, &c.," *DR*, 11 (August 1851), 212.

23   William E. Wiethoff, "Enslaved Africans' Rivalry with White Overseers in Plantation Culture," *Journal of Black Studies*, 36 (2006), 429–55; Breeden, ed., *Advice among Masters*, esp. 81–86, 170–78 and 291–304; William Van Deburg, *The Slave Drivers: Black Agricultural Labor Supervisors in the Antebellum South* (Westport, CT: Greenwood Press, 1979), esp. 3; Genovese, *Roll, Jordan, Roll*, 366–67; Starobin, *Industrial Slavery in the Old South*, 168–73.

Such claims, as W.E.B. Du Bois long ago observed, had far-reaching impact on the development of white supremacist thought far beyond the South. To the "watching world," a racism designed to manage what Du Bois called "slave industry" seemed "the carefully thought-out result of experience and reason." Indeed in other, and even more unlikely, areas as well, the seminal, if controversial, intellectual work of Professor Cartwright grew out of race management. His tortured foray into theology in order to develop the minority proslavery racist position that Africans were a pre-Adamic separate race who profited by enslavement under superior Caucasians, Cartwright read plantation management back into the Bible's earliest pages, hinging a circuitous argument on the retranslation of words that had made Ham the father of Cush and others as making him a "head man, manager, or overseer of the nacash [Negro] race." Thus, only those mastering and managing slaves could fully appreciate the ethnology and theology of the early Old Testament. Here Cartwright showed more respect for the wisdom of overseers. As Cartwright wrote in 1860, "The Bible tells us certain facts about negroes which none but the best informed planters and overseers know at the present day." As one agitated Southern critic of Cartwright put it in 1862, "How the theological world will be startled when they discover that what they looked on as important genealogical tables, turn out to be merely lists of negro slaves." Similarly Cartwright premised his scholarship in ethnology, squarely on the need managers of slaves had for racial knowledge. Those lacking such ethnological knowledge, he maintained, "have great trouble in managing negroes." He continued, "If their ethnology were better understood, their value would be greatly increased . . ."[24]

Cartwright's work is widely cited as foundational in scientific racism, though its place as a central text in the history of American management is seldom assayed. Indeed, his simple treatment for the slow-working "hebetude" accompanying dysaesthesia aethiopica was to make slaves work harder, therefore sending more oxygen to their brains. Management compelled Africans to work, to "inhale vital air," and to be transformed from the "*bipedum nequissimus* or

---

24   On Cartwright's use of work as a cure and on his managerial impulses for ethnology, see his "Diseases and Peculiarities of the Negro Race," 333–35, passim.

arrant rascal that he was supposed to be" to a healthy "good negro that can handle hoe or plow." Thus transformed and driven, the slave could produce effectively, accomplishing "about a third less than what the white man voluntarily imposes on himself" and not rebelling as whites "naturally would." Such an oxygenating prescription, and pseudo-quantified science of work captured much of the sense, nonsense, and circularity of race managements to come. Meanwhile, as Matthew Pratt Guterl writes, when reflecting on the supposed failure of emancipation in the West Indies, the proslavery consensus was "three freedmen equal one slave." The calculus of oppression and of race development could be quantified.[25]

Transnationalizing Race Management: From Confidence Men to Mining Engineers

For all of the attention of antebellum political economists and slave-drivers to race and productivity, Herman Melville's novel *The Confidence Man* remains the best source on the far-flung sources and implications of pre–Civil War race management. The ship on which the story is set crosses the confluence with the Ohio River as it proceeds down the Mississippi, leaving behind a stretch in which the water divides "free" and "slave" states. It enters—as the nation seemed about to do itself in 1857 when the proslavery Dred Scott decision and the novel both appeared—a place where all territory is slave territory. As the change occurs, at the novel's very center and after a playful and masterful section touching on race and mining, characters debate not only abolition and bondage but labor

25 W.E.B. Du Bois, *Black Reconstruction in American 1860–1880* (New York: Free Press, 1988), 39. For an important account of the disappearing of US slavery from the history of management, see Bill Cooke, "The Denial of Slavery in Management Studies," *Journal of Management Studies*, 40 (December 2003), 1895–1918. Cartwright's views on race and the Bible are laid out in "Unity of the Human Race Disproved by the Hebrew Bible," *DR*, 4 (August 1860), 131 and 129–36. For the long, rollicking critique of his views on Ham, see Unsigned, "Dr. Cartwright on the Negro—Reviewed," *DR*, 8 (May–August 1862), esp. 66–67; George Fredrickson, *The Black Image in the White Mind* (Middletown, CT: Wesleyan University Press, 1987), 87–88. For Guterl, see "After Slavery: Asian Labor, the American South, and the Age of Emancipation," *Journal of World History*, 14 (2003), 223.

generally. A contractor of unfree labor parading as a sentimental reformer (critics have generally taken him to be the shifty title character in disguise) offers to provide a "good boy" to a "misanthrope" soured on believing that any young worker would ever be able to satisfy his need for steady and honest help and, it is hinted, his desires for considerably more. In answer to the self-interested reformer's pieties regarding the essential goodness of all boys, the misanthrope lists a racialized litany of the young workers he has tried: "I speak from fifteen years' experience; five and thirty boys; American, Irish, English, German, African, Mulatto; not to speak of that China boy sent me by one who well knew my perplexities, from California; and that Lascar boy from Bombay. Thug! I found him sucking the embryo life from my spring eggs. All rascals, sir, every soul of them; Caucasian or Mongol."[26]

The multiplicity of types suggests the ways that a world labor market enlivened debates on race management, during a decade when calls to reopen the African slave became insistent and when the "coolie trade" from Asia to the Caribbean and elsewhere, already framed, as Moon-Ho Jung demonstrates, discussions of slavery and labor and the ways workers might be pitted against each other in the United States. By Reconstruction, pro-"coolie" planters and supporters, betraying what Jung calls an "unyielding fascination with race," saw importation of Chinese labor as a way to break "Sambo" from the sense that he was "master of the southern situation." One newspaper editorialized that most planters sought Chinese labor because they believed it to be "more easily managed, and do better work, although much slower." The writer praised racial competition as much as the virtues of any race, promising that entry of 100,000 Chinese workers would "make the negro a much more reliable laborer." Former slave-trader and slave-master, and literally murderous Confederate general, Nathan Bedford Forrest became an entrepreneur in new arenas and a railway manager after the war, as well as the leader of the terrorist Ku Klux Klan. He alternated between

---

26 Herman Melville, *The Confidence Man: His Masquerade* (Evanston and Chicago: Northwestern University Press, 1984 [1857]), esp. 15–28; Carolyn Karcher, *Shadow over the Promised Land: Slavery, Race, and Violence in Melville's America* (Baton Rouge: Louisiana State University Press, 1979). On slavery, race, and mining, see Starobin, *Industrial Slavery in the Old South*, 138, 214–19 and 223–24.

proclaiming African labor the world's best, and therefore seeking new importations of African guest-workers, and encouraging schemes to import Chinese labor, in both cases to compete with existing local labor supplies.[27]

Race management also opened the West, with the historic 1860s construction of the transcontinental railroad frankly structured as a competition, sometimes spilling over into violence, of Irish versus Chinese gangs on unspeakably dangerous jobs. The relatively cheap labor, and vulnerability, of the former group influenced even how the road was engineered, with inexpensive, imperiled labor substituting for wooden support structures. As with racialized gang labor elsewhere, the whole gang was paid, with management in one instance declaring that because Chinese were indistinguishable from each other, individual wage payments would have opened possibilities of the same worker drawing double pay.[28]

Indeed, while most such discourse was seemingly domestically produced, tied to North/South sectional conflict rooted in slavery, Melville rightly insisted on a context of trade and empire in framing all discussion of race and management. His section on labor in *The Confidence Man* lies in the shadow of that on the "metaphysics of Indian-hating," for example. In "The 'Gees," he offers a short, enigmatic and rollicking sketch of how whites, and particularly white managers of maritime work, claimed racial knowledge of the Afro-Portuguese from the island Fogo. Melville locates the production of

---

27   Moon-Ho Jung, *Coolies and Cane: Race, Labor, and Sugar in the Age of Emancipation* (Baltimore: Johns Hopkins University Press, 2006), 202–203; Unsigned, "A Picture of the West Indies," *DR*, 3 (June 1860), 729–38. Cf. Lucy M. Cohen, *The Chinese in the Post-Civil War South* (Baton Rouge: Louisiana State University Press, 1984), 53. See also Guterl, "Asian Labor, The American South and the Age of Emancipation," esp. 221–41 and, for the varied ways experiences of Southerners with Chinese workers in Cuba influenced the debates, 211–21. On Forrest and the KKK in the Piedmont, see Paul Ashdown and Edward Gaudill, *The Myth of Nathan Bedford Forrest* (Lanham, MD: Rowman & Littlefield, 2006), esp. 62–3, and Scott Reynolds Nelson, *Iron Confederacies: Southern Railways, Klan Violence, and Reconstruction* (Chapel Hill: University of North Carolina Press, 1999), 135–37.

28   Stephen Ambrose, *Nothing Like It in the World: The Men Who Built the Transcontinental Railroad* (New York: Simon and Schuster, 2000), 153, 327 and passim. On "race," immigration and the toleration of industrial accidents, see Michael K. Rosenow, "Injuries to All: The Rituals of Dying and the Politics of Death Among United States Workers, 1877–1910" (unpublished Ph.D. diss., University of Illinois, 2008), 32–33 and 81.

the racial knowledge that he ridicules within an Atlantic system of trade, folklore, and, above all, management. As Carolyn Karcher shows, the broader target of Melville's merciless satire is US ethnological writing on race, particularly that of Cartwright. Melville's over-the-top account undermines all claims of expert knowledge to scientific and managerial rigor, perfectly capturing its offhandedness, circularity, and selfishness without losing sight of its import. Ethnology regularly collapses in Melville's sketch into a ridiculous managerial how-to, advising captains on methods to capture the beam of evil in eyes of experienced 'Gee sailors attempting to pose as innocent and tractable "green 'Gees" in order to be hired. The most important judgments regarding 'Gees hinge on which ones to hire. Such decisions are best left to "'Gee jockeys," men "well-versed in 'Gees,"—that is, management experts—who then turn out to know nothing either.[29]

Nonetheless, the claim to have such knowledge, as Melville spelled out again in his even more bitter *Benito Cereno*, enabled US race managers to proceed across the continent and in the wider world (in that novella, the sea captain spouting elaborate US pretenses to racial knowledge manages to fully miss seeing the occurrence of a slave revolt). Well before the Philippine war, a striking number of former slave-owning or slave-trading Southerners found work and wealth by claiming expertise in the capture and management of Pacific Island forced laborers being brought into Fiji and Queensland.[30] Race was ultimately central to both industrial management at home and to imperial capitalist expansion. After the Treaty of Guadaloupe Hildalgo added much of Mexico to the United States, one US editor summed up what Ron Takaki has called the "metaphysics of Mexican-hating" as the triumph of the managerial:

> The nation that makes no outward progress . . . that wastes its treasures wantonly—that cherishes not its resources—such a

---

29   Herman Melville, "The 'Gees," in *Great Short Works of Herman Melville*, Warner Berthoff, ed. (New York: Harper & Row, 1969 [1856]), 355–61; Carolyn L. Karcher, "Melville's 'The 'Gees': A Forgotten Satire on Scientific Racism," *American Quarterly*, 27 (October 1975), 421–22.

30   Gerald Horne, *The White Pacific: US Imperialism and Black Slavery in the South Seas After the Civil War* (Honolulu: University of Hawaii Press, 2006).

nation will burn out [and] become the prey of the more adventur-
ous enemy.[31]

The old argument that the "English-speaking race" embodied
wise management continued to add its part to empire-building. In
1896, Andrew Carnegie, commenting on British actions in
Venezuela, would write of the "dubious" ways that indigenous land
had been seized, but conclude that nonetheless "upon the whole the
management of the land acquired by our race has been for the higher
interests of humanity." Indeed "civilization" made "the acquisition of
the land necessary"; it was "well that the Maori should fade away,
and give way to the intelligent, industrious citizen, a member of our
race."[32]

In large measure the cohabitation of race management and
management science matured among US managers outside the
country before it became so highly noticed at home. Arguably, the
greatest US export in the quarter century after 1890 was the mining
engineer, and with him US capital goods. Technically well trained,
such engineers replaced European experts in Asian, Mexican, South
American, Australian, and African mines in significant measure
because they could so loudly proclaim a knowledge gained at the
intersection of race and management. Such engineers often gained
experience in western US mines, where decisions regarding which
"races" (the term then marked differences of European nationality as
well as broad "color" divisions) could live in the "white man's camp"
were central to all management. In Columbia University's ambitious
1950s project interviewing mining engineers with far-flung careers,
Ira Joralemon was one interviewee who learned race (and gender)
management in the Southwest, and took it into wider worlds. In
Arizona's Ajo mine, he recalled, "a lot of Papago Indians" did the

31 Ronald Takaki, *Iron Cages: Race and Culture in Nineteenth-Century America* (New
York: Oxford University Press, 2000), 161; Herman Melville, "Benito Cereno," in *Great
Short Works* (New York: Harper Collins, 2004 [1854–55]), 238–315.

32 Andrew Carnegie, "The Venezuelan Question," *North American Review*, 162
(February 1896), 133. Cf. "Lo, the Poor Indian," *Barron's*, 4 (November 10, 1924), 9, for
an even more extreme sense that, whether in Australia, New Zealand, Canada, or the
United States, unless an "aboriginal race" is exterminated "it is hard to see more than a
sentimental reason for deploring its extinction. People die anyway."

dangerous and hard work of sinking the pit. Quickly Swedes from Minnesota, typed as "jackpine savages" when they mined in proximity to Indians in that state, joined the ranks of the mine's drill men. The Swedes, according to Joralemon's useful-to-management observations, were so tough that the "squaw men" around Ajo, who lived with their families out in the desert, called the new drillers "the savages."[33]

Men like Joralemon claimed an ability to know and to boss "native" and racially divided labor worldwide, with South African mines the site of the most spectacular influx of US management. In South Africa, where fully half of new gold mines had US managers by 1895, William Honnold was among the most powerful of the Yankee engineers. Holding that "some employers are unqualified or temperamentally unfit to manage crude labor," he held in 1908 that "to recall American experience" with the "efficiency of negroes" could clarify much in South African mines, where Honnold resisted proposals to bring in African-American miners with the judgment that "American niggers . . . would be the very worst thing that could be introduced."[34]

As central figures in the cult of the Yankee mining engineer, Herbert and Lou Hoover began to be publicized after 1900 as the nation's most "modern" transnational couple. Herbert gave the name "Golden Age" to the triumph of US engineers in the world's mines. Though press-agented as the "Doctor of Sick Mines" and the nation's "highest-salaried man" for his work as a transnational engineer

---

33   Clark C. Spence, *Mining Engineers and the American West: The Lace-Boot Brigade, 1849–1933* (New Haven and London: Yale University Press, 1970), 165–87 and 278–317; Shula Marks and Stanley Trapido, "Lord Milner and the South African State," *History Workshop Journal*, 8 (Spring, 1979), 61; Yvette Huginnie, "A New Hero Comes to Town: The Anglo Mining Engineer and 'Mexican Labor' as Contested Terrain in Southeastern Arizona, 1880–1920," *New Mexico Historical Review* (October 1994); Roediger, *Working Toward Whiteness*, 74–75. On Joralemon, see his interview with Henry Carlisle, "Arizona Characters and the Ajo Mine" from November 1959 and included in the Mining Engineer Project, vol. 1, part 1, in the Columbia University Oral History Project, Butler Library, Columbia University, dated November 1959. See also Steven G. Vick, *Degrees of Belief: Subjective Probability and Engineering Judgment* (Reston, VA: ASCE Press, 2002), 342.

34   Honnold as quoted in John Higginson, "Privileging the Machine: American Engineers, Indentured Chinese and White Workers in South Africa's Deep-Level Mines, 1902–1907," *International Review of Social History*, 52 (April 2007), 10 and 15.

whose most spectacular adventure capitalist exploits brought efficiency to Africa, China, and isolated areas of Australia, he might as
easily deserve the simpler title of "race manager." In Australia, he
thought that the "saucy independence" and "loafing proclivities" of
local white miners required a counterweight. Hoover ranked groups
of indigenous Australians eagerly but called all of them "niggers" and
judged even "superior" ones as having "too little intelligence to work
very much." He therefore pitted the "races" against each other by
importing crews of Italian immigrants and keeping them "in reserve"
in order to "hold the property" against the possibility of a general
strike. In the context of an Australian Labor Party–backed inquiry
into the use of Italian labor, Hoover's associate gave the fuller logic
of the choice. Italians, he reckoned, were more "servile" and "peace-
able"—Hoover himself put the advantage of Italian labor at a ratio
of 26:15 on one work gang—but the real benefit lay in the racial
competition itself. Management would be "in a mess if they had all
aliens or all British." It was "mixed labor" that provided the real
payoffs.[35]

An eager consumer and producer of reports judging the relative
efficiency of African, Chinese, and white miners on the Rand in
South Africa, Hoover was accustomed to calculating productivity by
weighing "colored shifts" and "colored wages" against the white. His
own most extensive calculations on race and management involved
Chinese workers. Hoover, who once extravagantly wrote that he had
strongly supported restriction of "Asiatic immigration" to the US
from the moment that he could "think and talk," made much of his
early career as an engineer in North China. He continually
commented on race and productivity there, at times spinning that
data to attract investment in China, and at others to explain why
more dramatic gains in efficiency had not been made under his
watch. In an early prominent appearance before an international
congress of engineers in London in 1902, for example, he wrote of

35 Spence, *Mining Engineers*, 278; George H. Nash, *The Life of Herbert Hoover: The
Engineer, 1874–1914* (New York: W.W. Norton, 1983), 72–73 and 330–33; Joan Hoff
Wilson, *Herbert Hoover: Forgotten Progressive* (Prospect Heights, IL: Waveland Press, 1992
[1975]), 33–37; Herbert Hoover Scrapbooks (Hoover Presidential Library [hereafter HL],
West Branch, IA); "Extracts from Letters Home" (Western Australia, 1897?) in HL, box
50, Pre-Commerce Papers.

the "mulishness" of Chinese miners and of a "capacity for thieving [that] permits the abstraction of nails, screws, nuts and even coal." However, he cheerily concluded, money could be saved on timbers supporting mines because the resulting tragedies only had to be compensated at thirty dollars per death, given what he perversely saw as "the disregard for human life" among the Chinese.[36]

Hoover mixed impressions and calculations in arriving at varied views of the Chinese worker, and could always claim knowledge, if not consistency. Chinese "thieving" was epidemic, but at other junctures judged as no worse than the world's norm. He could credit charges that Chinese cultural baggage regarding mining fatally interfered with operations, and then turn on a dime to offer the more plausible view that to dwell on "superstition" there was a "great mistake," adding

> The Chinese mine as fast as anyone if they believe that there is anything in it for them. The main reason for the riots against our mines and miners was the Chinese dislike of seeing foreigners make capital out of their soil.[37]

The ratios of race and productivity that Hoover fabricated, to the delight of commentators at international conferences, similarly varied wildly. In 1900, he supposed that Chinese in mining produced a fifth of what white workers did, since for the former group "to work, in the sense of Western miners, is an unheard-of exaction."

---

36 See, for example, "Rand Native Labor Committee" (1903) in HL, box 56, Pre-Commerce Papers; "Notes on Stopping on the Rand During 1907" in HL, box 55, Pre-Commerce Papers; Herbert Hoover, *Principles of Mining: Valuation, Organization and Administration* (New York: Hill Publishing Company, 1909), 161–65; "Hoover to Dear Mr. Congressman [John Baker]" (February 19, 1924) in HL, box 289, Commerce Papers, and the draft dated February 13, 1924 in the same box; Herbert Hoover, "The Kaiping Coal Mines and Coal Field, Chihle Province, North China" printed in the proceedings of the Eighth Ordinary Meeting of the Institute of Mining and Metallurgy (London, 1902), 419 and 426–27 in HL, box 50, Pre-Commerce Papers.

37 See Hoover, "The Kaiping Coal Mines and Coal Field, Chihle Province, North China," and Hoover, "Metal Mining in the Provinces of Chi-li and Shantung, China," printed in the proceedings of the Sixth Ordinary Meeting of the Institute of Mining and Metallurgy (London, 1900) in HL, box 50, Pre-Commerce Papers, and the clipping in box 56 of the same collection defending Chinese miners.

Two years later, the Chinese worker had "no equal" in the world for crude labor, though an accompanying chart counted him only a quarter as productive as the "American" in such work, and for a twelfth the pay. For miners, the newly calculated ratio of productivity was 1:8, with Chinese miners paid a sixth as much and therefore more expensive than whites. However, Hoover's mathematical mistake leads him to the opposite conclusion, and then to a disquisition on the "superintendence" of hidden costs and "eternal vigilance against fraud," to explain why working costs could be high in Chinese mines.[38]

When he published *Principles of Mining* in 1909, Hoover produced a chart on South African mines, amalgamating data on African and Chinese workers there. He also purportedly reflected on data from the Chinese in China to conclude that in simple tasks like shoveling "one white man equals from two to three of the colored races." In more highly skilled work "the average ratio is . . . one to seven, or . . . even eleven." Hoover's memoirs explained the productivity differences as racial, though all of his writings offer the possibility, common in progressive thought, that enduring cultural habits mattered as much as biology in making race. "Our inventions and machinery came out of our racial instincts and qualities," he held. "Our people learn easily how to make them work efficiently." The Chinese, "a less mechanical-minded people than the European-descended races . . . require many times more men to operate our intricate machines."[39]

Groping towards a kind of "white jointness" uniting interests of capital and labor around race, Hoover departed substantially from the editorial view of the influential *Engineering and Mining Journal*, which maintained that "mine operators find it economical to make the best of whatever native labor may be available," training it up to

---

38   Cf. the Hoover papers given in 1900 and 1902 (cited in n. 37 and 38 above) and the comment appended to the 1902 paper (427).

39   Herbert Hoover, *The Memoirs of Herbert Hoover: Years of Adventure, 1874–1920* (New York: The Macmillan Company, 1951), 69–71, and Hoover, *Principles of Mining*, 161–65. For a provocative exploration of the relationship of the use of race to organized management, to more contemporary concerns about technology and the control of workers, see Michael Perelman, "Preliminary Notes on Technology and Class Struggle," *Labor Tech: Bringing Technology to Serve the Labor Movement*, labortech.net.

"American or European" standards, rather than deal with sickly and entitled imported white miners. However, he never argued that nonwhite labor must be barred from unskilled work, only that wages, opportunities, expectations, and conditions of competition be adjusted by knowledgeable race managers, whose ability to calculate advantages aggrandized their roles. In South Africa, he closely associated with Honnold, with John Higginson's wonderful account terming the pair "formidable enemies of South Africa's black and white workers." Indeed, for all of his doubts as to their efficiency, Hoover played an active role with the Chinese Engineering and Mining Company in recruiting over 60,000 indentured Chinese to work in South African mines. At a time when African miners were massively withdrawing their labor from jobs in which wages had decreased and danger of accidents was rising, and when organized skilled white miners commanded great social power in the industry, the Chinese seemed to offer great opportunities to play races against each other. The particular task of sinking ever deeper mines rested on new technologies for recovery of less rich ore, but, as Higginson shows, it also hinged on "concealing death," and on management's role in producing it. Chinese and African miners were made to perilously drill into hanging walls in shafts insufficiently supported by timbering; Chinese miners were especially blamed for the resulting cave-ins, from which neither skill nor whiteness offered protection.[40]

When employing nonwhite labor, Hoover also indulged in paternal fantasies of generalized racial uplift. Hoover balanced racial competition with what was called "race development" in the early twentieth century. Such alternating currents of race management and race development helped give rise to a thoroughly modern US imperialism. Perhaps the firm who most practiced race management, in part via race development, was Ford Motor Company. Hoover's thinking in the world was mirrored by Henry Ford at home, whose foremen and managers set immigrant "races" against each other even as company-paid social workers could claim to develop "the race" as a whole through education in Americanism

---

40   T.A. Rickard, ed., *The Economics of Mining* (New York: Engineering and Mining Journal, 1905), 388; Higginson, "Privileging the Machines," 16 and 12–26.

and intrusive home visits from company "sociologists."[41] African-American workers at Ford outnumbered those in all other auto plants combined, yet rather than suggesting a lack of concern with racial justice in its plants, Ford's hiring of African Americans reveals a sophisticated—if contradictory—approach to management via race. That the flagship journal of modern US empire, *Foreign Affairs*, evolved from the tellingly titled *Journal of Race Development* suggests that few architects of US empire did their work outside a racial framework.[42]

Scientific Management, Racist Science, and the Studied Unstudiedness of Race Management

The ways in which race management coexisted with scientific management at home deserve our attention, as they are the clearest examples of how fully compatible with the innovations of capitalism were the atavisms of race. The come-and-go hopes of Melville's misanthrope as he sought the perfect racial and national types to produce the perfect worker seem utterly at odds with the science of management that Frederick Winslow Taylor is credited with inventing in the late nineteenth century. Yet Commons was able to maintain otherwise, in part because Taylor's ideas existed alongside crude practices of race management. More importantly, the famous example that Taylor himself used to educate the public regarding his system's ability to create "high-priced men" by selecting them studiously and regimenting their motions scientifically, suggests overlap between managerial science

41 Wilson, *Hoover*, 32–33; Hoover, *Memoirs of Hoover*, 71; on Ford, see Stephen Meyer III, *The Five-Dollar Day: Labor Management and Social Control in the Ford Motor Company, 1908–1921* (Albany: State University of New York Press, 1981), 156-92. See also Elizabeth Esch, "Shades of Tarzan! Ford on the Amazon," *Cabinet: A Quarterly Journal of Art and Culture*, 7 (Summer 2002), 76–79.

42 Jessica Blatt, "'To Bring Out the Best That Is in Their Blood': Race, Reform, Civilization, and the *Journal of Race Development*," *Ethnic and Racial Studies*, 27 (September 2004), 691–708; Thomas Bender, *A Nation among Nations: America's Place in World History* (New York: Hill and Wang, 2006), 210. The publication became the *Journal of International Relations* in 1919 and *Foreign Affairs* three years after that. On Ford and Hoover, see David Lanier Lewis, *The Public Image of Henry Ford* (Detroit: Wayne State University Press, 1987), 222.

and race management. In the example, even as he insisted that the key to effective management was to remake individuals, Taylor chose Schmidt as the first worker to retrain into a new regimen, in moving an abandoned stock of pig-iron suddenly made valuable by the Spanish–American–Cuban–Filipino War. He did so with "racial" attributes much in mind. Schmidt's name, and Taylor's description, emphasized that Schmidt's agreement to submit to the new system, and his ability to produce, flowed in part from his membership in the German "race." Schmidt embodied the strength, doggedness, and love of savings thought by Taylor to be peculiarly concentrated in the Pennsylvania Dutch, as Germans in the area were called.

Taylor's racial logic in the Schmidt example did not run through the whole of his writing. His desire to uproot the arbitrary power of foremen and other petty bosses placed Taylor among those management experts whose formal system left the least room for day-to-day uses of stormy racial competition to extract production. But more broadly, the race-thinking that informed Taylor's presentation of his new system, by introducing listeners and readers to Schmidt, did comport with larger patterns that saw race management survive, and even expand, in the early years of the era of scientific management. As David Montgomery has written of the period in which scientific management flowered, "all managers seem[ed] to agree" with International Harvester's H.A. Worman, who held that "each race has aptitude for certain kinds of work." However, Montgomery slyly—and as we shall see, weightily—adds that they could disagree utterly about "which 'race' was best for what." Montgomery further observed that the trend toward personnel management as a complement to Taylorism specifically "extended the purview of scientific management from the factory itself to the surrounding community," a development that "flowed directly from the concern with recruiting from specific ethnic groups."[43]

43   Frederick Winslow Taylor, *Principles of Scientific Management* (New York: Norton, 1967 [1911]), 41–47; David Montgomery, *The Fall of the House of Labor: The Workplace, the State, and American Labor Activism, 1865–1925* (Cambridge: Cambridge University Press, 1987), 242–43. See also Sanford M. Jacoby, "A Century of Human Resource Management," in Bruce E. Kaufman, Richard A. Beaumont, and Roy B. Helfgott, eds., *Industrial Relations to Human Resources and Beyond: The Evolving Process of Employee Relations Management* (Armonk, NY: M.E. Sharpe, 2003), 148–50.

Montgomery was right about both the ubiquity and durability of race management on the one hand, and its haphazardness regarding which races performed best in what jobs on the other. In 1915 an iron industry journal went so far as to challenge the adequacy of the very term "common labor" on the grounds that "such labor is racial," so that iron and steel actually did not compete in recruiting employees with other lines of work. "Immigrants of some races," it held, "turn chiefly to agriculture, some to the vending of fruit, others to the making of clothing, and others seek the coke works, blast furnaces and steel mills." At times, management literature recorded "how" races should be slotted into jobs. John Williams, who presided over the Philadelphia Association for the Discussion of Labor Problems, wrote during World War One that in fabricating steel grinders ought to be "Polish, Lithuanians, or Americans." Finishers were to be Italian or American girls (and, or perhaps therefore, "not flirty") and forgers either Americans or "American Poles." The elaborate chart ranking three dozen immigrant "races" according to their fitness for three dozen job types and conditions, posted at Pittsburgh Central Tube in 1925, assembled a much more impressive number of opinions systematizing a huge factory and the peoples in it in upwards of a thousand multicolored squares.

But in all of these cases, judgments were extremely crude, gathering up managerial and professional folklore and summing up existing prejudices and practices. Italians, according to the Pittsburgh chart, allegedly excelled with pick and shovel but could not handle serving as helpers for engineers. Armenians ranked "good" in none of the twenty-two job categories listed, and rose to "fair" only once: wheelbarrow. "Americans, White" could do any job, at least at a "fair" level and excelled in most. Jews supposedly fit well into no industrial jobs. Portuguese workers rated as poor in seven of eight "atmospheric conditions" and joined Mexicans and Filipinos in lacking capacity to work on the night shift, or the day one.[44]

Montgomery's second point is perhaps more interesting: the

----

44 "The Iron Industry's Labor Supply," *Iron Age*, 96 (July 8, 1915), 91; John M. Williams, "An Actual Account of What We Have Done to Reduce Our Labor Turnover," *The Annals of the American Academy*, 71 (May 1917), 64; John Bodnar, Roger Simon and Michael Weber, *Lives of Their Own: Blacks, Italians, and Poles in Pittsburgh, 1900–1960* (Urbana: University of Illinois Press, 1983), 240 reprints the chart.

constant glancing attention to race in management literature did not require close empirical investigation of which races produced best in what jobs. The Immigration Commission report of 1911 posited virtual unanimity among employers about the idea that Southern Italians were "the most inefficient of races." This coexisted with Pittsburgh Steel placing Italians in the most efficient third, above Canadians, of all "racial" groups shortly thereafter, revealing how even attempts at pragmatic application of such knowledge were contradictory. Nor did the fact that one steel manager might prefer "two Negroes" to "three Macedonians," while most ranked the "alien white races" above African Americans, provoke any urgent desire to systematically settle the issue. Not only the basic question of who was white, but even that of who was Black, remained unanswered by managers fixated on race. "The 'black races' cannot do the work in three days that a white man can do in one," an Iron Range mine superintendent told a government investigator, using the former term to connote Montenegrins, Serbs, Southern Italians, Greeks, and Croats. When rankings were hazarded, they reflected collections of existing prejudices, not investigation. Thus a 1911 *Iron Age* article placed the "races" in "about the following order: Slovaks, Poles, Magyars, Croatians, Italians," ranked according to "preferences of the employers."[45]

The Schmidt and Hoover examples, with Montgomery's commentary, remind us that scientific management and race management coexisted because they were not so utterly different after all. Scientific management, like Hoover's race management in the mines, was, as Bernard Doray wrote long ago, a "science" that could not escape "bear[ing] the scars of the social violence that characterized the society that gave birth to it." Replete with pro-management assumptions, it selectively drew on folk knowledge and crude observations

---

45   Roediger, *Working Toward Whiteness*, 75–77; for the Iron Range, "Industrial Progress and Efficiency," in vol. 16, part 18; "Iron Ore Mining," in "Reports of the Immigration Commission, Immigrants in Industries," Senate Documents, 61st Congress, 2nd Session 1909–1910, vol. 78, Washington, Government Printing Office, 1911, 339-41, with thanks to Thomas Mackaman; Lauck, "Recent Immigration," 899. For Commons's blithe ranking of European immigrants, in part based on their class consciousness, see his "The Sweating System in the Clothing Trade" in Commons, ed., *Trade Unionism and Labor Problems*, 332–33. On the use of "race" to refer to European groups later thought of as "ethnic," see Victoria Hattam, *In the Shadow of Race: Jews, Latinos, and Immigrant Politics in the United States* (Chicago: University of Chicago Press, 2007).

of existing work patterns in ways mercilessly unearthed in Harry Braverman's dissection of Taylor's methods. Scientific management was therefore broadly compatible with that other great scar-bearing, scar-causing science of the early twentieth century—the elaboration of racial hierarchies.[46]

Thus, even at their most ambitious pitch, purportedly scientific connections of race and productivity remained crude in the extreme. This crudeness turns out to be vital for understanding how race management worked. The most solid studies of immigrant workers surveyed their conditions off the job, teaching readers in 1921, for example, that only one Greek male immigrant in five, and one Spanish immigrant in seven, brought family members to the United States. The weightiest research on productivity and race tended to be assembled by investigators writing in the government journal *Monthly Labor Review*, and it often focused on demonstrating the falsity of negative stereotypes regarding Black workers. This data seems to have made scant impact against such stereotypes while the repetition of antiblack and xenophobic folklore took scholars to great academic heights. When the towering figure in American sociology, E.A. Ross, for example, urged slotting the Slavic "race" into filthy and unhealthy jobs because they were "immune" to dirt, he offered an opinion, not a study. Just the same should be said of Commons's own assessments, such as that "the Negro . . . works three days and loafs three [while the] Chinaman, Italian, or Jewish immigrant works six days and saves the wages of three."[47]

---

46 Bernard Doray, *From Taylorism to Fordism: A Rational Madness* (London: Free Association Books, 1988), 83–84, and Braverman, *Labor and Monopoly Capital*, 104–23.

47 Hugh Reid, "Why Bar the Door to Labor?" *Nation's Business*, 9 (January 1921), 31; Luther D. Burlingame, "Americanizing a Thousand Men," *Industrial Management*, 53 (June 1917), 385–92; "The Southern Negro in Cleveland Industries," *Monthly Labor Review (MLR)*, 19 (July 1924), 41–44; "Negro Labor During and After the War," *MLR*, 12 (April 1921), 853–58; "Working and Living Conditions of Negroes in West Virginia," *MLR*, 21 (August 1925), 256–59; "Industrial Employment of the Negro in Pennsylvania," *MLR*, 22 (June 1926), 224–227. Ross as quoted in Stanley Lieberson, *A Piece of the Pie: Black and White Immigrants since 1880* (Berkeley: University of California Press, 1980), 25; Roediger, *Working Toward Whiteness*, 54. Commons is quoted from his "Social and Industrial Problems," *The Chautauquan*, 39 (March 1904), 18 and 13–22; Ramstad and Starkey, "Racial Theories of John R. Commons," esp. 16–17 and 63–64 and, for the context, Bari Jane Watkins, "The Professors and the Unions: Academic Social Thought and Labor Reform, 1883–1915 (unpublished Ph.D. diss., Yale University, 1976).

As early as 1913, Hugo Münsterberg's classic *Psychology and Industrial Efficiency* identified the discontinuity between precise studies of workers' motions and seat-of-the-pants assumptions on "race" and productivity. Münsterberg set out to assess how far scientific management had gone and could go, and staked out a place for "scientific psychology" as congruent with the "revolutionary," but incomplete, innovations of Taylor. Race initially seemed to Münsterberg to present little difficulty in achieving such a synthesis. "If a man applies for a position," he wrote, "he is considered [for] the totality of his qualities, and at first nobody cares whether the particular feature is inherited or acquired, whether it is an individual chance variation or . . . common . . . to all members of a certain nationality or race." Crude reliance on race in the search for the "best possible man" for the job would be checked because even when the required "combination of mental traits" occurred in specific races, "psychical qualities may vary strongly in the midst of the group."[48]

But in further developing his analysis, Münsterberg acknowledged that the search for the best man for the job did often devolve into unexamined racial assumptions. That management at the plant level cared about race was not necessarily bad in his view, but that it cared so unsystematically and unscientifically clearly did bother him. At one factory with "twenty different nationalities," the employment officers might declare the Italians best for one job, the Irish for another, and the Hungarians for a third. At the next factory, he added, completely different conclusions would be reached. In one workplace, managerial race lore had the "hasty and careless" Italians and Greeks as undesirable in risky jobs, which were to go to the Irish. In the next, it was the Irish who were too prone to court danger to do risky work. Münsterberg himself was no critic of race-thinking—he tended to credit the stereotype of carelessness as applying to Italians, Greeks, and Irishmen. But he abhorred the lack of system in studying race and management. "American industrial centres," he argued, presented "extremely favorable conditions for the comparative study of nationality," but the opportunity was not being seized. "Much more thorough statistical inquiries," especially

---

48 Hugo Münsterberg, *Psychology and Industrial Efficiency* (Boston and New York: Houghton Mifflin Company, 1913), 27–28, 50, and 69.

into nationality and responses to piece rates, were needed to ground "race psychological statements."[49]

The fit between immigrant attributes and the needs of industry was, at other junctures, much more rapturously described. The management and industry journal *Iron Age* linked new immigrants from eastern and southern Europe not only to the ability to withstand heat, but to an "attraction" to "hot and heavy work"— in contrast to the Northern European "aversion" to such conditions. Mexicans, according to a 1930 account in *Nation's Business*, "are fond of outdoor life [and] easily enter a nomadic mode of living" making them almost natural farm workers. Other serendipities that management publications posited included among Slavs a "temperamental tendency toward being easily managed," toward being anti-union, and toward preferring "the lowest wage scale" to any extra effort, at least until Slavic-American militancy in the post–World War One mass strikes strained such assumptions.[50]

Ford English School's graduation ceremony paraded evidence of the ease of race development imagined in the hopeful moments before World War One and the strike wave that followed. The ceremony saw immigrant workers in "shabby rags" walk down a gang plank connected to the image of an ocean liner and into a huge cauldron. The script labelled them with the racial slur "hunkie" as they entered the cauldron to, as a 1916 account in *Ford Times* put it, "see what the melting pot will do for them." After teachers from the school ladled vigorously, race development occurred and graduates emerged in "neat suits" as Americans. Workers entered the melting pot as "Irish-Americans" or "German-Americans" but, according to

---

49   Münsterberg, *Psychology and Industrial Efficiency*, 129–31.

50   "Strong Support for Selective Immigration," *Iron Age*, 111 (January 11, 1923), 163; H.D. Minich, "The Value of Time Study," *100%: The Practical Magazine of Efficient Management*, 1 (November 1913), 6. See also James Howard Bridge, *The Inside History of the Carnegie Steel Company: A Romance of the Millions* (New York: Aldine, 1903), 81; Karl De Laittre, "The Mexican Laborer and You," *Nation's Business*, 18 (November 1930), 44ff; W.J. Lauck, "Recent Immigration: Its Significant Aspects to the Iron and Steel Industry," *Iron Age*, 87 (April 13, 1911), 898; cf. "The Filipino Problem in California," *MLR*, 30 (June 1930), 73–74; David Colcord, "A Beast That Nurtures Children," *Nation's Business*, 18 (November, 1930), 32–34 and 170–71. Cf. Frances A. Kellor, "Chambers of Commerce and Alien Workmen," *Nation's Business*, 3 (December 1915), 18–20.

the company, they emerged as just Americans, "having learned to view the hyphen as a minus sign."[51]

At its almost providential extremes, even after the race-based immigration restrictions of 1924, faith in the fit of immigrant traits and American workplaces was one factor obviating any need for close investigation of immigrants in production. Thus in a 1930 article the steel industry became "The Beast That Nurtures Children." The "fabrication of metal" pushed up successive waves of Irishmen, "dark Sicilians," and Slavic "hunkies" both "spiritually" and "materially," quickly freeing them from hard mill work so that even Slavs were supposedly gone from the plants by the time the article was written, all of them "foremen or assistant superintendents," if not self-employed. On this view, which reminds us how thoroughly race development coexisted with "playing one race against the other," it was time (in 1930!) for the "uplifting forces of steel" to work their magic on "the last of the steel immigrants—southern [N]egroes and Mexicans." In an industry like steel, management's institution of what Katherine Stone calls "minutely graded job ladders," enabled experts to point to acquisition of skills—albeit skills easily learned in a few weeks—to make a case for the racial development of white new immigrants. One industry leader connected the rise of the semi-skilled machine tender to the development of white independence, using the language of an older labor system. Writing in *Iron Age*, the rubber manufacturing executive Charles R. Flint held that "the American wage earner is raised to the dignity of an overseer, not over degraded humanity, but over a more reliable and effective slave—machinery." Since African Americans, immigrants of color, and Jews were often excluded from working with machines, their slavishness was reiterated.[52]

---

51   On Ford English School, see Daniel M.G. Graff, "Ford Welfare Capitalism in Its Economic Context," in Sanford G. Jacoby, ed., *Masters to Managers: Historical and Comparative Perspectives on American Employers* (New York: Columbia University Press, 1991), 98 and (for the quote) 99. For "hunkie" (or "hunky"), see Roediger, *Working Toward Whiteness*, 37–45. On the melting pot and Ford, see Elizabeth Esch, "Fordtown: Managing Race and Nation in the American Empire, 1925–1945" (unpublished Ph.D.diss., New York University, 2004).

52   Frank Julian Warne and J.R. Commons, "Slavs in Coal Mining," in John R. Commons, ed., *Trade Unionism and Labor Problems* (Boston: Ginn and Company, 1905), 346. Cf. Mark Pittenger, "'What's on the Worker's Mind': Class Passing and the Study of the Industrial Workplace in the 1920s," *Journal of the History of the Behavioral*

Ordway Tead, the coauthor in 1920 of the first textbook in the new field of personnel management, introduced his *Instincts in Industry* with the remark that "differences in race, climate and civilization . . . may so modify human organisms as to cause radical differences in what is the substance of our . . . human nature." Tead wrote of "employers who have a definite policy of hiring several different nationalities in one department of a factory in order that workers may be less able to communicate effectively and therefore less able to cause trouble." For Tead, that deliberate divisiveness focused, as in the Mr. Block cartoon, on keeping out unions. But he offered neither an investigation of how or whether such a strategy worked, nor of his contention that the southern and eastern European immigrants commonly exhibited an "instinct" to be submissive, albeit punctuated by the occasional "brave frenzy of self-assertion." In 1920, when the Social Science Research Council (SSRC) "mapped" industrial relations, enumerating well over a hundred disciplines poised to contribute to the new field, it set for anthropologists the task of investigating "inherited racial characteristics (not including nationality)" capable of "effecting work," offering the "alleged laziness of the negro" as an example. But the SSRC did not set out to solve the problem of, to use Montgomery's phrasing, "which 'race' was best for what."[53]

Sciences, 39 (Spring 2003), 153. On steel, see Katherine Stone, "The Origins of Job Structures in the Steel Industry," in Richard C. Edwards, Michael Reich and David M. Gordon, eds., *Labor Market Segmentation* (Lexington, MA: D.C. Heath and Company, 1975), 49. Flint's quote is from "Conference on Labor and Capital," *Iron Age* (May 16, 1901), 32–33, as quoted in Rosenow, "Injuries to All," (unpublished Ph.D. diss., University of Illinois, 2008), 26. On occupational color bars and machinery see David Roediger, "Gaining a Hearing for Black–White Unity: Covington Hall and the Complexities of Race, Gender, and Class," in *Towards the Abolition of Whiteness: Essays on Race, Politics, and Working Class History* (New York and London: Verso, 1994), 127–80; see also Amy L. Fairchild, *Science at the Borders: Immigrant Medical Inspection and the Shaping of the Modern Industrial Labor Force* (Baltimore and London: Johns Hopkins University Press, 2003), 191–220, for the role of Immigration Service and the Public Health Service in firming up distinctions that "tended to draw a line around Europe as a whole, setting it apart from Asian and Mexican (Chinese, Japanese, 'Hindoo', and Syrians)" (219).

53 Ordway Tead, *Instincts in Industry: A Study in Working-Class Psychology* (Boston and New York: Houghton Mifflin Company, 1918), 13, 89–90, and 143; the "map" is reproduced in Bruce E. Kaufman's excellent *The Origins and Evolution of the Field of Industrial Relations in the United States* (Ithaca, NY: ILR Press, 1993), 14–17. See also 19–63 for an account of the early evolution of industrial relations in which race and ethnicity are absent.

After the start of immigration restriction, more social scientists joined Münsterberg in ridiculing the lack of system in investigating the productivity of various "races." They saw such imprecision as the irrational underside of an avowedly rational industrial society. As the old opportunities to manage by race and nationality gave way in the face of world war and immigration restriction legislation of 1921 and 1924, retaining immigrant workers came to be seen as more critical than dividing them. Commons's remark that "when immigration suddenly stops we see a human being in those who are here and begin to ask them what they want" overstated the change grossly. To the extent that the unevenly developing trend toward personnel management identified the problem of labor turnover with what Sanford Jacoby calls "the foremen's hire and fire approach," it undermined the most potent material way in which the races were set against each other in daily managerial practice. Since, as Jacoby adds, "the vast majority" of workplaces retained the "foremen's drive system" throughout the 1920s, the extent and pace of change should not be exaggerated. However, the decline of immigration certainly did open further space for questioning race management's basis in science and its staying power in a post–immigration restriction economy. By 1926 questions of race and management were already being cast by the pioneering personnel management textbook as likely to devolve in future into a focus on African-American and Mexican workers. Commenting on the 1920s and 30s, the management experts Herman Feldman and T.J. Woofter rued the fact that manufacturers, so scrupulously careful in choosing raw materials, "rely on hearsay and rumor as to the grades of labor hired." Everett C. Hughes and Helen M. Hughes observed that off-the-cuff opinions on racial difference so pervaded managerial choices and language, while hard data comparing racial performance remained so rare, that it was worth questioning whether "modern society is really guided by the impersonal concepts of the market and efficiency in choosing ... its labor force." Taylor had written, "Under scientific management arbitrary power ... ceases; and every single subject ... becomes the question for scientific investigation." Where race was concerned, experts rightly argued, such a shift did not happen.[54]

---

54 Roediger, *Working Toward Whiteness*, 76; John R. Commons, "Introduction to the Edition of 1920," in his *Races and Immigrants*, xix; Jacoby, "Century of Human

Even attempts like those of Woofter and Feldman to cast race management as the exception to the general rationality of industry underlined the staying power of supposedly unscientific systems. Critics vacillated between ridiculing race management and calling for making its invidious distinctions more scientifically systematic. The deep roots of the practice of race management, as detailed above, go some distance to explaining its impressive durability. But to emphasize only such history leaves us in danger of seeing management by race as residual, even premodern, and therefore at odds with the longer rational logic of capitalism. Rather, it has been central to such logic.

The staying power of what has been called the "foremen's empire" in the face of scientific management might be considered as a triumph of one form of capitalist rationality intimately linked to race management. It is in this specific realm that Commons's remarks again become critical. As early as 1904, Commons heard from an employment agent at Swift and Company that the "playing" of races against each other had been "systematized" in his factory, which rotated favored groups week by week. Commons worried that such "competition of races," especially when it included workers from the "non-industrial" Negro race and too many immigrants from the "backwards, shiftless, and unintelligent races" of southern and eastern Europe and elsewhere, would lead to catastrophe. But he recognized that competition extracted productivity as well as exerted a downward pressure on wages. Commons regarded these same packing houses as also among the most "systematized" workplaces extant where the labor process was concerned. Even "the animal was laid off and surveyed like a map," he wrote, with (dis)assembly line innovations engineering efficiency and speed-ups. Systems of modern

Resource Management," 149, 154, and 148–55; for the textbook, see Ordway Tead and Henry C. Metcalf, *Personnel Administration: Its Principles and Practice* (New York: McGraw-Hill, 1926 [1920]), 48; Everett Cherrington Hughes and Helen Macgill Hughes, *Where Peoples Meet:: Ethnic and Racial Frontiers* (Glencoe, IL: Free Press, 1952), 67; T.J. Woofter Jr., *Races and Ethnic Groups in American Life* (New York: McGraw-Hill, 1933), 144; Reinhard Bendix, *Work and Authority in Industry: Ideologies of Management in the Course of Industrialization* (New York: Wiley, 1956), 273 and 278; Nyland, "Taylorism, John R. Commons and the Hoxie Report," 986. See also Nelson, *Managers and Workers*, 80–83.

management and race management coexisted cheek by jowl in the most advanced factories.[55]

Such a system of racial competition did not rest on the fixing of a scientific chart of hierarchy, but on the production, mostly by first-line management, of a series of contradictory and volatile, hierarchical managerial opinions. The sociologist Niles Carpenter found workers thinking that lower management's racial prejudices and slights often weighed heaviest, and Feldman's research suggested that they were exactly right. Since foremen in the 1920s tended to retain the ability to hire and fire in the face of challenges from personnel managers, great weight lay behind their prejudices, which could keep racialized workers productively on edge. Indeed, on the rare occasion when the adequacy of the racial knowledge possessed by foremen was directly questioned by management experts, the framing of the issue was likely to be that the races were being too much pitted against each other with the fear, especially after the wave of racial terror during and after World War One, that lower management would appear "unsympathetic" and foster racial hatreds.[56]

If, as Doray has written, scientific management involved at times a "rational madness," management also long deployed the seeming irrationalities of race in a calculating manner. Sometimes it did so by

55   John R. Commons, et. al., *History of the Labor Movement in the United States*, 4 vols. (New York: Macmillan, 1918–1935), 3: xxv and 322–33, esp. 328 for Don D. Lescohier's section on personnel management; Ramstad and Starkey, "The Racial Theories of John R. Commons," 16–18, quote Commons on the "competition of races." Their study is as acute on his antiblack racism as it is obtuse on his racial nativism. See also John R. Commons, "Industry," *The Chautauquan*, 38 (February 1904), 533–43 and Commons, "Social and Industrial Problems," 19 ("physical exertion") and 17–22; Harold M. Baron, *The Demand for Black Labor: Historical Notes on the Political Economy of Racism* (Somerville, MA: New England Free Press, 1971). For the last Commons quote, and a fine discussion of the labor process in packing, see James R. Barrett, "Immigrant Workers in Early Mass Production Industry: Work Rationalization and Job Control Conflicts in Chicago's Packinghouses, 1900–1904," in Hartmut Keil and John B. Jentz, eds., *German Workers in Industrial Chicago* (Dekalb, IL: Northern Illinois University Press, 1983), 105–09.

56   Herman Feldman, *Racial Factors in American Industry* (New York: Harper and Brothers, 1931), 147; Niles Carpenter, *Nationality, Color, and Economic Opportunity in the City of Buffalo* (Westport, CT: Negro Universities Press, 1970), 118–30; Fred H. Rindge Jr., "From Boss to Fore-Man," *Industrial Management*, 53 (July 1917), 511–12; Kaufman, *Origins and Evolution of the Field of Industrial Relations*, 15 and 17, and Tead and Metcalf, *Personnel Administration*, 48.

fixing categories and hierarchies, more often by leaving races not fixed in rankings and permanently in competition.[57] A brutally logical system kept their positions in play—in the cases of African Americans often keeping them out of jobs via color bars and judging their fitness as a reserve army of labor. Historians have long known that Taylorism's revolutionary changes often supplemented, rather than supplanted, the "hurry and push" tactics in which lower management bullied and threatened workers. But we have too often forgotten Commons's suggestion that the hurrying and pushing could be chronically infected by playing races against each other.

57   Doray, *From Taylorism to Fordism*, 83–84.

CHAPTER 6

Making Solidarity Uneasy: Cautions on a Keyword from Black Lives Matter to the Past

> Solidarity is always an active achievement, the result of active struggle to construct the universal on the basis of particulars/differences.
>
> —Chandra Talpade Mohanty

The important insurgencies that have matured in response to the vigilante murder of Trayvon Martin and to the many murders by police of mostly young Black women and men have brought outpourings of solidarity and important debates over what forms such solidarity should take. These developments, like the efforts of the American Studies Association (ASA) to be in solidarity with Palestine, challenge the ASA to approach the question of solidarity in a direct and sustained manner. The Ferguson, Missouri killing of Michael Brown quickly brought massive August 2014 demonstrations often explicitly expressing "Solidarity with Mike Brown."[1]

---

1   For the epigraph, see Chandra Talpade Mohanty, *Feminism Without Borders: Decolonizing Theory, Practicing Solidarity* (Durham: Duke University Press, 2003), 7; Holly Yan and Steve Almasy, "London Is Latest City to See Protests as Ferguson Dismay Spreads," CNN (November 26, 2014), cnn.com; Britni Danielle, "The Ferguson Revolution Is Happening in the Tweets and via Hacker Group Anonymous," *takepart* (August 14, 2014), takepart.com. Thanks to Donovan Roediger, Brendan Roediger, Elizabeth Esch, Jonathan Garlock, Tricia Rose, the late Joel Olson, Robin D.G. Kelley, Alberto Toscano, and the Chicago Surrealist Group for help with this article or ideas within it.

Thousands of young people were introduced to the idea and actuality of solidarity in these protests.

However, this solidarity was anything but simple and easy. In Ferguson, Minneapolis, Providence, upstate New York, and elsewhere, demonstrators collectively debated whether protesters who were not Black ought to raise their hands in "Hands Up, Don't Shoot!" chants or to participate in die-ins, given that whites are far less likely to suffer fatal attacks from the police. Debates over whites wearing "I Am Trayvon Martin" T-shirts—signaled especially by the widely circulated internet video "I Am Not Trayvon Martin" featuring the University of Kansas activist and American Studies major Emma Halling—troubled a too-easy discussion of unity by pointing out that some populations face threats of extralegal and unpunished violence in ways very different from what others face. Embryonic movement debates even developed over whether the word "ally" ought to give way to "accomplice" as a better description of the role best played in a Black-led movement by those who are white. The counter-position, that simply invoking a past golden age of solidarity could settle matters, was also put forward. Thus the often perceptive political philosopher Steven D'Arcy wrote less than convincingly that the loss of a language of solidarity, and the rise of "positionality" as a term, had derailed the left. He specifically held that "I Am Not Trayvon Martin" disabled whites from "identifying with African-American resistance." Solidarity, on the other hand, had treated "injuries to one" as "injuries to all" and succeeded in "resisting them in common."[2]

My giving the ASA presidential address, available online and significantly different in presentation from this chapter, unexpectedly underlined the difficulties of calling at once not only for more scholarly consideration of solidarity but also for more sober and uneasy reflection in thinking through its promises and difficulties. I began with just such a call but then played, for reasons clarified below, a video clip of Utah Phillips singing "Solidarity Forever." Despite my promptings toward an unease with solidarity, a fair share

2   For the Halling video "I Am Not Trayvon Martin" (March 31, 2012), see youtube.com; Steve D'Arcy, "The Rise of Post-New Left Political Vocabulary" from "The Public Autonomy Project," The Public Autonomy Project (January 27, 2014), publicautonomy.org.

of audience members sang along. Doubly complicating matters was my realization that, positions reversed, I would surely have been among the singers myself. Nevertheless, it remains critical to make a case for embracing solidarity while simultaneously being uneasy about the assumptions it sometimes evokes. The unease ought to make us wonder if solidarity is always a good thing, to recall what and whom solidarity leaves out, and how it is premised on those leavings out, to consider how solidarity works across differences in kinds and degrees of oppression, and to ask if the presence of solidarity is the logic of things or if for long periods it may be a treasured exception. This article also focuses on "solidarity" as a surprisingly neglected keyword in cultural studies and discusses how we ought to historicize and memorialize the word.[3]

The last twenty years of my career, roughly evenly split between service in the ASA and in the Working Class Studies Association (WCSA), inevitably shape my approach. In the ASA, talk of solidarity—at least using that word—has been almost absent in presidential addresses over those years, even when such great historians of working people as Vicki Ruiz and Michael Frisch delivered the talks. Digital searches return no more than a handful of such usages, more or less offhand, until the last two years. In the two presidential addresses before mine, in the wake of the ASA's attempts at solidarity with Palestine, "solidarity" came to appear several times in the presentations of presidents Curtis Marez and Lisa Duggan. Duggan vividly contrasted the "fun of solidarity" with the "fury of critique." Her remarks sparked a response from Scott Morgensen that anticipated themes within my contribution here. Morgensen explicitly addressed "relationality within solidarity" seeking, in tribute to the late José Muñoz, "a politics not yet known."[4] That so many young scholars experienced in graduate student labor activism invigorate

---

3 For my ASA presidential address "Making Solidarity Uneasy: Promises and Presumptions From Bacon's Rebellion to the Present" (October 16, 2016), see youtube.com.

4 Curtis Marez, "Seeing in the Red: Looking at Student Debt," *American Quarterly*, 66 (June 2014), 270 and 276–77; Lisa Duggan, "The Fun and the Fury of Transforming American Studies," *American Quarterly*, 67 (June 2014), 286 and 281–92; Scott L. Morgensen, "A Politics Not Yet Known: Imagining Relationality within Solidarity," *American Quarterly*, 67 (June 2014), 309 and 310–15. See also Jodi Melamed, "Dangerous Associations," *American Quarterly*, 66 (June 2014), 289–300 on Palestine and solidarity.

the ASA also argues for investigating and interrogating solidarity as an American Studies topic.

On the other hand, searches for an inspiring record of solidarity very much drive labor history and working class studies scholarship, though not always leavened by sufficient curiosity regarding what scholars are doing when we search hard for a usable past. My own 2009 WCSA presidential address shared this lack of curiosity, supposing that there was already an archive of solidarity answering our needs, needing only to rediscovered or perhaps just popularized. As Jana Lipman and Dan Bender have written in introducing their excellent recent collection on labor and empire, "Solidarity is one of the most evoked but least analyzed concepts in US labor history. [It] always has been a central assumption—rarely a topic of analysis . . . simultaneously a powerful ideal and a slippery category."[5]

Needing Solidarity and Keeping Balance

My own first hearing of "solidarity" was perhaps an exotic one. Although I was raised in a family of trade unionists in the 1950s and 60s, the "solidarity of labor" did not register with me through my teen years. By the time I heard "Solidarity Forever," probably first in the context of support for the United Farm Workers' grape boycott, the idea of "solidarity with the Vietnamese revolution" was familiar to me. Both examples matter in showing how modern learnings of the word are associated with coming to be on the side of angels. Indeed, they suggest the several dominant axes on which the recent and contemporary left has cherished solidarity—as labor unity, as (for example in the grape boycott) interracialism, and as internationalism. Solidarity's magnificent association with the good fights is thus well established in its recent past. To encourage an unease with the magic seemingly worked by such a word is therefore perilous. It

5   David R. Roediger, "The Unknown Worker: A Provocation," Presidential address. Working Class Studies Association, University of Pittsburgh (June 2009); Jana K. Lipman and Daniel E. Bender, "Introduction: Through the Looking Glass: US Empire through the Lens of Labor History" in Lipman and Bender, eds., *Making Empire Work: Labor and United States Imperialism* (New York: NYU Press, 2015), 14.

risks being misheard as defeatism and resignation in the face of division rather than as an appeal for sober reflection on the difference that differences make even in how unity is apprehended. Nevertheless, the magnificence of solidarity can hardly be realized if it is tethered to impossible expectations leaving us coming up forever short of an unexamined ideal.

A personal and a recent historical example will have to suffice to introduce these points. The personal one involves self-criticism and led to my sampling Utah Phillips in the presidential address. The book I was writing two years ago in celebration of the sesquicentennial of the general strike of the slaves, *Seizing Freedom*, included from its earliest drafts discussions of three songs sharing one tune. The first was the Union Army song "John Brown's Body," composed in 1861 and which quickly became a favorite of troops. Memorializing the eponymous Kansas freedom fighter and abolitionist martyr, but not his specific politics, "John Brown's Body" was soon given new lyrics by Julia Ward Howe in her nationalist anthem "Battle Hymn of the Republic." Connected to both feminism and abolition, Howe herself long supported antislavery causes. Her husband secretly funded Brown's raid on Harpers Ferry and went into exile during the repression that followed. Howe was soon to be president of the New England Woman's Suffrage Association. Fast forward fifty years from Howe's composition, and the labor organizer Ralph Chaplin borrowed the tune in writing "Solidarity Forever." I found myself listening to the songs—as performed by Paul Robeson, Janice Harrington, and Phillips respectively—in writing *Seizing Freedom*.[6]

The three songs brought together the emancipation of slaves, of women, and of wage workers in ways that resonated with that book's argument that the example of the slaves' general strike energized the reinvented women's suffrage and labor movements. The songs formed the soundtrack that led to my considering briefly whether to end *Seizing Freedom* at the high point of solidarity just after the war rather than continuing on to tell the bleak story that followed. But I

---

6 Franny Nudelman, *John Brown's Body: Slavery, Violence and the Culture of War* (Chapel Hill: University of North Carolina Press, 2004), esp. 16 and 165–67. For the music, see youtube.com (Paul Robeson, "John Brown's Body"; Janice Harrington, "Say Brother Will You Meet Us," and Utah Phillips, "Solidarity Forever").

knew that the music could only guide me so much in romanticizing matters, because the slaves themselves were absent in the songs and because the sharp divisions that almost immediately emerged among the African-American, white workers', and women's movements necessarily ended the story I ultimately needed to tell on a fully somber note.

Just as the manuscript was almost done, I read Harvard historian John Stauffer's introduction to the reissue of *Slave Culture*, the classic study by my wonderful mentor Sterling Stuckey. Stauffer answered a question that should have occurred to me: where did the creators of "John Brown's Body" get the tune? They heard it, Stauffer shows, in "Say Brothers," a camp meeting religious song. That song in turn originated as a "ring shout," a counterclockwise dance and call-and-response musical performance that Stuckey places at the center of African culture in the United States. Variously titled, it was sung and danced from the Carolina coastal areas all the way to Arkansas. Listening to Sparky and Rhonda Rucker sing "Say Brothers," I also heard their version of the "Marching Song of the First Arkansas," in which late in the war African-American troops fighting for emancipation sang of revolutionized social relations:

> They will have to pay us wages, the wages of their sin,
> They will have to bow their foreheads to their colored kith and
> kin.

While the tune is often now attributed to "John Brown's Body," some who sang it would have known it as the ring shout "Say Brothers."[7]

The timing of my learning all of this as the book was being completed seemed almost providential and rekindled my desire for a

---

7 John Stauffer, "Foreword" to Sterling Stuckey, *Slave Culture: Nationalist Theory and the Foundations of Black America* (New York: Oxford University Press, 2013 [1987]), x–xi; for Stuckey on the ring shout see in the same volume, xv, 11, 25, 88, 92–93, and 103–09; David Walls, "Marching Song of the First Arkansas Colored Regiment: A Contested Attribution," *Arkansas Historical Quarterly*, 66 (Winter 2007), 401–21, reproduces the lyrics and ably rehearses arguments over who wrote the Arkansas song, with Sojourner Truth as one possibility. For the Ruckers, hear "Glory Hallelujah Suite," youtube.com.

usable past making solidarity easy. The symmetries for a moment seemed so perfect, right down to the room for audiences to improvise new verses, present from the shout to "John Brown's Body" to "Solidarity Forever." I almost concluded the book with that neat symmetry, trying to make music seal an easy solidarity only undermined by the real lives of social movements, but opted instead for a closing meditation on the difficulties of solidarity.[8] There is such a pull towards believing so urgently that everything is connected that we minimize the disconnections that I hope to now make us uneasy about, especially as regards any argument that the Black solidarity of the ring shout became the supposedly broader class solidarity of "Solidarity Forever" in an unproblematic way.

Looking as well at the forms of solidarity that emerged after the killing of Mike Brown underscores another dimension of the difficulties involved in arriving at a sober assessment of the phenomenon. We confront, that is, not only the question of our own desires but also perhaps an erratic pattern of ways in which solidarity actually comes and fails to come into the world. In at least two particular areas, Black/Palestinian solidarity and Black/queer solidarity, the dramatic successes after Ferguson seemed almost simple in their triumphs—a matter of showing up and reaching out and waiting. And yet other efforts at solidarity, such as trade union solidarity with victims of white supremacist police violence, solidarity proceeds excruciatingly slowly and not always forward.

The connecting of Black and Palestinian issues moved forward from early in the Ferguson protests. The reaching out and showing up occurred through social media and physical presence. Activists in Palestine sent pictures of their demonstrations of support, some simply pictures of young people with a sign saying "FERGUSON WITH LOVE FROM PALESTINE." Palestinian activists sent advice about coping with tear gas; knowledge that some police deployed in Ferguson had received training in control of demonstrators from Israeli authorities brought points home. Above all pro-Palestine forces in the United States mobilized impressively for the Fall 2014 marches in Ferguson and St. Louis, joining locally based Palestinians. These forces came

8   David R. Roediger, *Seizing Freedom: Slave Emancipation and Liberty for All* (New York: Verso, 2014), 204–12.

to demonstrate and also to address questions of day-to-day interactions between Arab and Islamic owners of stores and their African-American customers. Within months African-American activists from St. Louis had nationally toured Palestine. Summer of 2015 saw solidarity flow from Black America with dozens of organizations and over a thousand movement leaders signing a statement declaring support for Palestinian freedom.[9]

Queer solidarity often seemed as charmed. From the beginning of the overnight presence of demonstrators near where Brown died, participants reflected on the presence of trans people and the impact of their bravery and their ideas. Thus central figures in Millennial Activists United and other movements were young African-American lesbians, so much so that Reverend Osagyefo Uhuru Sekou, a veteran organizer, recently told an interviewer, "I take my orders from twenty-three-year old queer women." In December 2014 local St. Louis leaders Brittany Ferrell and Alexis Templeton, took advantage of an opening for same-sex marriage. They went to St. Louis's City Hall, site of so many protests against police violence, to apply for a marriage license. The local African-American paper, the venerable and typically mainstream *St. Louis American*, headlined on page one "REVOLUTIONARY LOVE." The same issue included a guest editorial urging African-American advocacy of trans issues.[10]

Somewhat more caution could be useful in thinking about even such inspiring victories. If they seemed spontaneous, such examples of solidarity reflected prior and ongoing work across Black/queer,

9   Hamde Abu Rahma, "To Ferguson, with Love from Palestine" (August 22, 2014), hamdeaburahma.com; Bassem Masri, "The Fascinating Story of How the Ferguson–Palestine Solidarity Movement Came Together" *AlterNet* (February 18, 2015), alternet.org; Kristian Davis Bailey, "Dream Defenders, Black Lives Matter and Ferguson Leaders Take Historic Trip to Palestine," *Ebony* (January 9, 2015), ebony.com; Kenrya Rankin, "More than 1,000 Black Activists Sign Statement of Support for Palestine," *COLORLINES* (August 18, 2015), colorlines.com.

10   Sarah van Gelder, "Rev. Sekou on Today's Civil Rights Leaders: 'I Take My Orders From 23-Year-Old Queer Women'," *Yes! Magazine* (July 22, 2015), yesmagazine.org; Rebecca Rivas, "Revolutionary Loves: Protest Leaders Get Engaged at City Hall," *St. Louis American* (December 16, 2014), stlamerican.com; Sharon Lynn Pruitt, "Transgender Rights Are a Black Issue, Too" *St. Louis American* (December 16, 2014), stlamerican.com; on queer leadership in Black Lives Matter, see Mychal Denzel Smith, "A Q&A with Opal Tometi," *Nation* (June 2, 2015), thenation.com.

Black/Palestinian, and even Black queer/Palestinian differences. At times Ferguson protesters had to fight their ways on to the agendas of existing LGBTQ groups. Nor of course were debates and even fights over priorities absent. However, the larger point remains that groups who built solidarity by first showing up and reaching out stood the best chance of prevailing.[11]

In other instances, solidarities developed far more slowly. The very high rates of killings by police of American-Indian people generated an impressive Indian Lives Matter movement that gained traction only slowly before joint protests with groups focusing on Black lives disrupted the 2015 Twin Cities marathon. Immigrant rights, a movement in which Black Lives Matter founder Opal Tometi had organizing roots, nevertheless has come into alliance with anti–police violence initiatives only modestly. Nor, despite many rank-and-file participants being active in both movements, have ongoing ties with the "Fight for 15" minimum wage movement among fast food workers matured quickly along programmatic lines.[12] To comment on such matters is not to suppose that solidarities in these areas cannot or will not develop but it is to say that timing, spatial distance between groups, varied histories, and difference in the forms oppression takes can make the achievement of unity a large and long task. Nor in this instance could the overarching unity of class bind constituencies effectively. The heralded statement on Ferguson by the AFL-CIO head Richard Trumka turned out to offer a re-acknowledgment of the position that police unions are labor organizations just like any other. As Trumka had it,

> Lesley McSpadden, Michael Brown's mother who works in a grocery store, is our sister, an AFL-CIO union member, and Darren Wilson, the officer who killed Michael Brown, is a union

---

11   Noura Erakat, moderator, "Roundtable on Anti-Blackness and Black-Palestinian Solidarity," *Jadaliyya* (June 3, 2015), interviews.jadaliyya.com; Jenny Blair, "Black Trans People Address Creating Change Conference," Bilerico Project (February 7, 2015), bilerico.com.

12   Lydia Millet, "Native Lives Matter, Too," *New York Times* (October 13, 2015); Susan Du, "Black Lives Matter Takes on the Twin Cities Marathon," *City Pages* (October 4, 2015); Ben Smiff, "The Fast Food Workers' Movement and the Ferguson Rebellion," *The North Star* (February 15, 2015), thenorthstar.info; Smith, "A Q&A with Opal Tometi."

member, too, and he is our brother. Our brother killed our sister's son and we do not have to wait for the judgment of prosecutors or courts to tell us how terrible this is.

Mobilization of membership by the AFL-CIO for demonstrations in solidarity with Mike Brown was unsurprisingly meager.[13]

Solidarity's Checkered Origins

Beginning with the longer history of "solidarity" as what the American Studies tradition has called a "keyword" opens some space for reflection. From Raymond Williams's innovative 1976 volume in British cultural studies *Keywords: A Vocabulary of Culture and Society* to recent American Studies volumes of such words edited by Bruce Burgett, Glenn Hendler, and others, scholarship in this area has produced scores of essays on the shifting meanings of particularly resonant words around which Anglophone conceptions of power and social knowledge have coalesced. Ranging back especially to Latin and French origins, the contributions often establish that it is less the precision of a keyword than its various, even conflicting, resonances that underpin its power. Neither Williams nor American Studies scholars made "solidarity" a keyword, but in *Keywords for Radicals* Markus Kip contributes a fine entry on the word.[14]

The *Oxford English Dictionary* (*OED*) entry on "solidarity" reveals the jumble of meanings, historically and now, attached to the word. The first definition refers to the "fact or quality, on the part of communities, etc., of being perfectly united or at one in some respect, esp. in interests, sympathies, or aspirations," a meaning

---

13   Quoted in Kenneth Quinnell, "Trumka in Missouri Speaks on Confronting Racism," *AFL-CIO Now* (September 15, 2014), aflcio.org.

14   Raymond Williams, *Keywords: A Vocabulary of Culture and Society* (New York: Oxford University Press, 1985 [1976]); Bruce Burgett and Glenn Hendler, *Keywords for American Cultural Studies* (New York: NYU Press, 2007); Markus Kip contributes a full and thoughtful entry on "solidarity" to Kelly Fritsch, Clare O'Connor, and A.K. Thompson, *Keywords for Radicals: The Contested Vocabulary of Late-Capitalist Struggle* (Chico, CA: AK Press, 2016).

easily congruent with the unity of a preindustrial village, across lines of class. However, the *OED* quickly adds "*spec.* with reference to the aspirations or actions of trade-union members." Two further additions send us to older and newer meanings. First, a separate but related meaning sends us back to Roman civil law: a "form of obligation involving joint and several responsibilities or rights." Second, a recent example of usage points towards forms of solidarity absolutely transcending particular local communities, connoting instead inter-racialism and internationalism, as illustrated by "Afro-Asian Peoples Solidarity Committees."[15]

The origins of the term "solidarity," and even usage into the nineteenth century, are surprisingly entwined with impulses that, if not conservative, are seemingly at odds with the left uses of the word so common today. In the longest view, the word arose from Roman law, and specifically the enforcement of "*in solido*" obligations of debtors in common to each be responsible, if held to account, for an entire debt. As Gaius's *Institutionum Iuris Civilis* put it, "Every creditor is severally entitled to receive the whole object of the active obligation, and every debtor is bound to discharge the whole object of the passive obligation." The rearticulation of this principle in Napoleonic law after the French Revolution coincided with the opening of political space for a consideration of corporate obligations more generally, especially under the auspices of Catholic social thinkers. Thus the *OED* notes that the "French origin of the word is freq. referred to during the period of its introduction into English use."[16]

Well into the nineteenth century, the Catholic Church, not radicals, deployed "solidarity" most effectively, being better poised to survive repression and more able to combine a critique of bourgeois individualism with a hankering for older preindustrial regimes of rule, including at times even royalism. Even near the end of the 1800s, "*solidarité*" in France and elsewhere was elaborated as part of what Michael Hoelzl described as "the exchange

---

15   "solidarity, n." *OED Online*. Oxford University Press, September 2015 (accessed December 3, 2015).

16   Ibid., for Gaius; J.E.S. Hayward, "Solidarity: The Social History of an Idea in Nineteenth-Century France," *International Review of Social History*, 4 (August 1959), 265–82.

between theological and political ideals" and its emergence at times in mainstream discourses bespoke elite attempts to arrive at a response within capitalism to heightening class divisions. None of this reveals "solidarity" to be devoid of social critique. Even as they favored creditors over groups of debtors in the main, "*in solido*" obligations (nominated in English as "solidarity obligation") were part of precapitalist discourses on debt that were at times able to take community norms and even moral economies into account. Catholic emphases on solidarity both underpinned the Church's episodic commitments to the poor and were expanded, especially after Pierre Leroux's 1840 *De l'humanité*, in secularizations animating a variety of political positions. Two years later Hippolyte Renaud's *Solidarity*, a brief study of utopian socialist Charles Fourier, became the first book explicitly taking its title from the ideal of "solidarity." However, it is worth emphasizing that into the early twentieth century key ideas of solidarity in France and elsewhere had much to do with both the internationalism of Catholicism and that of socialism, if only to remind us that what the historian of France J.E.S. Hayward calls the "mystique" of solidarity cut in many directions.[17]

Laboring Solidarity

In the second half of the nineteenth century, the connection between solidarity and labor became firm for the first time at the level of both practice and theory. Ironically, Marxist practice, far more than Karl Marx's theoretical writings, spread the use of "solidarity"—often in its English rather than in its French form—across national boundaries. The elaboration in theoretical work came principally from the

---

17   Michael Hoelzl, "Recognizing the Sacrificial Victim: The Problem of Solidarity for Critical Social Theory," *Journal for Cultural and Religious Theory*, 6 (December 2004), 50 ("exchange"), 51 ("solidarity obligation"), and 45–64. Hoelzl's work is also especially valuable for its elaboration of the idea of solidarity in German sources; J.E.S. Hayward, "Solidarity: The Social History of an Idea in Nineteenth-Century France," 265–82 and Lawrence Wilde, *Global Solidarity* (Edinburgh: Edinburgh University Press, 2013), 19–21; Markus Kip, "Solidarity," in Fritsch, O'Connor, and Thomspon, *Keywords for Radicals*.

French sociologist Émile Durkheim. Both Marxist thought and Durkheim predicted, in very different ways, that industrial society would make possible wholly new forms of solidarity. Both traditions also missed, at times, the extent to which existing patterns of racial divisions and uneven development produced solidarities compromised by their creation within industrial capitalism and imperial expansion. The empire-inflected work of the great radical artist Walter Crane, who attempted to "labor solidarity" in drawings at about the same time that Marx and Durkheim did so in words, will illustrate some of the complications.

At the time of the 1848 revolutions, Marx and Engels had maintained that the growth of industry created the conditions for solidarity, though they did not use the word. Machines and new divisions of labor minimized distinctions based on skill and flattened wage differences, they argued in *The Communist Manifesto*. Thus "equalized," though in desperation and alienation, not in freedom, workers could move together in new ways. Moreover, "National differences and antagonism between peoples are daily more and more vanishing, owing . . . to the world market, to uniformity in the mode of production." By 1864, with Marx as a leading force, the newly formed International Workingmen's Association (IWA) decided on its "General Rules." Their drafting made "solidarity" stand among the first words of an organization uniting communists, anarchists, and trade union leaders. The four brief rules insisted that solidarity could not be left to the processes set in motion by capital but that it could be organized. The last of these rules described the stakes, at home and internationally: "That all efforts aiming at the great end [of labor's emancipation] hitherto failed from the want of solidarity between the manifold divisions of labor in each country, and from the absence of a fraternal bond of union between the working classes of different countries." A year later when the IWA issued cards to members, their text described the International's goal as "complete emancipation, economical and political, of the Working Classes." The means to reach such an end included to "promote the establishment of solidarity between the manifold divisions of labour in each country, and the co-operation of the Working Classes of different countries." In 1872, Marx would speak of "the basic principle of the International: Solidarity," which doubled also as the "great lesson of the [defeat of the] French Commune."[18]

While a passionate concern of the Marxist political project, solidarity did not centrally figure in Marx's main theoretical work. The word appears not at all in the first volume of *Capital*, published in German in 1867 alongside Marx's concerted activism on solidarity's behalf, and was subsequently translated into English. The Canadian Marxist economist Michael Lebowitz made this point powerfully from a related angle. Lebowitz wrote of the lack of any theorizing of the necessity for capital of producing differences among workers in order to maintain hegemony within the process of production. He named that difference-generating variable the "x-factor." X, "the tendency to divide workers," functions as "part of the essence of capital, indeed, an essential aspect of the logic of capital." Lebowitz allowed that Marx "recognised well," as for example in his famous writings on the role of anti-Irish prejudices of English workers in weakening the movement of the latter group, that fostering disunity was a "secret . . . by which the capitalist class maintains its power." However, at the level of theory "the importance to capital of dividing workers" remained unaccounted for by Marx. Specifically, Lebowitz continued, "racism and sexism [do] not appear as part of the essence of capital in Marx's *Capital*."[19] Within the American Studies tradition such a critique of, or (as I'd prefer) supplement of, Marxism has been powerfully advanced by Lisa Lowe, Grace Kyungwon Hong, and others.[20]

The flip side of Lebowitz's insights is what interests me here: namely the extent to which Marx's relative disinterest in theorizing

18   For the *Communist Manifesto* (1848) quotes see marxists.org, Chapters 2 and 3; for the IWA's "General Rules" (first published November 1864), see marxists.org; for the IWA's 1865 cards, see marxists.org; for Marx's 1872 "La Liberté" speech, first published in French, see marxists.org.

19   Michael A. Lebowitz, "The Politics of Assumption, the Assumption of Politics," *Historical Materialism*, 14 (2006), 29–47, all quotes from 39, save the last two, on 38 and 40. For the Marx passage on Ireland, see "Marx to Sigfrid Meyer and August Vogt in New York" (April 9, 1870), marxists.org.

20   Lisa Lowe, *Immigrant Acts: On Asian American Cultural Politics* (Chapel Hill: Duke University Press, 1996), esp. 27–28; Grace Kyungwon Hong, *The Ruptures of American Capital: Women of Color Feminism and the Culture of Immigrant Labor* (Minneapolis: University of Minnesota Press, 2006).

how solidarity operates simplifies matters, but at a cost. We inherit the rather different stops of the *Manifesto*, seeing labor unity as produced by capitalism, and of the IWA writings, casting solidarity as needing to be urgently built across difference by the purposeful voluntary actions of workers. These are the poles in thinking about solidarity that this article seeks to trouble: first, that our success in producing unity lies in the logic of capital; second, that our own voluntary action can easily secure solidarity's triumph.

Durkheim's far less globally ambitious work nevertheless made him the nineteenth-century thinker most explicitly articulating a theory of solidarity, particularly in *The Division of Labor in Society* (1893). Specialization in industrial society played for Durkheim an almost magical role in creating the basis for new human bonds. He was not very interested in specific configurations of productive processes, and far more apt to write about legal codes than factories even in a volume ostensibly centered on the possibilities opened by the modern division of labor. However, Durkheim hinged big ideas about a more dynamic and meaningful solidarity on new labor processes, differentiated political and social roles, urbanization, and the consequent rise of complex personalities able to see that others had necessary skills and roles that they did not. He twinned that hopefulness with a very constricted view of the possibilities of meaningful solidarity in preindustrial and especially in kin-based societies. Durkheim termed the constricted "solidarity by similarities" that applied in such societies as mere "mechanical solidarity."[21] His metaphors to describe such societies and their solidarities came often from science. The people caught in them lacked individuality and the societies resembled segmented worms accreting in webs of sameness. At another juncture Durkheim regarded the persons in village or tribal settings as being like molecules fixed in "inorganic" objects. Thus it was possible to name the meaningful solidarity that he saw as being enabled by modern of divisions of labor as "organic solidarity." This made logical the counterintuitive terminology in which

---

21   Émile Durkheim, *The Division of Labor in Society*, W.D. Halls, trans. (Houndmills, Hampshire: Macmillan, 1984), 31 ("solidarity by similarities"), and esp. 31–67; Christopher K. Ansell, *Schism and Solidarity in Social Movements: The Politics of Labor in the French Third Republic* (Cambridge: Cambridge University Press, 2001), 11.

Durkheim had the age of capitalist mechanization supplanting "mechanical solidarity" with a manufactured "organic solidarity."[22]

Aspects of Durkheim's thought, on "slotting" into jobs for example, suggest ways in which to think about how the division of labor was also racialized and gendered, but his central arguments do not address how solidarity might apply in a highly uneven world. Durkheim's analysis of mechanical solidarity does usefully describe reciprocities based on likeness and reminds us that the word "solidarity" might apply to also describe insularity. However, positing such a deep gulf between the premodern and the industrial leaves little room for his considering the xenophobic but thoroughly modern solidarities of, for example, the racially exclusionary "sundown town" and the imperial state.[23]

Moreover, as Lawrence Wilde's very generous appraisals of Durkheim's work on modern solidarity observe, the latter's theorizing of solidarity assumed the nation as its unit of analysis, though it did offer some musings on what a broader framework would look like. Durkheim was very active as a French liberal reformer and an associate of Léon Bourgeois, the politician and author of the wildly popular 1896 volume *Solidarité*; room for him to reflect on global inequality was, however, scant. Nor did his framework of seeing history as a triumph of civilization and productivity over backwardness expand the possibilities for such an analysis. Whereas the late work of Marx had moved decisively towards an appreciation of what Native American and Russian village society offered to those prizing solidarity, Durkheim held that industrial society excelled in both individualism and solidarity. Such a formulation by Durkheim also absented the extent to which modern working-class solidarities continued to be lived out in small communities and kin networks. Nor did Durkheim provide a strong alternative to views that regarded solidarity as "natural" given the existing division of labor. While he recognized that class struggle, economic crises, and something like

---

22   Durkheim, *The Division of Labor in Society*, 84 ("inorganic"), 127 ("worms"), and 68–175; Wilde, *Global Solidarity*, 36–41.

23   For an especially important use of Durkheim and slotting in this regard, see Richard Williams, *Hierarchal Structures and Social Value: The Creation of Black and Irish Identities in the United States* (Cambridge: Cambridge University Press, 1990); James W. Loewen, *Sundown Towns: A Hidden Dimension of American Racism* (New York: New Press, 2005).

alienation attended the division of labor, these were "abnormalities" born of an "extreme division of labor," not structural features of a system he saw as normally producing "happiness."[24]

Picturing Empire and Solidarity

A recent discovery in the history of cartography dramatically shows how race and uneven economic development across the globe burdened the laboring of solidarity. The map itself was made in 1886 for the Imperial Federation League (IFL), which commissioned it for the Colonial and Indian Exhibition of that year. The IFL had the map published as a lavish special supplement to the liberal weekly *The Graphic*. Huge and colorful, the map included inset facts, prepared by Captain J.C.R. Colomb, the Conservative MP, on the value of empire. His essay on the IFL and empire appeared in the same issue of *The Graphic* as the map. Within the pro-imperial run-up to Queen Victoria's Golden Jubilee celebrations in 1887 and in the early stages of the "New Imperialism" period and the attendant "Scramble for Africa," the map shaded the Queen's realm in pink. It demands being read as an artifact publicizing empire's appeals and showing support for expansion, and for the IFL's plans to modernize and reform imperial rule, across party lines. A Mercator projection, the map made Britain the center of the world. Orientalist imagery, exotic animals, partially clad women, and racial stereotypes abounded. The links among the peoples pictured were trade routes and a shared turning towards the

---

24 Durkheim, *The Division of Labor in Society*, 4 ("extreme"), 62 ("civilization"), 179–81 ("happiness"), and 291–328 ("abnormalities"). In providing assurance that segmented societies had utterly lacked individuality, for example, Durkheim believed that the practice of slave traders who allegedly asked only about ethnic origins of those purchased and not about their personal characteristics reliably reflected realities in the societies whose members were enslaved rather than the views of slave traders (89–90); Kenneth Surin, "On Producing (the Concept of) Solidarity," *Rethinking Marxism*, 22 (2010), 452, uses Raymond Williams' own life to describe the persistence of older forms in working class solidarity; Hayward, "Solidarity," 280; Wilde, *Global Solidarity*, 35 and 39. For Marx's evolution, see Franklin Rosemont, "Karl Marx and the Iroquois," *Arsenal/Surrealist Subversion*, 4 (1989), 210–12; Teodor Shanin, *Late Marx and the Russian Road* (London: Routledge & Kegan Paul, 1983).

reclining figure of Britannia, bottom center, who seems in turn to watch out for all. Three banners at the map's top proclaim the promise of the reformed and expanded empire: "FREEDOM," "FRATERNITY," and "FEDERATION."[25]

Figure Two.
Walter Crane, "Imperial Federation Map Showing the Extent of the British Empire (1886),*" Graphic* (July 24, 1886), supplement.

Just over a decade ago a graduate student geographer, Pippa Biltcliffe, spotted a signature of sorts on the 1886 map and recognized its import. In the lower left corner, the artist had signed with a tiny rebus, or pictogram, depicting a crane and adding the still tinier stylized letters "W" and "C." Such was the mark of Walter Crane, known as the "artist of socialism" and a major figure with William Morris in the radical Arts and Crafts Movement. For the purposes of this article, the most significant of Crane's drawings was the 1890

---

25 Pippa Biltcliffe, "Walter Crane and the Imperial Federation Map Showing the Extent of the British Empire (1886)," *Imago Mundi: The International Journal for the History of Cartography*, 57 (2006), 63–69. See also Felix Driver, "In Search of the Imperial Map: Walter Crane and the Image of Empire," *History Workshop Journal*, 69 (2010), 146–57.

frontispiece to an American edition of William Morris's, *News from Nowhere*. Titled "Labour's May-Day," but proclaiming "Solidarity of Labour," it is the first major artistic work to name "solidarity," in English, as its theme.

LABOUR'S MAY-DAY.

Figure Three.
Walter Crane, "Labour's May-Day," in William Morris, *News from Nowhere* (Boston: Roberts Brothers, 1890), frontispiece.

It too shows a Britain-centered globe, held up by an Atlas figure, labelled "Europe" and here joined by clasped hands with the workers of the world. Nature and a liberty-inspiring woman again feature prominently and the three banners topping the image change in only one instance: "FREEDOM" and "FRATERNITY" survive but the IFL's beloved "FEDERATION" yields to "EQUALITY" in the socialist internationalist version.[26]

Both of the main writers on the 1886 imperial Crane map, Biltcliffe and the curator and geographer Felix Driver, situate it amid Crane's socialist and eventually strongly anti-imperialist works. They specifically consider "Solidarity of Labour" in counterpoint to the IFL-commissioned map and rightly refuse to regard the two works as completely separate in their politics. This Crane scholarship notes that as an artist needing paid work he could hardly have created only revolutionary art, emphasizing that the 1886 map was very much produced with the demands of the employer in mind. Crane's textiles reproducing imperial and Orientalist images might be considered in the same light. Moreover, both authors find in the 1886 map a certain success by Crane in smuggling subversions into a work commissioned to praise the possibilities of empire. The three draped women at the top, for example, sport headwear "distinctly reminiscent . . . of the red Phrygian cap" worn by liberated Roman slaves, which had become a symbol of liberation and specifically of opposition to colonialism, figuring as it did in the flag of revolutionary Haiti. Asian labor is pictured as both bowed down by exploitation, "struggling in midst of plenty" as Driver writes, but also as powerful. Atlas, holding up all, wears a belt reading, albeit in tiny letters, "HUMAN LABOUR." A plausible case can be made for seeing the map as containing subterranean critique. Indeed, the IFL seems to have quickly lost interest in promoting it, preferring a simple version with the empire colored in a far more dramatic dark blue.

The problem, revealingly enough, lies more in the 1890 map and its easy assumptions regarding solidarity across difference. In it, women all but disappear with what Driver calls "masculine

---

26   Ibid. For an illuminating study of Crane's relations to anarchism and socialism, see also Morna O'Neill, "Cartoons for the Cause: Walter Crane's *The Anarchists of Chicago*," *Art History*, 38 (February 2015), 108–37.

brotherhood" carrying the message instead. Indigenous people of both North America and the Antipodes are present in 1886 but not in 1890. The figure representing the labor of Africa appears to be a white, if sun-drenched, worker in Crane's later depiction of the "solidarity of labour." Perhaps most significantly, the idea that images can simply be borrowed in a drawing of global solidarity from a paean to empire suggests that Driver is correct when he writes that Crane at times thought "that empire is potentially a vehicle and not an obstacle to socialism." Driver further argues that despite his unearthing of subversion in the iconic 1886 map, it remains "in some ways a troubling image." As much can also be said for Crane's likewise iconic representation of solidarity in 1890.[27]

A United Statesian Keyword

The 601 uses in 480 published works between 1843 and 1901, returned from searching Cornell University Library's "Making of America" digitized website for the word "solidarity," reveal a great variety of usages; many simply suggest a commonality among all manner of things.[28] However, the chronologically first citation retrieved is very important for our purposes and some patterns do emerge. In June 1843, Orestes A. Brownson, making his way from liberal Christianity to Catholicism—his conversion would be completed the following year—wrote of "the mutual solidarity of the human race" in an article on "Universal History." He traced the language to a "French legal term"; a few months later he offered further complications, based on individualism and access to property. In 1853, scholar and merchant Charles Eliot Norton connected "Communism" and "solidarity"

---

27   Driver, *"In Search of the Imperial Map,"* 154 ("masculine" and "vehicle"), 151 ("troubling"), and 150–57. Driver likewise reads the African pictured as being white (154); Biltcliffe, "Walter Crane and the Imperial Federation Map Showing the Extent of the British Empire (1886)," 63–69; see also Jo Briggs, "The Second Boer War, 1899–1902: Anti-Imperialism and European Visual Culture," BRANCH (2015), branchcollective.org. For the general problems of globality and the representation of labor see Michael Denning's fascinating, "Representing Global Labor," *Social Text*, 92 (Fall 2007), 21–45.

28   The Making of America site of Cornell University Library, library.cornell.edu (accessed November 28, 2015).

briefly, rejecting both in favor of faith in his *Considerations on Some Recent Social Theories*. Nevertheless the central fact regarding the usage of "solidarity" through 1860 was its infrequency. As measured by Google Ngram, the last forty years of the nineteenth century saw a thirteen-fold increase in usage of the word over 1860 levels, and by the 1920s that increase was nearly forty-fold.[29]

Writing in 1874, the New York lawyer and literary critic Richard Grant White regarded the word "solidarity" as exemplifying that "we [in the United States] have adopted a few very expansive French words."[30] Generally true, White's observation cannot account, however, for what may be the earliest usages of solidarity as a pro-labor noun in the United States. The militant abolitionist Richard Hinton, who fought in support of John Brown in Kansas and later joined the International Workingmen's Association borrowed from English-language publications of the IWA as he publicized the organization to readers of *Atlantic Monthly*. Hinton wrote of a "new and imposing politico-social organization" acting on the belief that "it is useless for the working people of one nation to attempt to remodel society; there must be a combination of all the nations." Combining the labor and internationalist strands of solidarity's modern meanings, he quoted an IWA resolution from its Brussels meeting: "The Congress reckons upon the solidarity of workingmen of all countries for [a] strike of the people against war."[31]

The Knights of Labor rightly and wrongly enjoys a reputation for advancing the cause of solidarity in its practice as the leading

---

29 Orestes A. Brownson, "Universal History," *The United States Magazine and Democratic Review*, 12 (June 1843), 578; Brownson, "The Origin and Ground of Government," *The United States Magazine and Democratic Review*, 13 (October 1843), 357; Charles Eliot Norton, *Considerations on Some Recent Social Theories* (Boston: Little, Brown, and Company, 1853), 20. The searches using Google Ngram were made on November 28, 2015. On Brownson, see Arthur M. Schlesinger, *Orestes A. Brownson: A Pilgrim's Progress* (Boston: Little, Brown, and Company, 1939), esp. 112–83.

30 Richard Grant White, "Literary and Linguistic Notes and Queries," *The Galaxy*, 17 (February 1874), 185.

31 Richard J. Hinton, "Organization of Labor: Its Aggressive Phases," *Atlantic Monthly*, 27 (May 1871), 544–59, first quotation from 551, the latter two from 552. On Hinton's radicalisms, see Timothy Messer-Kruse, *The Yankee International: Marxism and the American Reform Tradition, 1848–1876* (Chapel Hill: University of North Carolina Press, 2000), 62–63, 115, and 251, and Mark Lause, *Race and Radicalism in the Union Army* (Urbana: University of Illinois Press, 2009), 1, 16, 86.

nineteenth-century US mass organization of working people, and one that was particularly willing to organize across lines of skill, gender, nationality, and race. Its powerful slogan, "An injury to one is the concern of all," has resonated widely in changing forms in subsequent labor movements as one basis of solidarity. Nevertheless, in its 1880s heyday the organization used the term "solidarity" scantily and, contradictorily, much more often described its own ideal as "fraternity." Indeed, even the celebrated "injury to one" motto dated from the early days of the Knights as a secret fraternal brotherhood and was unevenly used during its heyday as an openly organizing labor organization.[32] In the six fat volumes of the Knights' *Journal of United Labor* published in the early and mid 1880s, only two articles used the word "solidarity." In the first, "The Present Slavery— The Coming Freedom," the cooperative leader Justus O. Woods reflected the tendency to use "solidarity" to mean Christian brotherhood: "The solidarity of human interests may be safely assumed. One part of our race cannot be permanently elevated and happy while the other is degraded and miserable." The line resonated with Marx's famous pronouncement that "labor cannot emancipate itself in the white skin while in the black it is branded"—but without the labor. Christian faith, Woods held, furnished "the noblest ideal of human society," that of a "grand brotherhood of the race." Countering the individualism of social Darwinians, he used solidarity to establish the right to legislate for social good.[33]

Woods's usage built on a strong tradition of Protestant humanitarianism, and at times internationalism and egalitarianism, that in the United States often pioneered the explicit use of "solidarity" to breach racial lines. In 1886, for example, the editorial "Daniel Webster and Caste" in *The American Missionary* reproduced a small

---

32   Robert E. Weir, *Beyond Labor's Veil: The Culture of the Knights of Labor* (University Park, PA: Pennsylvania State University Press, 1996), 236; Alex Gourevitch's sometimes able *From Slavery to the Cooperative Commonwealth* (Cambridge: Cambridge University Press, 2015), esp. 138–70, makes "solidarity" the hallmark of the late nineteenth-century labor republicanism of the Knights. However, the term very seldom emerges in the sources he cites. Thanks to the great scholar of the Knights of Labor Jonathan Garlock for conversations on the languages of labor in the organization.

33   Justus O. Woods, "The Present Slavery—The Coming Freedom," *Journal of United Labor*, 5 (September 25, 1884), 795 and 796; Karl Marx, *Capital*, v. 1 (Chicago: Charles H. Kerr Publishing Company, 1906), 329.

part of Webster's 1820 Plymouth Rock oration. The editors praised it as a speech that "declares for the solidarity of the race" and "frowns upon the spirit of caste at all times and everywhere." Solidarity here was their word, not Webster's, and the evidence that Webster was a determined foe of caste is less than impressive. However, the editorial deploys a usage of "solidarity" later quite firmly developed in *The American Missionary*, which used the word nine times in the late nineteenth century, almost always in support of human brotherhood and in supporting Christian education abroad and/or African-American and American-Indian education at home. In one remarkable 1894 article chronicling racial oppression in the United States, the author glories specifically in the "racial solidarity" forming around the term "Afro-American."[34]

The other *Journal of United Labor* article using "solidarity" shows that there was at least some use of the word to signify labor unity within the Knights. The piece was part of the long, unsigned "Chapters on Labor" series, and titled only as "Chapter VI." It defended the tactic of going on strike even when immediate results were poor—most Knights of Labor actions had resulted in defeat according to the author—because the experience "*has taught us the power of unity; it has shown us that all our interests are identical; it has enabled us to understand solidarity.*" The author looked forward, after the growth of cooperatives, to "a general strike, which will be the last strike, the great strike, the universal strike." The major novel reflecting the experience of the Knights from a member's—albeit a lawyer whom the order's formal rules technically barred from membership—point of view, T. Fulton Gantt's 1887 *Breaking the Chains*, echoes this usage. As Maud Simpson, a leading female character and the novel's best spokesperson for the logic of labor organizing, puts it, "The Knights have learned that they are powerless to accomplish anything individually and so labor for their whole class. It is the correct idea—solidarity."[35]

---

34 Unsigned editorial, "Daniel Webster and Caste," *The American Missionary*, 40 (February 1886), 35; Rev. C.W. Hiatt, "Addresses at Annual Meeting: Negro Education," *The American Missionary*, 48 (January 1894), 4.

35 Unsigned, "Chapters on Labor, Chapter VI," *Journal of United Labor* 6 (October 10, 1885), 1094; For Simpson on solidarity see the reprint in Mary C. Grimes, ed., *The Knights in Fiction: Two Labor Novels of the 1880s* (Urbana: University of Illinois Press, 1986), 99, italics original. Weir, *Beyond Labor's Veil*, 217–21.

On the other hand, the same novel winds its way toward culminating scenes that offer an occasion for unease about the power of solidarity that Maud Simpson evokes. The strand of anti-Chinese racism that animated a subplot of the story compounds into a deadly brew of opium addiction, elite decadence, and anxiety regarding interracial sex as a Chinese servant provides drugs to a young rich woman. That such casual racism did not seem to the author to clash with phrasings regarding solidarity underlines how wary we should be of seeing solidarity at this point in time as merely incomplete, awaiting further inclusions. Generations of workers died with almost no impulse toward even the beginnings of movement beyond reflexive Chinese exclusion.[36] The most honest and exemplary study in this regard, Alexander Saxton's *The Indispensable Enemy: Labor and the Chinese Exclusion Movement in California*, argues that an important part of the labor movement was built not despite a commitment to anti-Chinese racism but through such a commitment. Critical in modeling the productive uneasiness regarding solidarity urged in this article is Saxton's repeated inclusion in his study of the anti-racist barber and seaman's organizer Sigismund Danielewicz. Long fighting a lonely crusade against overwhelming forces that either believed in Chinese exclusion or thought themselves able to use it tactically, Danielewicz lost again and again. His brilliance as an organizer could not overcome his insistence on principle. His last appearance in the book finds Danielewicz making a statement against anti-Chinese racism knowing "beforehand that his comrades would permit him to be guffawed and howled and booed from the podium." His presence hardly signaled for Saxton that there was always a saving remnant of the labor movement seeking a broader solidarity. In this case, there was not.[37]

Full use of "solidarity" within a language of US labor awaited the twentieth century, and specifically the rise of the Industrial Workers of the World (IWW). That organization would in 1909 launch the publication *Solidarity* so that when Chaplin's anthem "Solidarity

---

36 Grimes, ed., *The Knights in Fiction*, 132–33; see David Montgomery's afterword to the volumes at 327 on the Knights and Chinese immigration. See also Laura Hapke, *Labor's Text: The Worker in American Fiction* (Rutgers University Press, 2000), 61–62.

37 Alexander Saxton, *The Indispensable Enemy: Labor and the Chinese Exclusion Movement in California* (Berkeley: University of California Press, 1995 [1971]), 267; see also 164, 198, 221–23 and, on the Knights and the Chinese, 40.

Forever," appeared six years later its lyrics debuted in the publication. Two years later the idea that solidarity might be represented by a clenched fist appeared, again in *Solidarity*, with a striking cartoon in which (white male) workers form strong underground roots of a powerful fist emerging above the ground. Signed with his pen name "Bingo," the cartoon was also the work of Chaplin, then an editor of *Solidarity*. In both song and image the desire for solidarity is touching but hardly interested in portraying difference or in thinking, beyond a spirited reliance on a language of class, about what produced unity. [38]

Solidarity, June 30, 1917. The Hand That Will Rule the World—One Big Union.

Figure Four.
"Bingo" [Ralph Chaplin], "The Hand That Will
Rule the World," *Solidarity* (June 30, 1917).

---

38   *Solidarity* (January 9, 1915) includes the song. See Joyce Kornbluh, ed., *Rebel Voices: An IWW Anthology* (Chicago: Charles H. Kerr Publishing Company, 1988), 26–27; Lincoln Cushing, "A Brief History of the Clenched Fist Image," Docs Populi, docspopuli.org, which includes the cartoon from *Solidarity* (June 30, 1917). Cf. David R. Roediger, "Gaining a Hearing for Black–White Unity: Covington Hall and the Complexities of Race, Gender and Class," in *Towards the Abolition of Whiteness: Essays on Race, Class and Politics* (London and New York: Verso, 1994), esp. 139–48.

Solidarity, History, and Memory

As someone trained in history, I want to explore, in closing, three instances concerning how remembering the past reflects a sometimes enervating desire for solidarity to be easy. To raise this set of issues is not to disavow the pull towards what the French geographer, anarchist, antislavery travel writer on the United States, and Communard Élisée Reclus described as solidarity with "those who are no longer here." Such an aspiration was beautifully apparent when freedpeople sang of the "many thousand gone" in contemplating their liberation and their future.[39] Such a sensibility challenges, among other things, too-firm separations of mechanical solidarity from organic solidarity. However, to imagine ourselves in solidarity with social *movements* of the past challenges us to remember them as presenting both ways forward and ways in which broad solidarities have often been elusive and difficult.

Perhaps the leading case in which historians have rewritten the history of solidarity in the last fifty years, Bacon's Rebellion in Virginia in 1675 and 1676 provides the first of these examples. Before the late 1960s, two connecting interpretations informed the thinking about how the armed revolt led by the plantation owner Nathaniel Bacon and followed by common people presaged later anticolonial and democratic initiatives. In the first interpretation, Bacon was the "torchbearer" for a revolution a century away. The second interpretation, reading the historical record with perhaps less license, emphasized the rebellion's anti-Indian character.[40] When one of the leading US liberal historians, Edmund S. Morgan, and one of our leading radical historians, Theodore Allen, reinterpreted Bacon, they placed his revolt in the context of many other insurgencies in Maryland and

---

39 On Reclus, see Kristin Ross, *Communal Luxury: The Political Imaginary of the Paris Commune* (London: Verso, 2015), 127; Sterling Brown, Arthur Davis, and Ulysses Lee, eds., *The Negro Caravan* (New York: Dryden Press, 1943), 441.

40 See, respectively, Thomas Jefferson Wertenbaker, *Torchbearer of the Revolution: The Story of Bacon's Rebellion and its Leader* (Princeton: Princeton University Press, 1940) and Wilcomb Washburn, *The Governor and the Rebel: A History of Bacon's Rebellion in Virginia* (Chapel Hill: University of North Carolina Press for the Institute of Early American History and Culture, 1957).

Virginia between 1660 and 1680. Turning on questions of land and labor, these class conflicts united the "giddy multitude," indentured and formerly indentured workers of both African and European ancestry, and shook the colonial order's foundations. Allen in particular argued forcefully that the result of threats to elite control was "the invention of the white race." Elites reacted not only by turning to more slave labor but also to strategies drawing a color line, enlisting the white poor, accorded petty privileges, in the defense of a slave system soon also functioning as a racial system. Though not quite an example of interracial solidarity of labor—on Allen's argument racial categories came after the rebellion—Bacon's insurgency stood as a shining example of class solidarity.[41]

For many radical historians of race, myself certainly included, the reinterpretations of Bacon were profoundly attractive and remain so. So much is this the case that what they have left out has been minimized. Where gender was concerned the important work of Kathleen Brown quickly pointed to a critical omission, but one that the revisionist and traditional historians of Bacon's Rebellion had themselves shared. More recently historians have reasserted and detailed an older anti-Indian story that ought also to complicate our understanding of the solidarity of the "giddy multitude." Both James Davis and the late Ethan Schmidt have weighed in with powerful reminders that while Bacon's forces came into class solidarity around a desire for land, their more precise goal was speedy movement onto Indian land: Davis demonstrates that the setting was not simply a colony but rather "Indian country"; for Schmidt, the emphases are equally on "social conflict and Indian hatred." Indeed, in concert with new work establishing some materially based pre–Bacon's Rebellion impulses towards white supremacy and preference for slave labor, the question could be raised whether class solidarity in a settler alliance led by Bacon actually served the interests of African-descended poor people.[42]

---

41   Edmund Morgan, *American Slavery, American Freedom: The Ordeal of Colonial Virginia* (New York: W.W. Norton, 1975); Theodore W. Allen, *The Invention of the White Race*, 2 v. (1: *Racial Oppression and Social Control*; 2: *The Origin of Racial Oppression in Anglo-America*) (New York: Verso, 1994 and 1997).

42   Kathleen M. Brown, *Good Wives, Nasty Wenches, and Anxious Patriarchs: Gender, Race and Power in Colonial Virginia* (Chapel Hill: University of North Carolina Press, 1996); Ethan Schmidt, *The Divided Dominion: Social Conflict and Indian Hatred in Early Virginia*

In the city where I live, a monument particularly exemplifies how memorializing an historic impulse towards solidarity against one form of oppression can coexist with a refusal to acknowledge another. The striking twenty-three-ton reddish pink rock, with a plaque affixed, sits across from the Lawrence, Kansas city hall. The text rightly recalls the heroism of those who founded the town as an antislavery outpost: "TO THE PIONEERS OF KANSAS WHO IN DEVOTION TO HUMAN FREEDOM CAME INTO A WILDERNESS, SUFFERED HARD-SHIPS AND FACED DANGER AND DEATH TO FOUND THIS STATE IN RIGHTEOUSNESS." Disappeared in the plaque's words is the fact of settlement on native land, so tragically a part of the story of the monument itself. The stone anchoring its plaque was a Shunganunga boulder, an oddity among the region's yellowish-white stone, carried from the Dakotas on a glacier during the last Ice Age.[43] Its distinctiveness was not lost on the Kanza Indians living near its location at the intersection of Shunganunga Creek and the Kaw River. Having incorporated the boulder into water worship rites, the Kanza recalled it as a source of collective identity long after their removal to Oklahoma in the wake of the Civil War. In 1929, as part of Lawrence's seventy-fifth anniversary celebration, the Santa Fe Railroad helped to move the stone from its centuries-old resting place. It went from marking a sacred native place to becoming Founders Rock in Lawrence. In 1989, the Kanza asked that the Shunganunga boulder be restored to its former place in the river. A Lawrence Sesquicentennial Commission member justified rejecting the proposal on grounds clarifying that a monument to abolition could also be deeply embedded in long, unacknowledged histories of colonialism: "To the Kanza, these things had a life and a spirit," the commission member said. "In some ways, the spirituality of the rock has been shifted to a

(Boulder: The University Press of Colorado, 2015); James D. Rice, "Bacon's Rebellion in Indian Country," *Journal of American History,* 101 (December, 2014), 726–50; Carmen Pecola Thompson, "'Twenty and Odd Negroes': Virginia and the International System of Slavery" (Unpublished Ph.D. diss., University of Illinois, Urbana-Champaign, 2012).

43   James R. Shortridge and Barbara G. Shortridge, "Yankee Town on the Kaw: A Geographical and Historical Perspective on Lawrence and Its Environs," in Dennis Domer and Barbara Domer, eds., *Embattled Lawrence: Conflict and Community* (Lawrence: University of Kansas Continuing Education, 2001), 8. In the same study, see 23–77 on Lawrence's antislavery history; Jay Senter, "Boulder, Plaque Pay Homage to Pioneers," *Lawrence Journal-World* (September 19, 2004).

Figure Five.
Pepsy M. Kettavong's "Let's Have Tea," Rochester, New
York (2001), bronze. Photo © Wendy Gilmore.

different area. The boulder was very important to the residents of Lawrence who brought it here—it was kind of like their Plymouth Rock."[44]

The last of the cautions regarding memory and solidarity directly returns us to my doubts regarding how to write *Seizing Freedom*. In "Let's Have Tea" the Laotian-born American artist Pepsy M. Kettavong pays tribute to the friendship of Rochester, New York's two great feminist-abolitionists, Frederick Douglass and Susan B. Anthony. The decades of their collaboration, also commemorated by their names jointly gracing a spectacular bridge near the sculpture, richly deserve remembering. In an interview the artist cast his own role in producing the work and its subject matter as exemplifying US democracy at its best. All of that granted, the installation implies an ease in solidarity that the lives of Douglass and Anthony both exemplify and contradict. Their long and fruitful collaborations before and during the Civil War ought to be recalled, but so, too, should the fact that in the immediate postwar years, when the questions of African-American and women's rights emerged with unprecedented intensity, bitter political splits utterly divided the two leaders.[45]

To insist that school children who visit the park would benefit from knowing both stories is not to deprecate the plain heroism and the capacity for alliance Anthony and Douglass often displayed. Nevertheless profound structural differences in the ways in which African-American men and middle-class white women experienced both misery and the possibilities for redress left them in different and even opposing organizations. Indeed the fine eponymous

---

44   Senter, "Homage to Pioneers," including quotation; Shortridge and Shortridge, "Yankee Town," 8; Ronald D. Parks, *The Darkest Period: The Kanza Indians and Their Last Homeland, 1846–1873* (Norman: University of Oklahoma Press, 2014), 87–89. On water and the Kanza, see Dennis Domer, "Water in Willow Springs Township," *Kansas History*, 19 (Spring 1996), 67–69.;

45   Entry on "Let's Have Tea," Rochester Public Art, rochesterpublicart.com; Anne Klaeysen, "An Enduring Friendship," New York Society for Ethical Culture (February 2009), rochesterpublicart.com. Amid a vast and superb literature, for a study expertly treating the structural logic behind post–Civil War splits within the women's movement and between the women's movement and some African-American leaders, see Ellen C. Dubois, *Feminism and Suffrage: The Emergence of an Independent Women's Movement in America 1848–1869* (Ithaca: Cornell University Press, 1978).

documentary film based on the "Let's Have Tea" sculpture makes just that point.[46] To understand the power of those pressures working against solidarity is also a usable part of remembering the past, alerting us to structural differences between forms of domination in the present and allowing activists to know that not all fallings out of coalition are the result of bad faith.

Expressing an unease with the solidarity we nevertheless desire intersects with a variety of recent rethinking of the questions of optimism. These include Terry Eagleton's *Hope without Optimism*, the excellent new British journal *Salvage*, and Lauren Berlant's work on the perils of "cruel optimism." In a related way, the surrealist concept of "miserabilism," which animated the call for papers of the 2015 ASA conference, holds that the terrible miseries social systems produce can at times reinforce the ability of elites to rule. Such different warnings against easy optimisms are far from calls for quietism.[47] Instead they reflect on the extent to which the desire for reassurances that social motion is proceeding in our favor can lead in practice to immobilization, especially when defeats accumulate and hollow victories are extolled. They urge that we realize what we are up against and how uneasy the road ahead is bound to be. We ought to be willing to make solidarity uneasy as well, seeking it by owning its difficulties.

---

46   *Let's Have Tea* (2006), film, available at youtube.com.

47   David R. Roediger, "Miserabilism," *xcp: Cross Cultural Poetry*, 15/16 (2006), 237; Lauren Berlant, *Cruel Optimism* (Durham: Duke University Press, 2011); Terry Eagleton, *Hope without Optimism* (New Haven: Yale University Press, 2015). For *Salvage*, whose call includes "*Salvage* has earned its pessimism. *Salvage* yearns for that pessimism to be proved wrong," see salvage.zone.

Index

Colorblind racism, 34–35

Commons, John R., 113, 115, 117–119, 122–124, 143, 146–147, 150, 152–155

Communism and communists, 28, 52–55, 57, 62, 80–81, 169–170, 177

Congress of Industrial Organizations, 53

Cotton, 21, 102, 104–107, 109, 111–113, 124, 128–129

Crane, Walter, 169, 174–177

Critical whiteness studies, 47

Curti, Merle, 82–83, 85–88

D'Arcy, Steven, 158

Danielewicz, Sigismund, 181

Darder, Antonia, 6–7, 33, 35–36, 40–43

Davis, Adriene, 113

Davis, Angela, 91

Davis, Mike, 44–45, 59

Dawson, Michael, 4, 24

De Guzman, Orlando, 2

Debs, Eugene Victor, 33, 36, 43, 46

Doray, Barnard, 146, 147, 154, 155

Double consciousness, 69

Douglass, Frederick, 187

Drapetomania, 130

Driver, Felix, 174, 176, 177

Du Bois, W.E.B., 4, 33, 38, 40, 45, 50, 61–66, 69–71, 101–102, 132, 133

Dubilet, Alex, 1–3, 27, 29

Duggan, Lisa, 159

Durkheim, Emile, 169, 171–173

Dysaesthesia Aethiopica, 130, 132

Eagleton, Terry, 188

Elkins, Stanley, 86–87, 90

Emancipation, 63–64, 113, 133, 135, 161–163, 169

Empire, 33, 40, 61, 92, 113, 135, 137, 143, 150, 153, 160, 169, 173–177

British, 137, 173–177

and class, 8, 36, 39

Foreman's, 153

and indigeneity, 40, 137

and labor solidarity, 33, 160, 169, 172–177

and management, 135–137, 142–143, 172

and race, 5, 8, 33, 36, 39–40, 61, 135–137, 142–143, 169, 172–173

and slavery, 40

United States, 40, 61, 142–143, 160

Engels, Friedrich, 20, 59, 168

Engineers, 123, 133, 137–139, 145

Esch, Elizabeth, vii, x, 26, 29, 71, 102, 115, 143, 150, 157

Ethnic cleansing, 45

Ethnology, 131–132, 136

Facing Reality, 72, 79, 87–96

Fanon, Frantz, 38, 67–68, 70

Fasce, Nando, 76

Feldman, Herman, 152–154

Feminism and Feminists, 1–2, 23, 91, 113, 157, 161, 170, 187

Fenichel, Otto, 69